Cambridge Introductions to Music

Renaissance Polyphony

This engaging study introduces Renaissance polyphony to a modern audience. It helps readers of all ages and levels of experience make sense of what they are hearing. How does Renaissance music work? How is a piece typical of its style and type; or, if it is exceptional, what makes it so? The makers of polyphony were keenly aware of the specialized nature of their craft. How is this reflected in the music they wrote, and how were they regarded by their patrons and audiences? Through a combination of detailed, nuanced appreciation of musical style and a lucid overview of current debates, this book offers a glimpse of meanings behind and beyond the notes, be they playful or profound. It will enhance the listening experience of students, performers and music lovers alike.

FABRICE FITCH is a composer and musicologist specializing in Renaissance polyphony and its performance. His monograph *Johannes Ockeghem: Masses and Models* remains the only full-length book in English on the composer, and he has published widely on Obrecht, Agricola, other composers of that generation, and the Eton Choirbook. His compositions have been performed by leading soloists and chamber ensembles and broadcast internationally. He has been a reviewer with *Gramophone* for over twenty-five years. He is currently Senior Research Fellow at the Royal Conservatoire of Scotland.

A complete list of books in the series is featured at the back of this book.

Cambridge Introductions to Music
Renaissance Polyphony

FABRICE FITCH

CAMBRIDGE
UNIVERSITY PRESS

University Printing House, Cambridge CB2 8BS, United Kingdom

One Liberty Plaza, 20th Floor, New York, NY 10006, USA

477 Williamstown Road, Port Melbourne, VIC 3207, Australia

314–321, 3rd Floor, Plot 3, Splendor Forum, Jasola District Centre, New Delhi – 110025, India

79 Anson Road, #06–04/06, Singapore 079906

Cambridge University Press is part of the University of Cambridge.

It furthers the University's mission by disseminating knowledge in the pursuit of education, learning, and research at the highest international levels of excellence.

www.cambridge.org
Information on this title: www.cambridge.org/9780521899338
DOI: 10.1017/9781139017299

© Cambridge University Press 2020

This publication is in copyright. Subject to statutory exception and to the provisions of relevant collective licensing agreements, no reproduction of any part may take place without the written permission of Cambridge University Press.

First published 2020

A catalogue record for this publication is available from the British Library.

Library of Congress Cataloging-in-Publication Data
Names: Fitch, Fabrice, author.
Title: Renaissance polyphony / Fabrice Fitch.
Description: [1.] | New York : Cambridge University Press, 2020. | Series: Cambridge introductions to music | Includes bibliographical references and index.
Identifiers: LCCN 2020004220 | ISBN 9780521899338 (hardback) | ISBN 9781139017299 (epub)
Subjects: LCSH: Music – 16th century – History and criticism. | Counterpoint – History – 16th century. | Music – To 1500 – History and criticism. | Counterpoint – History – To 1500.
Classification: LCC ML172 .F57 2020 | DDC 781.2/8609031–dc23
LC record available at https://lccn.loc.gov/2020004220

ISBN 978-0-521-89933-8 Hardback
ISBN 978-0-521-72817-1 Paperback

Cambridge University Press has no responsibility for the persistence or accuracy of URLs for external or third-party internet websites referred to in this publication and does not guarantee that any content on such websites is, or will remain, accurate or appropriate.

To my students at Durham University (1994–2009) and the Royal Northern College of Music (2009–2018), especially L. M. I., J. A. H., and L. K. T. (F.)

Contents

List of illustrations   [*page* x]
List of figures   [xi]
List of tables   [xii]
List of music examples   [xiii]
Acknowledgements   [xvi]
Note on the music examples   [xviii]
Note on the bibliography   [xix]
List of abbreviations   [xx]

Chapter 1   Introducing Renaissance polyphony   [1]
            A musical Renaissance?   [2]
            A starting point: the *Missa Caput*   [4]
            Overview   [7]

Chapter 2   Making polyphony: sources and practice   [9]
            Polyphonic manuscripts: choirbook format   [9]
            Polyphonic prints: partbook format   [13]
            Extemporized polyphony   [18]
            From composed to extemporized polyphony (or vice-versa?)   [22]

Chapter 3   Makers of polyphony   [24]
            Renaissance attitudes towards music: theory and practice   [24]
            Singer-clerics before 1500   [28]
            A sense of corporate identity   [31]
            Singers or composers?   [34]
            Composers in the age of print   [36]
            Instrumental ensembles and soloists   [39]
            Women and polyphony: cloth and court   [43]

Chapter 4   Pitch: an overview   [46]
            The gamut: measuring musical space   [46]
            Species and modes   [49]
            Measuring musical space with syllables: the hexachord   [52]
            Contrapuntal practice: polyphony and modal classification   [54]
            The cadence (*clausula*)   [56]
            Cadence and mode   [58]

vii

A short note on *musica ficta*   [60]
Signature flats and expanded hexachords ('*conjunctae*')   [61]
Enhanced chromaticisms   [63]
An even shorter note on dissonance treatment   [64]

Chapter 5   Voice-names, ranges, and functions   [66]
What clefs mean (and what they don't)   [67]
Cadential function and the principal voice-types   [68]
Registral tiers: the English *Caput* Mass and the contratenor bassus   [70]
From four voice-ranges to *chiavette*   [74]
Another look at cadence   [78]

Chapter 6   Mensural notation, duration, and metre   [83]
The four prolations   [83]
Mensural usage and musical style   [88]
Tempo and proportions   [94]

Chapter 7   Genre, texts, form   [96]
The genre problem   [96]
Words and music   [102]

Chapter 8   'Cantus magnus': music for the Mass   [109]
The Mass cycle   [109]
Propers, Requiem Masses, and other liturgical forms   [116]

Chapter 9   'Cantus mediocris': the motet   [120]
A snapshot of the motet repertory: the Medici Codex   [122]
Stylistic markers   [123]
Motets for private and public devotion   [124]
Penitential music   [127]
Occasional motets   [128]
Towards the motet of the later Renaissance   [128]

Chapter 10   'Cantus parvus': secular music   [130]
Formes fixes: Ockeghem, *Ma bouche rit*   [131]
Strophic song: Senfl, *Lust hab' ich g'habt zur Musica*   [133]
Epigram: Lassus, *En un chateau*   [134]
Descriptive and narrative songs: Flecha, *La bomba*   [135]
Instrumental music: Tye, *Sit fast* and *O lux*   [137]
Madrigal: Cipriano, *Da le belle contrade*   [138]

Chapter 11   Scoring, texture, scale   [141]
Scoring: fifteenth-century experiments and beyond   [142]
Texture types: polyphony with and without cantus firmus   [146]
Varietas: texture types and the role of imitation   [151]
English exceptionalism: the Eton Choirbook and beyond   [155]

                Pervasive imitation and its aftermath   [158]
                'O che nuovo miracolo': scale as exploration   [163]

Chapter 12   Understanding musical borrowing   [168]
                Chant paraphrase and cantus firmus   [169]
                Masses: from cantus firmus to model   [172]
                The aesthetics of borrowing: the model as analogy   [174]
                Homage, exchange, and competition: the *L'Homme armé* story   [177]
                The Mass cycle and 'peak borrowing' circa 1500   [181]
                The imitation Mass and the listener   [185]
                The limits of borrowing   [191]

Chapter 13   Canons, puzzles, games   [197]
                Playing with syntax: cadence   [197]
                Playing with material: hexachord games and ostinato   [200]
                Playing with pitch   [205]
                Fugal canon   [208]
                Non-fugal and enigmatic canons   [212]
                Puzzles and *Augenmusik*   [215]
                Playing with numbers   [217]

Chapter 14   Performance practice: a brief introduction   [223]
                What the sources don't tell us: aspects of pitch   [223]
                Tempo and modern performance practice   [226]
                Scoring and texting, voices and instruments: a historical view   [227]
                'The past is a foreign country': strategies of de-familiarization   [232]

Notes   [237]
Glossary   [245]
Bibliography   [249]
Index of compositions   [259]
General index   [263]

Illustrations

2.1 La Rue, *Ave sanctissima Maria*, Brussels, Koninklijke Bibliotheek/ Bibliothèque Royale, Ms. 228, ff. 1^v–2 (reproduced with permission)   [*page* 10]

2.2 Isaac, *La mi la sol la sol la mi* (beginning), Sankt Gallen, Stiftsbibliothek, Cod. Sang. Ms. 461, pp. 42–3 (reproduced with permission)   [14]

2.3 Isaac, *Rogamus te, piissima virgo*, *Motetti C* (Venice: Petrucci, 1504), discantus partbook, f. 26^v, Bayerische Staatsbibliothek München, Musikabteilung, 4 Mus.pr. 160#Beibd.2 (reproduced with permission)   [16]

2.4 Isaac, *Missa O praeclara*, 'Patrem', *Liber quindecim missarum* (Nuremberg: Petreius, 1539), discantus partbook, LL[i^v], Bayerische Staatsbibliothek München, Musikabteilung, 4 Mus.pr.159 (reproduced with permission)   [17]

4.1 Guidonian hand, Brussels, Koninklijke Bibliotheek/Bibliothèque Royale, Ms. 1758, f. 117^r (reproduced with permission)   [48]

13.1 La Rue, *Missa L'Homme armé*, 'Agnus dei II', Brussels, Koninklijke Bibliotheek/Bibliothèque Royale, Ms. 9126, f. 42 (reproduced with permission)   [211]

13.2 Michael Maier, *Atalanta fugiens*, fuga/emblema XLV (Oppenheim: Johann Theodor de Bry, 1617), pp. 188–9, Bayerische Staatsbibliothek München, Musikabteilung, Res/4 Alch. 54 (reproduced with permission)   [218]

Figures

4.1 The gamut   [*page* 47]
4.2 The eight church modes and the species of fourth and fifth   [50]
4.3 The gamut and the hexachords   [53]
4.4 Voice-ranges of Du Fay, *Le Serviteur*, showing the constitutive species of fourth and fifth   [56]
5.1 (a) Modern SATB clefs and voice-ranges; (b) Old-style SATB clefs   [67]
5.2 Four-part cadence, two-tier texture (pre-1400)   [70]
5.3 (a) *Chiavi naturali*; (b) *Chiavette*   [75]
6.1 Mensural levels and the four prolations   [84]
13.1 Obrecht, *Hec Deum celi*, discantus II: numerical structure   [222]
13.2 Obrecht, *Hec Deum celi*, discantus II: alternative numerical structure   [222]

Tables

5.1 Voice-names and functions in the Renaissance   [*page* 71]
6.1 Normative mensural usage in the Renaissance   [88]
8.1 The Ordinary and Propers of the Mass   [110]

Music examples

1.1 Anon., *Missa Caput*, Kyrie (beginning), (a) bb. 1–13; (b) bb. 20–27   [*page* 6]
2.1 Plainchant hymn, *Veni creator spiritus* in faburden (first two phrases)   [20]
3.1 Compère, *Omnium bonorum plena*, second part (excerpt)   [32]
3.2 Du Fay, *Ave regina celorum III*, second part (excerpt)   [33]
4.1 Anon., *L'Homme armé* (in Dorian and Mixolydian) with solmization syllables   [51]
4.2 Two-voice cadential motion   [57]
4.3 Cadential ornaments   [57]
4.4 Three-voice cadences on modal finals, (a) Dorian, (b) Phrygian, (c) Lydian, (d) Mixolydian   [58]
4.5 (a) Delahaye, *Mort, j'appelle de ta rigueur* (excerpt); (b) Du Fay, *Bien veignés vous, amoureuse lyesse* (beginning); (c) Ockeghem, *Missa Quinti toni*, 'Kyrie II' (beginning)   [62]
5.1 Du Fay, *Je requier a tous amoureux* (complete)   [69]
5.2 Anon., *Missa Caput*, Sanctus (first tenor entry)   [72]
5.3 Busnoys, *Quant ce viendra*, second part (beginning)   [73]
5.4 Gaspar, *O salutaris hostia* (complete)   [75]
5.5 Willaert, *Saluto te, sancta virgo Maria* (beginning)   [76]
5.6 Gombert, *Media vita in morte sumus* (beginning)   [77]
5.7 Four-voice cadences on modal finals, (a) Dorian, (b) Phrygian, (c) Lydian, (d) Mixolydian   [79]
5.8 Phrygian cadences   [79]
5.9 'Fermata' cadence   [80]
5.10 (a) '*Satzfehler*' cadence; (b) 'English' cadence   [81]
5.11 Arcadelt, *Il bianco e dolce cigno* (conclusion)   [81]
6.1 Original notation (upper stave) transcribed according to C (middle stave) and O (lower stave)   [86]
6.2 Anon., *Confort d'amours* (beginning)   [89]
6.3 Busnoys, *Noel, noel* (beginning)   [91]
6.4 Janequin, *Toutes les nuictz* (beginning)   [93]

6.5	Lassus, *Lagrime di San Pietro*, no. 16, 'O vita troppo rea' (beginning)	[93]
7.1	Isaac, *La mi la sol, la sol la mi* (beginning)	[99]
7.2	Ockeghem, *S'elle m'amera/Petite camusette* (beginning)	[101]
7.3	Lassus, *Prophetiae Sybillarum*, 'Sybilla Cimmeria' (excerpt)	[104]
7.4	Wert, *Ascendente Jesu in naviculam*, (a) first part (excerpt); (b) second part (excerpt); (c) second part (excerpt)	[107]
8.1	Du Fay, *Missa L'Homme armé*, (a) Kyrie (beginning); (b) 'Et in terra' and 'Patrem' (beginning); (c) Sanctus and Agnus dei (beginning); (d) 'Kyrie II' (conclusion); (e) 'Christe' (excerpt); (f) 'Agnus dei III' (excerpt)	[113]
8.2	Isaac, *Salve sancta parens* (beginning)	[118]
9.1	Agricola, *Si dedero* (beginning)	[121]
9.2	Mouton, *In omni tribulatione* (complete)	[126]
11.1	Josquin, *Que vous madame/In pace in idipsum* (beginning)	[144]
11.2	Agricola, *Revenez tous regretz/Quis det* (beginning)	[144]
11.3	Ockeghem, *Missa Au travail suis*, 'Et resurrexit' (conclusion)	[145]
11.4	Du Fay, *Ave regina celorum III* (beginning)	[147]
11.5	Obrecht, *Salve crux* (second part, excerpts)	[150]
11.6	Josquin/La Rue (?), *Absalon fili mi* (beginning)	[155]
11.7	Tallis, *Lamentatione Jeremiae I*, 'Plorans ploravit' (excerpt)	[161]
11.8	Palestrina, *Dum complerentur* (beginning)	[162]
12.1	(a) Du Fay, *Alma redemptoris mater* (beginning); (b) Ockeghem, *Alma redemptoris mater* (beginning)	[170]
12.2	(a) Du Fay, *Se la face ay pale* (excerpt); (b) Du Fay, *Missa Se la face ay pale* 'Confiteor' (excerpt)	[173]
12.3	(a) Busnoys, *Missa L'Homme armé*, 'Agnus dei III' (excerpt); (b) Josquin, *Missa L'Homme armé sexti toni*, 'Agnus dei III' (excerpt)	[179]
12.4	(a) Ockeghem, *Ma maistresse* (beginning); (b) anon., *Si vous voullez* (beginning)	[184]
12.5	(a) Gombert, *Ego sum qui sum* (beginning); (b) Rogier, *Missa Ego sum qui sum*, Kyrie (beginning); (c) Rogier, *Missa Ego sum qui sum*, 'Et in terra' (beginning); (d) Rogier, *Missa Ego sum qui sum*, 'Patrem' (beginning); (e) Rogier, *Missa Ego sum qui sum*, Sanctus (beginning); (f) Rogier, *Missa Ego sum qui sum*, Agnus dei (beginning)	[187]
12.6	Victoria, *Dum complerentur* (excerpt)	[194]

12.7 (a) Rogier, *Missa Ego sum qui sum*, 'Kyrie II' (conclusion); (b) Monteverdi, *Missa In illo tempore*, 'Kyrie II' (conclusion)   [195]
13.1 Evaded cadences (four-voice)   [197]
13.2 Evaded cadences (two-voice)   [198]
13.3 Agricola, *Allés regretz* (excerpt)   [198]
13.4 Agricola, *Comme femme desconfortée I* (beginning)   [199]
13.5 Lassus, *Psalmi David poenitentiales: Beati quorum*, 'Nolite fieri' (conclusion)   [200]
13.6 Ockeghem, *Missa Quinti toni*, 'Agnus dei II' (contratenor bassus, excerpt)   [201]
13.7 Josquin, *Ut Phebi radiis*, tenor and bassus: canonic pitch materials   [202]
13.8 Josquin, *Ut Phebi radiis*, first part (excerpt)   [203]
13.9 Josquin, *Missa Faisant regretz*, 'Agnus dei III' (beginning)   [204]
13.10 Obrecht, *Missa Libenter gloriabor*, 'Kyrie II' (conclusion)   [207]
13.11 Le Jeune, *Qu'est devenu ce bel œuil* (beginning)   [207]
13.12 La Rue, *Missa L'Homme armé*, 'Agnus dei II' (beginning)   [210]
13.13 De Orto, *Missa L'Homme armé*, Sanctus, tenor in original notation (beginning)   [215]
13.14 Obrecht, *Hec Deum celi*, 'canonic' voices   [221]

Acknowledgements

Given how long this book has been in preparation, my first thanks must go to its prime mover, Victoria Cooper, who commissioned it; Kate Brett, her successor at Cambridge University Press; and their assistant, Eilidh Burrett, all of whom have shown me boundless kindness and patience. I hope that what follows fulfils Vicky's long-expressed wish to see in print the book she would like to have read as a student. Professor Barbara Kelly was instrumental in securing a period of research leave from the Royal Northern College of Music, without which the final campaign of work would not have begun, and the Research and Knowledge Exchange Department of the Royal Conservatoire of Scotland brought about the material circumstances that enabled its completion, as well as providing financial assistance.

I thank colleagues and publishers who have granted permission for their editions to appear as supporting materials on Cambridge University Press's website: Jane A. Bernstein, Adam Knight Gilbert, Scott Metcalfe, Mariacarmen Gómez Muntané, the late Alejandro Enrique Planchart, University of Chicago Press, Institut Valencià de Música, BREPOLS, A-R Editions, and the Koninklijke Vereniging voor Nederlandse Muziekgeschiedenis. Anna Maria Busse Berger, Iain Fenlon, Richard Freedman, Jesse Rodin, and Richard Wistreich generously helped in the compilation of the bibliography. For other practical advice and support I am indebted to Simon Clarke, Roger Mathew Grant (who kindly set and allowed me to reproduce Figure 4.3), Ann Kelders, Jesse Rodin, and Stephen Broad. I thank Paul Archbold, my former colleague at Durham University, for his painstaking work in setting the musical examples, with financial support from the *Music & Letters* Trust (Oxford University Press), which I gratefully acknowledge. Last but not least, I thank my copy-editor, Kilmeny MacBride, who steered the text through its final stages expertly and with unfailing good humour, and Bonnie J. Blackburn for her eagle-eyed reading of the proofs, compilation of the index, and generous advice.

This book bears the traces of countless discussions and convivial exchanges with friends and colleagues alongside whom I have grown up (or, at any rate, grown older), in particular Jane Alden; Sean Gallagher; Andrew Kirkman; and the late Philip Weller (1958–2018), who is much missed by so many; all of whom have helped shape and sharpen my thinking about music of all kinds. Specific chapters draw on the work of Philippe Canguilhem, Ruth DeFord, Warwick Edwards, and Katelijne Schiltz. Warwick Edwards, David Fallows, Alastair Harper, and Martin Iddon read the entire typescript, and Ruth DeFord, Lois Fitch, Stefano Mengozzi, Scott Metcalfe, and Keith Polk read individual chapters, making valuable suggestions and sparing me innumerable blushes. I also thank the organizers of conferences I attended while writing this book, for providing creative stimulation and much-needed respite from a hermitic existence: Andrea Lindmayr-Brandl, Paul Kolb, Agnese Pavanello, Klaus Pietschmann, Immanuel Ott, Wolfgang Fuhrmann, João Pedro d'Alvarenga, Bart Demuyt, David Burn, Christiane Wiesenfeldt, Stratton Bull, Klaartje Proesmans, Jesse Rodin, and Emily Zazulia.

Finally, my debt to David Fallows remains incalculable, as also the support over many years of Jaap van Benthem, Warwick Edwards, and Brian Ferneyhough. Above all, I thank my family, especially my wife, Lois, and our daughter, Livia Aliénor, without whose love and support in especially challenging times, I could not have seen this project through.

Note on the music examples

For reasons of space, musical examples are presented in as compact a form as possible, including short-score and reduced note-values. During the Renaissance, the notation of durations underwent gradual change; for this reason, it is impractical to reduce note-values by the same proportion throughout the book. The ratio is indicated at the start of each example, with the exception of those in Chapter 6, which deals with mensural notation. There, musical examples are trancribed in original note-values so that the reader can follow the development of mensural practice throughout the period. Because the barring of individual pieces varies from edition to edition, no bar numbers for musical examples are given, except in the case of complete pieces.

In choosing musical examples to illustrate key points, I have sought as far as possible to ensure that editions of the complete piece are accessible through online databases (such as Petrucci IMSLP). Where this is not the case, rather than reproduce the piece in full, I direct the reader to www.cambridge.org/9780521899338, where complete editions of the pieces concerned (indicated with an asterisk on their first mention in the book) may be found, along with transcriptions of music examples with original note-values. This applies to several works discussed in Chapter 9 (particularly from the Medici Codex) and all those discussed in Chapter 10. Translations of texts are supplied, except for those from the Mass Ordinary.

Note on the bibliography

The bibliography is primarily intended as a guide to further reading. For reasons of space I have excluded primary sources (including theoretical writings) and modern editions of the music. (As a rule it is best to consult published scholarly editions rather than online ones unless these derive from specific research projects.) I have also (reluctantly) limited the citation of online resources to those cited in the text and the endnotes. For primary sources of the music, DIAMM is an essential resource, and it is worth noting that most major libraries have digitized their holdings of primary sources or are in the process of doing so.

Abbreviations

AM	*Acta Musicologica*
BHR	*Bibliothèque d'Humanisme et Renaissance*
BTM/RBM	*Belgisch Tijdschrift voor Muziekwetenschap/Revue Belge de Musicologie*
CD	*Comparative Drama*
EM	*Early Music*
EMH	*Early Music History*
JAF	*Journal of the Alamire Foundation*
JAMS	*Journal of the American Musicological Society*
JM	*Journal of Musicology*
JRMA	*Journal of the Royal Musical Association*
(K)TVNM	*Tijdschrift van de Vereniging voor Nederlandse Muziekgeschiedenis/Tijdschrift van de Koninklijke Vereniging voor Nederlandse Muziekgeschiedenis*
M&L	*Music & Letters*
MD	*Musica Disciplina*
MQ	*Musical Quarterly*
RM	*Revista de Musicología*
RQ	*Renaissance Quarterly*
SM	*Il Saggiatore Musicale*
YAF	*Yearbook of the Alamire Foundation*

Chapter 1 | Introducing Renaissance polyphony

In tackling such a vast topic in so concise a format, my aim is not so much to supersede existing studies as to complement them. Since Gustave Reese's magisterial *Music of the Renaissance* (1954), approachable surveys of the principal genres and composers have been increasingly accessible, to say nothing of more specialized, culturally or socially oriented readings.[1] More recently, the wealth of online resources (from search engines and encyclopedias like *Grove Music Online* and its German equivalent, *Die Musik in Geschichte und Gegenwart*, to editions and digital archives such as the Digital Image Archive of Medieval Music or CESR Programme Ricercar) presents both an opportunity and a challenge to re-imagine what a book like this can offer.

First, the title signals a difference from anthologies with names like 'Music in the Renaissance', which locate the subject within broader social, intellectual, or artistic contexts. These all have a place, but the focus of this book is squarely on the music, and specifically, polyphony. This is not a matter of exclusion but of emphasis: a study of Renaissance music more broadly would take in entirely unwritten practices, dance music, solo instrumental music, sacred and secular forms of monody – all of which pose very different questions. The fact that so much polyphony survives in notation marks it out from most of these other forms of music making, but in recent years the prevalence of extemporized polyphony within the Renaissance has become increasingly apparent. The recovery of these practices has only just begun, but already it has opened up fascinating new perspectives. It confirms the view of polyphony as a specialized activity, meriting investigation on its own terms.

There is another reason to focus so specifically on polyphony as musical practice. The popularity of Renaissance polyphony with modern audiences is due – at least in part – to its sonic appeal, added to its relative proximity to tonal music (particularly with later Renaissance figures such as Palestrina, Lassus, Byrd, and Victoria). That seeming familiarity masks all sorts of features that may be quite unfamiliar: genres, formal expectations, and habits concerning performance. The further removed in time, the greater the sense of unfamiliarity, extending to ever more basic features of musical language (the relationship between the voices, the disposition of cadences, the sense of pacing, and so on). Perhaps because the music easily lends itself to being enjoyed at a surface level, an appreciation of its more distinctive qualities can prove elusive. Yet there is a world of difference between Masses by Palestrina and Du Fay; between chansons by Lassus and Busnoys, and between two motets written by the same composer in different circumstances. What, then, makes a given piece tick; what makes it exceptional, or, on the contrary, typical? How does it relate to other pieces it resembles? How might the composer or musicians have approached the task of composing or performing it? In this book I seek to give interested listeners and students (in the broadest sense) the means to address these questions for themselves.

The distinction between performance and composition is crucial, for there is a dimension of polyphony that is expressed in the musical notation, an aspect by definition hidden from view of modern audiences, both figuratively and literally. The heart-shaped and circular notation of songs by Baude Cordier (*fl.* 1400) are earlier examples of this idea, but the phenomenon truly takes off during the Renaissance and is expressed in all sorts of ways. Often it takes the shape of riddles and codes in which the musical notation does not directly express the intended sounding result. Historians of the eighteenth and nineteenth centuries were suspicious of such features, sometimes because they misunderstood the notation and transcribed the music incorrectly, but also because the idea of notation as anything other than a transparent signifier was alien to them. Yet it is one of the most fascinating aspects of Renaissance polyphony. Far from being abstract or forbidding, it can be a source of delight, even humour.

In short, there is more to Renaissance polyphony than meets the ear.

A musical Renaissance?

So far, I have used the term 'Renaissance' without qualification. First used by the artist and writer Giorgio Vasari (d.1574), it was subsequently adopted for the historical period in Jacob Burckhardt's *The Civilization of the Renaissance in Italy* (1860). But its application to music is problematic. Many of the practices with which this book is concerned – including some of the most fundamental – trace their origins back decades and even centuries, in some cases back to the origins of documented polyphony. As a consequence, assigning a point of division between 'medieval' and 'Renaissance' music is an even more artificial exercise than usual.

Following Vasari, the classic art-historical definition of the Renaissance begins with the maturity of the painter Giotto di Bondone (d.1337), but no writers on music nowadays would advocate so early a date. After 1500, changes in musical style, forms, and notation are easier to describe and perceive, but a cut-off date at that point leaves several generations of composers stranded in a periodic no-man's-land, since few commentators, conversely, would extend the medieval period so late. Ironically, the idea of a musical 're-birth' was invoked not long after Vasari coined the term, but it was used to designate a very different phenomenon from what we mean by 'Renaissance'. The so-called 'academies' consisting of intellectuals, literary figures, and musicians in Italy and France sought to recover the supposed perfection of ancient Greece (specifically its synthesis of text and music in the domain of theatre). Their debates eventually found expression in accompanied monody, which led to opera. By their reckoning, there had been no musical Renaissance to speak of before the 're-birth' of Greek drama: in other words, 'our' Renaissance more or less collapses into the Baroque. In fact, the term's applicability to music history has divided writers on music from the nineteenth century onwards.[2]

A number of recent anthologies situate the start of the Renaissance in music with the early career of Guillaume Du Fay (c.1397–1474) and his first stay in Italy in the early 1420s, culminating in the composition of his motet *Nuper rosarum flores* (1436) for the consecration of the *duomo* (cathedral) of Florence and its newly completed dome, designed by Filippo Brunelleschi (d.1447).[3] This view runs the risk just mentioned of aligning the musical Renaissance too closely with its Italian art-historical origins. Brunelleschi's dome is so central to the narrative of Florence as the 'cradle of the Renaissance' that we ought to be wary of interpreting *Nuper rosarum* too strongly in terms of the circumstances of its composition. Put another way, it may be asked whether we would interpret its musical features quite so strongly in the absence of the connection with Brunelleschi and Florence.[4] After all, the piece's form (the tenor or 'isorhythmic' motet) was inherited from previous generations, and its style is not so different from his other pieces of this type; besides, attempts to link aspects of Du Fay's style with contemporary Italian music are too general to be fully convincing.

Another possible starting point takes its cue not from art history but from contemporary writings about music (historiography). Two statements are involved: in his lengthy poem *Le Champion des dames* (c.1440), the poet Martin le Franc (d.1461) credits Du Fay and his contemporary Gilles Binchois (c.1400–60) with reinventing their musical language in response to the 'frisque concordance' (lively sonority) and other innovative stylistic features of contemporary English music, notably that of John Dunstaple (c.1390–1453). A generation later, in his *Book on the Art of Counterpoint* (c.1477), the great music theorist and composer Johannes Tinctoris (c.1430–1511) names Dunstaple as the 'fons et origo' ('wellspring') of a new style, which Du Fay's generation and those after him adopted.[5] Among the most discussed in all Renaissance music, these two passages constitute another 'foundation myth' of Renaissance music: Dunstaple and his English contemporaries (notably Leonel Power, c.1380–1446) also feature prominently in the early sections of several anthologies.[6] But Le Franc's memorable term for this new English style ('contenance angloise') is difficult to interpret, since any poetic description is strongly conditioned by the demands of rhyme and scansion; for his part, Tinctoris does not say exactly which aspects made such a vivid impression on continental composers. In some ways, the known works of Power and Dunstaple are as deeply rooted in medieval models as those of their continental colleagues.

A starting point: the *Missa Caput*

My solution to the problem 'where to begin' is framed not in terms of contemporary developments in other spheres but of a concretely musical one.

Sometime around 1440, a clutch of anonymous English Mass cycles began circulating in mainland Europe.[7] They had several features in common, which marked them out from what continental composers were doing: the five movements of these Masses were in the same mode and based on the same plainchant (called 'cantus firmus', henceforth c.f.), which was treated similarly or even identically in each movement; all five movements began with a recognizable melodic tag (known as 'head-motif'), audibly linking them from the start. These were not the first c.f. Masses to find their way to the continent, where composers had been experimenting with similar unifying devices for some years, though less consistently. Two of them stood out because of their scoring: they were for four voices, the lowest of which was in a range of its own, below the tenor (the voice that 'held' the c.f.). This new voice-type was labelled 'contratenor bassus' (soon shortened to 'bassus'). Exactly why this novel feature so caught the attention of continental composers can only be guessed at, but soon it became standard in written polyphony.

Why does this matter? It is a question of style. In earlier music the tenor, with its slow-moving pitches pre-determined by the plainchant, was often the lowest-sounding voice, limiting the pitches the composer could place above it. A lower voice whose pitches were chosen by the composer meant a greater number of possible sonorities to choose from. All this will be explained in more detail in Chapter 5; but while this was not the functional bass of tonality, it is possible to draw a stylistic line from these English Masses to the music of Palestrina, Lassus, and their contemporaries; beyond that, the establishment of a free-standing bass line is a point of rupture signalling the new aesthetic priorities of the Baroque. The turn of the seventeenth century, just after the deaths of Palestrina and Lassus in 1594, is a much less contested end point for our period, and for this book; that said, the 'old' polyphonic style continued to be cultivated well into the new century, particularly on the Iberian peninsula, where the innovations from Italy were slower to take hold, and in England, notably due to the exceptional longevity and influence of William Byrd (c.1539/40–1623).

Of these English Mass cycles, one was especially popular: in fact, the *Missa Caput* is transmitted in more sources than any other Mass composed before 1480 (with the lone exception of the considerably later *Missa L'Homme armé* by Antoine Busnoys (c.1430–92)). Though little known today, choosing it as a notional starting point seems appropriate for a number of reasons. In common with the vast majority of music written before 1600, we do not know when it was written, and as with most of the music before the age of print, it is anonymous. Nor is it the only work of its kind: another English cycle, the *Missa Veterem hominem*, reached the continent at the same time, and is its twin in stylistic terms. All these things usefully suggest a gradual emergence of Renaissance polyphony, rather than a grand creation myth. (That said, its presumed date of composition tallies with another judgement in Tinctoris' *Book of the Art of Counterpoint* that only the music composed in the last forty years was worth hearing.) Fittingly, also, the *Missa Caput* set the seal on a new phenomenon, the cyclic Mass, which engaged composers throughout the Renaissance and stands today as one of its iconic artistic statements. Furthermore, the *Missa Caput* was significant not merely as an example of a new style but also in its own right: two leading fifteenth-century composers, Johannes Ockeghem (c.1425–97) and Jacob Obrecht (c.1457/8–1505), wrote Masses that not only used the same plainchant but whose structure is closely modelled on their English predecessor. When Obrecht wrote his response, it would have been about fifty years old. The re-working of pre-existing polyphony is a mainstay of Renaissance music, and the *Missa Caput* was one of the earliest pieces to be used in that way.

Most importantly, the significance of the *Missa Caput* is due to its intrinsic musical qualities. By the standards of previous music with a c.f., it is faster moving. The greater mobility of the lowest voice gives the musical texture a dynamism that is immediately audible. The music alternates sections where the long notes of the c.f. are present and others where the tenor pauses: sections without the tenor ('reduced texture') tend to be more active than those where it is present. The principle is inherited from the isorhythmic motet,[8] but in the *Missa Caput* reduced sections are typically longer, the number of shifts from full to reduced texture is greater, and the combination of voices sounding at any one time is more varied. This alternation audibly parses the music, like breaths inhaling and exhaling, or like structural upbeats (in reduced texture) and downbeats (when the tenor enters or re-enters). This formal clarity focuses the dynamism made possible by the new scoring and is further reinforced across the cycle by the recurrent features just mentioned. The very first entry of the tenor in the opening Kyrie (Example. 1.1b) gives rise to a startling sonority. It is not

Example 1.1 Anon., *Missa Caput*, Kyrie (beginning), (a) bb. 1–13; (b) bb. 20–27.

so much the tenor's pitch b as the e beneath it that is unusual (a sonority on g would have been the more obvious choice: see Example 5.2, p. 72 below). This bold gesture follows on the heels of an introductory duo that is far more extended than was typical in continental music. The calculated impact of this initial burst of full scoring strikes the listener even today.

Just as the novelty of its scoring was quickly adopted by continental composers, so the formal plan of these new English Masses was widely imitated. Within a few years, the implications of both were being explored and extended in all sorts of directions – not just in the nascent phenomenon of the Mass cycle but in motets and secular music as well.

Overview

This first look at the *Missa Caput* introduces several of the issues that inform this book. Unlike most historical surveys, which offer detailed information on composers' biographies, evaluations of their outputs, and histories of the most significant genres, my approach is not strictly chronological but thematic. (Given the breadth of resources now available, Reese's exhaustive coverage is neither possible today nor perhaps even necessary.) The main concern here is not with composers and works but with aspects of musical style and technique that shape the listening experience, and with issues that lie just beneath or beyond it, whose appreciation returns the listener to a deepened sense of that experience. The choice of chapter headings inevitably reflects my own preferences; it goes without saying that a survey with a different focus would have resulted in very different ones. (Space prevents me from discussing the migration of polyphony into the New World, for example.) A secondary aim is to make readers aware of some underlying issues and recent debates within research so that they can engage with and critique them for themselves. The most far-reaching is the distinction between what ethnomusicologists call 'emic' and 'etic' approaches to musical culture – that is, the attitudes shared by those within the culture being observed ('emic') and of those observing it from the outside ('etic'). A simple example: my use of the word 'sonority' in preference to 'chord' reflects the fact that modern notions of functional harmony were not pertinent to Renaissance musicians. Historical research into music now embraces the distinction, whose usefulness is evident throughout this book. Beyond these broad aims, each chapter draws on a substantial literature (in some cases a vast one). The bibliography cannot be exhaustive either but is primarily intended as a guide to further reading.

The individual chapters of *The Cambridge History of Fifteenth-Century Music* and *The Cambridge History of Sixteenth-Century Music* offer alternative insights on many of the topics explored here, along with up-to-date and detailed bibliographies.

This book reflects twenty-five years of teaching, thinking about, and performing Renaissance polyphony. My purpose in writing it is to enhance the experience of those who encounter this music.

Chapter 2 | Making polyphony: sources and practice

That making music is an activity is obvious, but in classical music the concert ritual, with its strict division between composer, performer, and audience, obscures the fact. These three functions typically exist in a hierarchical relationship (with the composer on top), and it is rare for any one function to be shared by the same person or group of people at the same time. But the concert ritual characterizes most modern performances of Renaissance polyphony: an audience listens to performers playing or singing a piece of music by a composer, typically from a score. In fact, such a strict division of roles is relatively new within Western music. (Some modern writers use the term 'musicking' to reflect the wealth of possibilities outside this traditional hierarchy.[1]) In this chapter, I consider the principal types of evidence that exist concerning polyphony as an activity, starting with the sources that transmit it in written form, before examining other types of information.

Polyphonic manuscripts: choirbook format

In the modern-day concert, the musical score is the currency of exchange between composer and performer (and, through the latter, the audience). During the Renaissance, score format was rarely used. More commonly, the layout of polyphony reflected its essentially contrapuntal conception, with parts copied out individually. This took two forms, known respectively as 'choirbook' and 'partbook' format.[2] The other essential distinction is technological: before 1501, polyphony was not printed but hand-copied. As with the written word, the shift between manuscript and print culture was gradual: the presentation of music in parts persisted well into the seventeenth century.

In choirbook format, the four voices are laid out separately: the uppermost voice is at the top left-hand side of the double page and the lowest at the bottom right.[3] Illustrations 2.1 and 2.2 show openings from two early sixteenth-century chansonniers (songbooks), the first for three notated voices and the second for four. In music for more than three

Illustration 2.1 La Rue, *Ave sanctissima Maria*
Brussels, Koninklijke Bibliotheek/Bibliothèque Royale, Ms. 228, ff. 1ᵛ–2 (reproduced with permission)

voices, the voice beneath the top one is usually the tenor, which sings the c.f. when there is one. It is distinguished by its longer note-values, and the consequently greater use of 'ligatures', notational shapes that combine several pitches in one symbol. In choirbook format, this layout of

Illustration 2.1 (Cont.)

the voices on the double page (called an opening) is the norm, and presentation is standardized in other ways: voice-names are nearly always given at the start and signalled by a large initial (with the exception of the top voice), and, where the cantus firmus is known, the scribe usually identifies it. In three-voice music, the top voice is often on its own on the left side of the opening, but the same basic principles apply. Sources in choirbook format range from tiny (about the area of a smartphone when closed) to big enough to be read by a dozen singers standing round a lectern. As a rule, those containing sacred music tend to be larger than song sources, and manuscripts destined for use by larger choirs could exceed two square metres when opened.

Destination or intended purpose was the determining factor in a manuscript's appearance. Some manuscripts were intended for use, and others for presentation. In the latter case, parchment (made from treated animal skins) tended to be used in preference to paper. Special care and expense were lavished on appearance, from the neatness and regularity of the copying to the beauty of the decorated initials for voices and the surrounding illuminations. These luxury items were produced to a very high standard by workshops of copyists and illuminators. (Perhaps the best documented is the so-called 'Alamire' workshop active in Flanders in the early sixteenth century, which produced the manuscript shown in Illustration 2.1.[4]) For most sources destined for actual use, paper was the usual medium, but elaborate parchment manuscripts were made for the chapel choirs of wealthier ecclesiastical institutions or courts: it is estimated that the skins of about 112 calves went into making the Eton Choirbook, one of the largest sources of the early sixteenth century.[5] Being much more durable than paper, parchment continued to be preferred for plainchant sources, since the repertoire they contained had far greater longevity and usage.

A few comparatively large chansonniers were clearly made for nobility, but most were small. Possibly the most famous is the astonishing 'Chansonnier Cordiforme', a heart-shaped songbook copied in Savoy in the 1470s for a notoriously dissolute member of the clergy. It surpasses all other surviving songbooks in conception and execution, an ingenious feature being that its shape when opened can be read simultaneously as a larger, stylized heart and as two hearts joined together – singularly appropriate given the repertoire's focus on matters of the heart. Most of the smaller sources in choirbook format were made for private use: a group of parchment songbooks copied in central France in the 1460s and 70s (known collectively as the 'Loire Valley chansonniers') was produced for members of the aspiring middle class, specifically the clerks and notaries who served the courts of the French nobility.[6] In common with many chansonniers, most are too small for several singers to perform from; possibly their owners read the music to themselves or followed the performances of professional musicians.

Another significant category of private user is the professional or semi-professional musician who copied music for personal use or instruction. Copied on paper, such collections vary considerably in size. Some are the work of known individuals working over several years or even decades and spanning hundreds of folios. Many of the collections that survive in this way originate in Germanic territories. A much-studied example is the group of so-called Trent Codices, compiled over a period of twenty years in the mid-fifteenth century, substantially by one Johannes Wiser. The Italian town of Trento, very near the Austrian border, was under Habsburg rule at the time, and 'Wiser' is a Germanic name. Illustration 2.2 shows another of these collections, made by the Swiss organist and composer Fridolin Sicher (c.1490–1546). Typically for this kind of personal archive, Sicher enters the name of the composer at the head of the left-hand leaf. The habit of ascribing pieces to named composers seems to have been the exception rather than the rule in fifteenth-century manuscripts, but it gradually became more widespread, and by the start of the sixteenth century it was commonplace.

This last category raises the question of the sources' circulation and survival. Typically, polyphonic manuscripts consisted of 'gatherings' made up of a number of pages placed on top of each other and folded in two. If the outer-facing sides were left blank, the resulting gathering (also called 'fascicle') could be easily transported without damaging the written pages on the inside. This is the format in which polyphony circulated throughout Europe, transported by riverboat and packhorse along the trade routes that connected the international trade fairs that fuelled European commerce. There are many recorded instances of travelling musicians offering to send music they have just got hold of on their travels to a colleague or employer, and it is from such people that Wiser or Sicher obtained their 'exemplars' (the copies from which they made their own). The annual and seasonal fairs were also key points of dissemination for the nascent print trade, playing a major role when the new technology eventually diversified into polyphony: Trento, for example, was located along one of the most active North–South trade routes, and thus exceptionally well suited to Wiser's purposes.

Polyphonic prints: partbook format

The first polyphonic prints were the initiative of the Venetian printer Ottaviano de' Petrucci (1466–1539), who issued his first collection,

Illustration 2.2 Isaac, *La mi la sol la sol la mi* (beginning)
Sankt Gallen, Stiftsbibliothek, Cod. Sang. Ms. 461, pp. 42–3 (reproduced with permission)

Odhecaton, in 1501.[7] It was the first of three publications showing the influence of manuscript production in two important ways: first, the use of choirbook format and the conventions associated with it, and second, the choice of a sacred work (a motet) to begin what is otherwise a collection of secular music. (This reflects the general habit of placing daily activities under divine protection, such as the saying of 'Grace' before meals.) Within a few years (beginning with *Motetti C* (1504),

Illustration 2.2 (Cont.)

shown in Illustration 2.3), Petrucci began using partbook format as well, where each voice has its own book. While this method of presentation was not unknown to copyists, they much preferred the choirbook format, which retained an allure all of its own. By 1510 Petrucci had a rival in Italy, Andrea Antico, some of whose volumes of sacred music mimicked the layout and appearance of actual choirbooks (for example the *Liber quindecim missarum* of 1516). Whereas Petrucci had adapted the moveable type method for musical characters, printing the musical staves and symbols separately, Antico used the older and more laborious process of

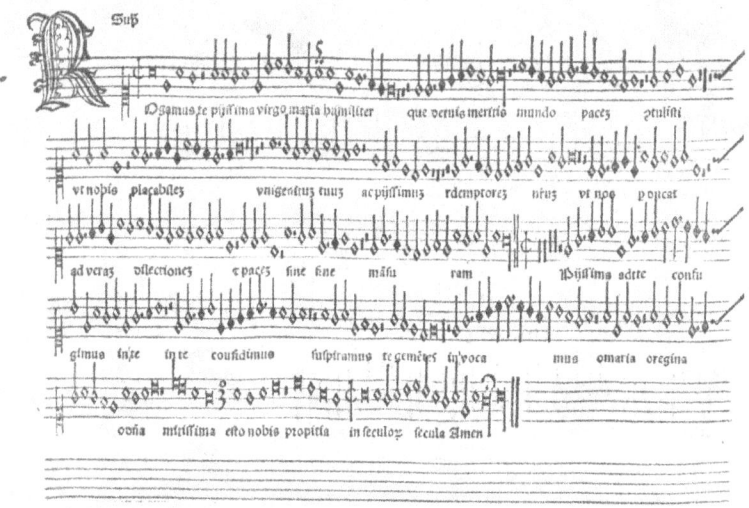

Illustration 2.3 Isaac, *Rogamus te, piissima virgo*
Motetti C (Venice: Petrucci, 1504), discantus partbook, f. 26ᵛ, Bayerische Staatsbibliothek München, Musikabteilung, 4 Mus.pr. 160#Beibd.2 (reproduced with permission)

printing from woodblocks, which allowed for more elaborate presentation. Ultimately, both technologies were superseded with the invention of single-impression printing, in which staves and symbols were printed together (Illustration 2.4). Though not as consistently attractive as double-impression or woodblock printing, it was far more cost-effective and allowed greater quantities of music to be published. The first printer to benefit significantly was the Paris-based Pierre Attaingnant (from 1528), and within a decade several others had joined the fray, in France (Jacques Moderne in Lyons from 1532), Germany (Christian Egenolff in Frankfurt from 1532 and Hieronymus Formschneider in Nuremburg from 1534), and Italy (the Scotto family firm from the mid-1530s and Antonio Gardano in Venice from 1538). Between them they issued hundreds of volumes, setting the pace for music printing throughout the Renaissance. But the elegance of choirbook format guaranteed its survival in print, albeit sporadically; Morales and Palestrina both chose it for their first books of Masses, printed at Rome in 1544 and 1554, respectively.

The advent of music printing was a game changer, not least in establishing the composer as the 'maker' of polyphony par excellence. Some printers had privileged relations with composers whose works they published – Gardano

Illustration 2.4 Isaac, *Missa O praeclara*, 'Patrem'
Liber quindecim missarum (Nuremberg: Petreius, 1539), discantus partbook, LL[i^v],
Bayerische Staatsbibliothek München, Musikabteilung, 4 Mus.pr.159 (reproduced with permission)

with Willaert in Venice, or the Parisian firm Le Roy & Ballard and the Munich printer Adam Berg with Lassus.[8] Print culture also changed the way in which music was consumed. It coincided with growing urbanization and the rise of a city-dwelling class for whom music became a commodity. This is not only borne out by the number of music printers active throughout the Renaissance and the quantity of volumes they produced but also by significant anecdotal evidence of domestic music making. One conversation-book portrays a family taking its music books out after a meal and deciding who should sing which part; in another, two laymen debate the merits of contemporary composers on the way home from hearing Mass.[9] From a relatively specialized activity requiring time and expertise to copy and years of training to perform, polyphony became a pastime and entertainment across a much wider social sphere. The vogue for popular genres (such as the so-called 'Parisian chanson' or its Italian counterpart, the madrigal) did not exclude performance of sacred music in the home; some publications offered pieces in a variety of genres and languages, sacred and secular, sometimes by one named composer (in France, where such collections were especially popular, these were known as *meslanges* or 'miscellanies'). The change in audience is also reflected in the music itself: like the Parisian chanson, early madrigals tend towards directness of expression, with the melodic interest centred on the top voices, minimal contrapuntal outlay in the lower ones, and comparatively narrow ranges. That they are easy to sing and sight-read accounts for their popularity; broadly speaking, music after about 1520 lends itself more readily than earlier music to amateur performance.

But manuscript culture did not cease because of print. Some members of the nobility affected to disdain printed books because they could afford to pay scribes and illuminators to produce luxury items for their exclusive use. Greater and lesser ecclesiastical institutions continued to produce choirbooks for their liturgies, and musically literate individuals for instruction and pleasure; but tellingly, these copies were sometimes taken from prints – a trend noticeable even from the time of Petrucci's early publications.

Print culture brought with it new habits that significantly shape our knowledge of Renaissance music. By 1500, music scribes were more likely than before to name the composers of the music they copied; print culture accentuated the tendency, as printers became aware that the names of the more celebrated composers helped sell their wares. The number of anonymous pieces diminished as less scrupulous printers made ascriptions with little regard for accuracy. (For this reason, ascriptions in printed volumes – especially those to famous composers – tend to be treated with greater caution than manuscript ones.) On the other hand, because the overwhelming majority of prints include a date of publication, they provide a terminal date of composition for the pieces they transmit. In comparison, dating manuscripts is far more complicated and nearly always conjectural, for music scribes rarely dated their work. Whereas our knowledge of musical style before 1500 is based on a web of interdependent hypotheses, from the onset of print culture we are on somewhat surer ground.

Other ways in which sources reveal information about the music they contain will be considered in the following chapters; but as witnesses to the activity of making polyphony, they cast the matter of extemporization in a singular light (and vice-versa).

Extemporized polyphony

So much polyphony was printed and copied during the Renaissance that it comes as a surprise to learn that polyphony was also routinely extemporized.[10] Perhaps it is the sheer volume of extant polyphony that has led modern commentators to downplay the evidence in this direction until very recently. Another contributory factor is the marginalization of improvised practices within Western music, which coincided historically with the growth of interest in early repertories. That marginalization is a relatively new phenomenon; the age of the composer-improviser is not so far removed from our own. But there is plenty of evidence for extemporized practice in the Renaissance.

Broadly speaking, contemporary witnesses use relatively few terms to designate composed polyphony. One of the most common is the Latin *res facta*, meaning 'a thing that is [or rather, has been] made'. Significantly, the term emphasizes the end product (notated polyphony) rather than the activity that gives rise to it (composing). By contrast, the number of terms designating extemporized polyphony is vast: in English alone, there is 'faburden', 'square', 'descant', 'gymel', and 'counter', to name just a few. These last three indicate the singing of a new voice in relation to a given one: 'descant' refers to a voice above, 'gymel' to a voice in the same range (derived from the Latin word for 'twin'), and 'counter' to a voice below. In other words, they emphasize the activity rather than the product. Some of them have equivalents in other languages, but others do not; another telling sign is the comparative difficulty with which they were absorbed into Latin, the 'professional' language of singers of polyphony (the phrase 'singing *super librum*' ['on the book'] is one of few exceptions). The same term may occur in contexts that clearly imply distinct things, or equivalent terms may denote practices that must have sounded very different; other terms survive with definitions so vague that we can only guess at what was involved, let alone how they might have sounded. All this points to the existence of localized practices with no known equivalents elsewhere.

Although teachers throughout the Renaissance clearly recognize a distinction between composition and extemporization, many state that the two forms of polyphony are not separate but complementary. (I use the term 'extemporization' rather than the more common 'improvisation' because the latter is often taken to imply that music is made up on the spot, without any written support.) The vast majority of extemporized performances involved a degree of preparation and conformed to the contrapuntal rules that apply in written polyphony, which performers had absorbed from childhood. Many extemporized practices also used written aids as a point of reference. The distinction between extemporizing and singing from notation is therefore less clear-cut than may first appear. Renaissance musicians regarded polyphony not as a single practice but as a complex or a continuum of related ones. Some writers just say that composition and extemporization, though distinct, are 'essentially one and the same'. Of course, the most important distinction between the two is that composed polyphony survives in a form that is recoverable to a greater degree, and in far greater quantity, than its extemporized equivalents. It is sometimes said that the surviving sources for composed polyphony are like the visible tip of an iceberg because of the amount of music known to have been lost; the comparison is truer still if one takes account of extemporized practices.

The 'given voice' against which others were extemporized was most often plainchant, a repertory in which singers were trained from childhood and would have known from memory.[11] For the vast majority of extemporized practices, notated chant was almost always the point of reference, for example in the English method known as 'sighting', in which imperfect consonances were sung by mentally transposing the pitch-level of the plainchant in front of them. The resulting music might be very simple and could easily have been extemporized from memory, and yet the term 'singing on the book' is so widespread that the visual support was plainly seen as integral, not to say essential. The simplest example of extemporization (according to contemporary writers) is faburden, which involves a voice singing consistently a fourth above the chant and another alternating thirds and fifths below it (Example 2.1). This style had a continental equivalent, 'fauxbourdon' (a transliteration from English). Other methods involved more complex mental gymnastics against the chant. Although certain writers record these processes clearly (especially the Portuguese composer and theorist Vicente Lusitano (d.1561) and the Italian Pietro Cerone (1566–1625)), the descriptions of church records throughout Europe suggest a wealth of local practices whose distinctions went beyond those described by contemporary writers. In general, the style or technique used depended on the importance or solemnity of the occasion, but it is not always clear how this was reflected (that is, whether polyphony was more complex on special occasions or just sounded fuller). The perceived

Example 2.1 Plainchant hymn, *Veni creator spiritus* in faburden (first two phrases). Translation: Come, Holy Ghost, Creator/Visit the minds of those who acknowledge you...

hierarchy among extemporized techniques reflects not just their degree of difficulty or adherence to contrapuntal rules but also social factors: some church authorities looked down on fauxbourdon because it too closely resembled the polyphonic singing of the peasantry and 'common people'. Genres that deliberately imitate popular idioms, such as the villanella and the strambotto, feature linear progressions otherwise avoided in composition. Their infiltration into print culture shows that the boundaries between different registers of polyphony were porous; equally, polyphony was not the sole preserve of trained specialists.

Much of the information concerning extemporization comes to us in the form of church records. All too often these are frustratingly vague since, like most other documents we scrutinize for information about polyphony, they were not drawn up for the purpose. On the rare occasions when they have been, we get a sense of the proficiency and specialization of which expert polyphonists were capable. In 1604, the cathedral of Toledo was auditioning for a new chapel-master.[12] The church officials drew up a list of twenty tests to which each candidate would submit. Opening a choirbook with a four-voice piece, for example, he would be asked to extemporize a fifth voice while four singers sang the notated parts; another exercise was to extemporize a voice against a plainchant while 'signing' a third and a fourth voice to other singers in real time (by means of hand-signals using the so-called 'Guidonian Hand', discussed in Chapter 4); yet another involved extemporizing a canon against a written voice. Such feats are widely echoed in other testimony. A century earlier, a musician at the court of Mantua reported from Venice in c.1494 and 1505 on instrumental performances of pieces by named composers, to which he had added extra voices for the occasion.[13] (Evidently, these skills were not the sole preserve of singers.) It is not uncommon for pieces to be transmitted with an extra voice in one or more sources: one of the copies of Josquin's *Miserere* has an added voice by the renowned singer Antoine Colebault (nicknamed Bidon). Clearly, it is not the feat itself that is exceptional but the fact that it was written down and survives. These additions were very likely the result of extemporization, which was not an exceptional skill but part of a professional musician's armoury. Hair-raising they may seem to us, but might not Renaissance musicians be equally astounded at modern-day conductors or repetiteurs reading or playing a Mahler score at sight, with its multiple key signatures, transpositions, phrasings, dynamics, and other performance instructions? One should remember that Renaissance singers were trained from an early age in the systems that made such things possible, performing them day in, day out.[14]

The audition tests at Toledo Cathedral and other comparable situations had a practical purpose: should singers lose their place in the performance, the chapel-master could instantly step in. Effective extemporization was a matter of internalizing the melodic formulae appropriate to one's voice part and matching them to the plainchant. Contemporaries tell us that the most successful ensembles were those whose singers had been together a long time and were familiar with each other's ranges and vocal habits, as in any chamber music. Depending on the type of technique, a greater or lesser degree of co-ordination was required, which was entrusted to a singer (usually called 'tenorist', regardless of his actual voice-type) who led the performance.

From composed to extemporized polyphony (or vice-versa?)

The question of preparation and co-ordination leads back to the relationship of composition to extemporization. Contemporary writers held different views; some regarded extemporization as the lynchpin of proficiency in polyphony while others valued composition more highly. The latter attitude was especially prevalent in German-speaking lands, where extemporization was seen as opening the doors of church and court to the 'uncouth' polyphony of the lower classes. (German writers' disapproval of extemporization is confirmed by the lack of documentary evidence for it in church records, in contrast to the situation in the rest of Europe.) In the end we are left with the chicken-and-egg question: given the amount of written music in circulation, why was extemporization considered necessary? A clue is the fact that these church documents stipulating how and when polyphony should be sung usually refer to a manner of extemporized performance but almost never to a written piece, and, as we shall see, not until the close of the fifteenth century did composition become a salaried activity. So perhaps it is more to the point to reverse the question: since polyphony was routinely extemporized, why the need to write anything down? (Plenty of the music that comes down to us could easily have been made up on the spot.) The later chapters of this book offer some answers to the question, but there is still much to learn about how these techniques of extemporization were taught. It may be significant that so many of them relied on notated cues of one sort or other: the visual dimension was plainly essential in shaping musicians' conception of aural practice. Then there are numerous examples of written polyphony throughout the Renaissance that refer, whether implicitly or explicitly, to extemporization.[15] Early examples are the Communion of the *Missa Sancti Jacobi* (c.1425) by Guillame Du Fay (c.1397–1474), for which the source gives the indication 'fauxbourdon', and the initial sections of the *Requiem* of Johannes Ockeghem (c.1425–97). Fauxbourdon texture in particular (in modern terms, consecutive 6-3 chords) persists throughout Renaissance polyphony and is frequently associated with lamentation or representations of antiquity. The meaning of these references, which has been debated for decades, is easier to interpret when we consider that extemporization was routine: reference to it was not a matter of laziness or expediency but a reflection of written and extemporized composition as two sides of the same coin. Where extemporization required singers to reproduce internalized contrapuntal procedures in live performance, composing allowed musicians to refine or sharpen musical ideas, 'inventions' (the closest one can get to the Italian term *fantasie*) that went beyond those internalized procedures and required working out in detail. Conversely, several teachers advise that singers wishing to gain proficiency in extemporization should compose as much as possible and that the best composers made the best improvisers. For all that the two sorts of polyphony were viewed differently by different writers, the distinction between them was perceived as qualitative but not essential.

Chapter 3 | Makers of polyphony

In the previous chapter we considered polyphony as an activity; here the focus shifts to the people who made it. Who were they, what lives did they lead, and what was their place in society? How did that society regard their music and what was its place in society more generally? How did these issues evolve in the course of the Renaissance? These questions are especially pertinent, since many of the social and cultural assumptions about music and musicians that took shape in the Renaissance resonate to this day.

Renaissance attitudes towards music: theory and practice

The fundamental distinction between music before and after the Renaissance is its status as a science.[1] This conception was transmitted to the Middle Ages primarily through the writings of the Roman philosopher and statesman, Boethius (d.524).[2] Medieval pedagogy recognized seven 'liberal arts': the language-based *trivium* (grammar, logic, and rhetoric) and the *quadrivium* (arithmetic, geometry, astronomy, and music), governed by number and measurement. Music's membership of the group was founded on the observation that the most perfect consonant intervals are related by simple arithmetic ratios – a basic acoustic fact that can be verified by any string player. To play the octave above an open string, the string is stopped at its midpoint so that the proportion of whole string to stopped string is 2:1; for the perfect fifth the proportion is 3:2, for the perfect fourth it is 4:3, for the major third (5:4), the minor third (6:5), and so on. According to classical teaching, the same simple proportions governed the relationships between planetary orbits in astronomy (a notion expressed in the well-known phrase 'the music of the spheres'); thus, music was regarded as an audible manifestation of cosmic order and, by extension, divine creation. This audible dimension encompassed pitch, rhythm, and duration: thus, the simple proportion 3:2 could be expressed as an interval (the perfect fifth), a rhythm (the simultaneous sounding of three subdivisions of the beat against two), or a tempo relationship (between adjacent sections of a piece). The Florentine polymath Leon Battista Alberti (d.1472) referred to architecture, a practical discipline based on the same numerical proportions, as 'frozen music', and he gave music first place among the liberal arts. Its place in the *quadrivium* conferred on music tangible social prestige: the highly influential training manual for gentlefolk, Baldassare Castiglione, *The Book of the Courtier* (pub. 1528), named a working knowledge of polyphony, no less than familiarity with literature, as the hallmark of good breeding and education.[3] Perhaps the most eloquent testimony to the status of music is the number of crowned heads whose musical interests extended to performance and even composition, not least the Tudor monarchs Henry VIII (r.1509–47) and Elizabeth I (r.1558–1603) as well as Charles the Bold, Duke of Burgundy (r.1467–77), and his descendants of the Habsburg dynasty. Their patronage fuelled the wider fashion for music in the growing urban environment, especially among the aspiring classes of merchants and notaries. In no period of Western history has music been regarded more positively.

Throughout the Renaissance, the numerical basis of music remained a point of reference, especially in the universities, which were founded on the primacy of the seven liberal arts. But it was not uncontested. The universities themselves were criticized for their unwillingness to move beyond medieval scholasticism. Some teachers pay little more than lip-service to the 'music of the spheres', being more concerned with music's effects on humans, bodily, intellectually, and spiritually. Tinctoris devoted an entire treatise to the beneficial effects of music on its hearers. This gradual shift in focus from the cosmic to the individual subject is a key feature of the period, which led to several challenges to music's position in society. The mathematician Luca Pacioli (d.1517) advocated music's removal from the *quadrivium* altogether. A more nuanced but equally radical view is that of his direct contemporary Leonardo da Vinci (d.1519). While clearly valuing music, he was keen to stake the claims of his favoured medium, painting, as the superior art. He did so on the grounds that painting pertained to sight, in his view a more important sense than hearing, and that unlike painting, which permanently fixes a point of view, musical sounds vanish once sounded. Leonardo's argument is remarkable for the importance he attached to the senses as both the means and the object of intellectual enquiry (implicitly disregarding music's theoretical claims as a numerical science) and for his claim that a practical art could be considered superior to music – both radical positions. As in much else, Leonardo was ahead of his time, for these lines of questioning were fundamental to attitudes towards music in later periods. In the later Renaissance, the promotion of music as an agent of public morals (in the broadest sense) was a central premise of the influential artistic and intellectual circles known as 'academies' (notably in Florence,

Rome, and Paris). Others considered music's capacity to excite the passions, linking different modes to different moods and the four bodily 'humours' that were held to determine people's personalities. But this physiological line of enquiry was not necessarily to music's advantage: ever since Plato, the power of music to rouse the emotions was as much suspected as applauded. At the turn of the seventeenth century, some writers went further, denying music any moral value. This sowed the seeds of a more general suspicion of music as an intangible category of uncertain moral quality, culminating in the ambivalent evaluations of Immanuel Kant (d.1804) and Wilhelm Friedrich Hegel (d.1831). During the Renaissance, research into the 'four humours' was closely related to alchemy, and thus the study of magic, which co-existed alongside what we would regard as properly 'scientific' investigations (a distinction that most contemporary thinkers would not have recognized). Music's power 'to charm the sense and captivate the mind' (in the words of Purcell's 1692 *Ode to St Cecilia*) related as much to supernatural phenomena as to the rational world.[4]

While music's standing in the Renaissance rested on its membership of the *quadrivium*, Tinctoris' writings emphasize that it was equally valued for what would later be called its aesthetic properties. Alongside its theoretical dimension, music fulfilled as many functions across all classes of society as we recognize today. This practical dimension was implicit in post-Boethian terminology, which distinguished between 'musica mundana' (also called 'musica universalis', the 'music of the spheres'), 'musica humana' (the harmony of the human body in a physical and spiritual sense), and 'musica instrumentalis' (sounding music, including – rather confusingly – vocal music). But the Platonic tension between music as a science of number and as cultural practice is a persistent undercurrent throughout the Middle Ages and the Renaissance. One manifestation of this was social: the lower class (the 'third estate') was distinguished from the nobility and the clergy (the 'first' and 'second estates') by having to work for a living, and the menial status associated with manual labour applied (theoretically at least) to even the best-paid and renowned painters or sculptors, and by extension to most instrumentalists and popular entertainers. Most makers of polyphony held positions within the church, and were thus notionally exempt from this prejudice, but only up to a point. Writers (known as *musici*), who typically held church positions, affected to disdain their singer colleagues (*cantores*), portraying them as uneducated. A second point of tension concerned the role of music in religious observance: echoing the church's disapproval of sensual enjoyment, some regarded any music other than plainsong (traditionally ascribed to divine inspiration of Pope Gregory I (r.590–604)) as a 'gateway' to more suggestive pastimes such as dancing. In 1324–5, Pope John XXII (r.1316–34) had denounced the use of the most recent polyphonic style in church. Two centuries later, the influential Dutch thinker and essayist Desiderius Erasmus (d.1536) echoed these criticisms, alleging that paying for polyphony was an unconscionable waste of church funds.[5] Certain Reformation thinkers put these concerns into action, Jean Calvin (d.1564) the most prominent among them: in his order of service, anything other than unison congregational singing was banned.

But the extent of hostility directed at polyphony and its practitioners can be overstated. The musical literacy of the nobility extended to prominent churchmen and religious leaders. Pope Leo X (r.1513–21), a member of the ruling Medici family of Florence, received an excellent musical training. On the side of the Reformation, Calvin's hostility was counterbalanced by the enthusiastic advocacy of Martin Luther (d.1546). Himself a more than competent singer and lutenist (and occasional composer), he corresponded with both Catholic and Reformed composers. For him, the use of simple chorale melodies in congregational singing was motivated by practical considerations (the faithful needed to memorize the music easily and recognize the words); he would surely have agreed with Tinctoris that 'music [including polyphony] excites souls to devotion'.[6] The Catholic Church's response to the challenge of the Reformation in musical matters was nuanced. On the one hand, the deliberations of the Council of Trent (1545–63) acknowledged that the insistence of Reformed faiths on textual intelligibility in music for worship was reasonable. On the other, the music of the Counter-Reformation represents a negation of the Reformation's functional attitude: whereas the latter was geared towards the congregation's conscious participation, the aesthetic of the Counter-Reformation transports the faithful to rapt contemplation of the divine presence (and, not coincidentally, the splendour of its earthly representatives). Both responses find musical expression in the music of the time, be it Palestrina's *Missa Papae Marcelli*, or Byrd in his more optimistic moments. Despite the hostile climate in which he worked (or rather precisely because of it), Byrd's settings of Propers for the feast of Saints Peter and Paul proclaim a church universal and triumphant.

The social status of those who made polyphony has been mentioned several times in passing; it is time to take a closer look at them.

Singer-clerics before 1500

In common with most people not born into the nobility, little is known of the early lives of Renaissance musicians (let alone their birthdates), but some patterns are discernible.[7] From the early fifteenth century, the training of choirboys within religious foundations gathered momentum. Many of the boys were from social classes affluent enough to donate to the church to fund their education. Many were illegitimate: Du Fay was probably the son of a priest, a not uncommon occurrence. The arrangement benefited nearly all concerned: the father provided for offspring he could not raise himself, and the church washed its dirty linen in-house (the mother's interests seldom figured in the equation). Being received into the church gave the boys an education and the possibility of a career. At an early stage, those with special aptitudes were singled out for further training – whether musically or through study at university (and in some cases, both).

When his voice broke (which happened later than nowadays), the young man might continue at his home institution, but the more gifted often sought positions elsewhere. There were two principal alternatives: the first was to remain in the church, which provided for its singers through a range of positions, some of them rather onerous (the duties of a 'succentor', responsible for the provision of music, could include training and housing the choirboys and teaching local children). Especially valued singers were allocated 'benefices', which notionally involved responsibility for a parish or other administration.[8] Crucially, the church allowed such positions to be held *in absentia*, whereby a local cleric was paid a portion of the income to do the work 'on the ground' and the beneficiary pocketed the rest. What had begun as an exceptional measure quickly became a huge loophole; the higher a cleric rose in the church, the more benefices he accumulated. He could even swap them with others, as in a game of Monopoly. Surviving documents show that these exchanges could involve several individuals and multiple posts, and that the means used to secure a coveted benefice were not always in keeping with ideals of Christian charity. (They do however make entertaining reading.[9]) These machinations often had a practical goal: it was usual for singers to retire to their homeland, having secured one or several local benefices. The second alternative was to join the court or retinue of a prince, lord, or high-ranking cleric. A well-appointed private chapel (including singers) was regarded as a status symbol among the high nobility. By 1400, the royal and ducal chapels of France, England, and Burgundy, the Imperial Court, and the papal chapel were already well established. In the following decades, their example was copied throughout Europe – particularly in Italy, where city-states came under the control of strong, rich, or influential families (the Sforza in Milan, the Medici in Florence, the Este in Ferrara) who bought or bluffed their way into nobility. Fabulously wealthy but insecure, these colourful princelings compensated for their status envy with ostentatious displays of artistic patronage, promising huge salaries to the best singers or poaching them from fellow princes (at the risk of diplomatic incidents: only hunting dogs attracted greater competition). The chapels of Galeazzo Maria Sforza of Milan (r.1466–76) and Ercole d'Este of Ferrara (r.1471–1505) rivalled those of more established courts. But a ruler's death or sudden financial difficulties could cause a renowned chapel to be disbanded or drastically curtailed almost overnight, as happened after Galeazzo's assassination. Though less lucrative, a church position was more secure, since the church sprang eternal and never went bankrupt.

Court and church were distinct institutions but part of the same broad system of patronage. Senior prelates were typically the younger sons of noble families, with their own courts and private chapels. Singers working at court were also clerics – not necessarily priests, but members of the orders below priesthood, which allowed them to hold benefices obtained for them by their princely patrons. The high nobility also founded religious institutions, creating sustained ties over centuries: founded by King Louis IX (r.1226–70), the Sainte-Chapelle in Paris maintained a regular exchange of personnel with the royal chapel throughout the Renaissance. The most significant fifteenth-century composers were on familiar terms with their noble patrons. Until his death, Du Fay remained attached to Cambrai Cathedral, where he had been a choirboy, but in his will he left several books of his works to Charles the Bold. The most prominent composer of the next generation, Johannes Ockeghem, divided his time between court service as the head of the French royal chapel and the duties of treasurer of the wealthiest abbey in Christendom, Saint-Martin of Tours.[10] This latter position was in the gift of the king, who must have appreciated his musical accomplishments, since on two recorded occasions the composer presented King Charles VII with new music (including a 'richly illuminated song') as a New Year's gift. Whether Ockeghem owed the appointment to his musical reputation is uncertain (the post was purely administrative), but he must have had considerable charm and the skills of a diplomat, for he participated in at least one embassy to Spain. One court document names him as a royal counsellor.

All this suggests a degree of worldliness. We should not infer too much about the religious beliefs and personal attitudes of our singer-clergymen from their education and career. Some may have been genuinely devout and others more conventionally pious, but standards of morality among the clergy were notoriously lax. The chapter acts of religious institutions relate numerous instances of absenteeism, drunkenness, gambling, keeping concubines, ball games during church services, not to mention neglect or outright mistreatment of choirboys in their charge. The penalties for misbehaviour in princely chapel regulations suggest that things were not much better there. A disincentive to good behaviour was the fact that the clergy were exempt from civil law. A particularly juicy case is that of Ockeghem's colleague, Antoine Busnoys (c.1430–92), excommunicated in 1461 for having repeatedly instigated the group beating of a fellow priest in the cloister of Saint-Gatien of Tours 'until the blood ran' (according to the record of excommunication). This was not the only instance of Busnoys behaving badly: a clutch of his songs relates to a probable affair with one Jacqueline de Hacqueville, the wife of a Parisian member of parliament.[11] Again, this was hardly atypical of Renaissance clergy; Busnoys' case is exceptional only because it concerns one of the most significant composers of the fifteenth century; but the Hacqueville episode reminds us that this red-blooded cleric was also a fine poet, who corresponded in verse with one of the foremost writers of the day, Jean Molinet (also a composer of some ability). Jacobus Clemens (c.1510–55/6) was turned down as a prospective employee by the Emperor Maximilian II on grounds of dissolute behaviour (hence the composer's tongue-in-cheek nickname, 'non Papa' – 'not the Pope', though it must be said that most Renaissance popes were very far from being saints).

At the Reformation, some composers were forced to declare for one religion or another, regardless of their personal beliefs, or risk losing a lucrative post. Before the use of the vernacular within worship became peculiarly associated with Reformed ideas, interest in it extended to the arch-Catholic Imperial and French courts. Thomas Stoltzer (c.1480–1526), one of the period's finest German-speaking composers, reported having written a polyphonic setting of Psalm 37, *Erzürne dich nicht*, at the request of the Habsburg Queen Mary of Hungary (d.1558), sister of the arch-Catholic Emperor Charles V (r.1519–56). In the same document he expressed admiration for the beauty of the words, but, as his comments were addressed to a prospective Lutheran employer, this cannot be taken as firm evidence of Protestant convictions. In England, the three surviving children of Henry VIII succeeded each other in just over a decade, first the proto-Puritan Edward VI (r.1547–53), then the arch-Catholic Mary I (r.1553–8). Each change of regime led to fresh upheaval in church music, and it was only under their more pragmatic half-sister Elizabeth I that stability returned. Byrd famously stuck to his Catholic convictions, and it was only Elizabeth's protection that saved him from serious trouble. Others, like the Huguenot Claude Goudimel (d.1572), murdered in the St Bartholomew's Day Massacres, were not so lucky.

A sense of corporate identity

For many singer-clerics, then, taking holy orders was often a means to an end – a career as a singer. It is no accident that the vernacular terms describing extemporized polyphony should spring up in greatest number during the fifteenth century, when the number of choir schools increased exponentially. The fact that so many of these terms resisted translation into Latin marks them out as the parlance of the singers themselves. This 'singers' jargon' is an expression of corporate identity, related to the urban guild culture of the late Middle Ages and Renaissance (it is worth recalling that instrumentalists already had guilds of their own and that singers of plainchant and polyphony were regarded as distinct groups). This sense was shared with others, not least by church officials with whom they came into daily contact and whose comments are not always flattering; one often gets the impression that the singers were left to choose what they should sing with little outside interference.[12] Bonnie J. Blackburn has drawn attention to a contemporary manuscript copy of a motet by Pierre de La Rue (c.1460–1518), *Ave sanctissima Maria* (see Illustration 2.1 above, pp. 10–11), which includes a depiction of the Virgin on a crescent moon with the sun at her back, surrounded by angels. Blackburn relates this iconography to a dispensation of Pope Sixtus IV (r.1471–84) granting anyone who said the prayer *Ave sanctissima Maria* while gazing at such a picture 11,000 years' remission from purgatory. This papal 'indulgence' (as it was known) therefore applied to the singers every time they performed La Rue's motet from this choirbook.[13] The surprising conclusion that singers sang for themselves as much as for their patrons or coreligionists provides a context for the notational codes, riddles, and other games that would have been unintelligible to any but them.

Example 3.1 Compère, *Omnium bonorum plena*, second part (excerpt). Translation: And Ockeghem, Desprez, Courbet, Hemart, Faugues and Molinet/Also Regis, all those who sing [to you], along with me, the praying Loÿset Compère...

There is also plenty of musical evidence for the singers' sense of themselves as a group. Clearest of all is the series of so-called 'singers' motets' stretching back to the previous century. Renaissance examples included *Omnium bonorum plena/De tous biens plaine* by Loÿset Compère (c.1445–1518) and *Mater floreat, florescat* by Pierre Moulu (c.1484–c.1550), which list well-known figures alongside others who cannot be identified (Example 3.1). These pieces were probably intended for gatherings attended by at least some of those named. Josquin's *Illibata Dei virgo nutrix* concludes with a plea to the Virgin Mary to protect 'those who sing her name'; although no individual is identified, the composer's name appears in the text as an acrostic. A unique case of a living individual being memorialized is Busnoys' motet, *In hydraulis*, dedicated to his elder colleague Ockeghem, who is likened to 'a new Orpheus'. (It is no coincidence that the structure of Josquin's *Illibata* is closely modelled on *In hydraulis*.) Still more common is the commemoration of composers at their deaths, which dates back at least to Machaut (1377). Ockeghem's ballade *Mort tu as navré* is a tribute to his

Example 3.2 Du Fay, *Ave regina celorum III*, second part (excerpt). Translation: Have mercy on the suppliant Du Fay.

older colleague (and possible mentor), the poet and composer Binchois. Josquin's lament for Ockeghem, *Nymphes des bois/Requiem*, enjoins a group of colleagues, 'Josquin, Brumel, Pierchon [i.e. Pierre de La Rue], [and] Compère', to mourn the dead master. In turn, there were several laments on Josquin's death, and a chain of memorials thereafter: Antoine de Févin by his colleague at the French royal chapel, Jean Mouton; Clemens non Papa by the chapel-master of the Imperial Court, Jacobus Vaet; Adrian Willaert by Cipriano de Rore; and Thomas Tallis by William Byrd. An especially well-documented case of self-memorialization is that of Du Fay, several of whose late works were intended to facilitate his passage to the afterlife. He requested that his Requiem Mass (now lost) be performed on the day after his death; and for his actual deathbed he composed an especially elaborate motet, the four-voice *Ave regina celorum*, whose text includes a number of interpolations, requesting the Virgin to 'have mercy on the beseeching Du Fay' (Example 3.2).[14] His *Missa Ave regina celorum* (*c*.1472) draws substantially on this motet, including the key passage just mentioned, which is quoted exactly in the Agnus dei. This was to be sung at his annual commemoration, for which he left a substantial sum in his will. To modern sensibilities this may smack of self-aggrandizement, but making preparations for death and the afterlife was expected of any Christian of substance. And Du Fay, the friend of princes, plainly saw himself in those terms.

Singers or composers?

Their clerical status notwithstanding, our singers typically defined themselves as singers first and foremost: it is what they were paid to do.[15] What they were *not* paid to do (at least not contractually until the turn of the sixteenth century) was compose. As clerics, they differed from craftsmen (painters, sculptors, and the like) who engaged in manual work, but there was a further distinction: even where a regular salary was involved, a craftsman's employment stipulated the production of objects whose ownership and use were transferred to a patron or institution. In the era before music printing, the notion of musical work was in its infancy and had neither the force nor the connotations that it later acquired (I explore this idea further in Chapter 7). Consequently, the notion of its ownership simply did not apply. Because polyphony could be copied, it could be performed far from its place of origin. A Mass could be performed anywhere, and if the text of a motet or chanson referred to people or events that had no local relevance, it could simply be changed. (Thus, Josquin's renowned *Missa Hercules dux Ferrariae*, composed in honour of Duke Ercole d'Este of Ferrara, had its name changed to 'Philippus rex Castiliae' and even 'Federicus dux Saxoniae' when copies were made for those rulers, even though the inscription of Ercole's name within the music itself was integral to the Mass's design (see Chapter 13). (The notion that the Mass 'belonged' to Ercole in the sense that he might own an altarpiece had little pertinence.) Besides, polyphony could be extemporized and require no composer at all. Essentially, composition was a by-product of the singer's trade. Payment records confirm this: the highest-paid members were not those who composed but those who had the best voices or held the role of 'tenorist'. Although paid commissions are not unheard of (a payment is recorded to Francesco Landini (c.1325–97) for composing five motets in 1379), these appear as generic gifts in exchange for services rendered. Most tellingly of all, only after 1500 does the term 'composer' gain common currency.

That is not to say that composers were not valued. The fame of Guillaume de Machaut (c.1300–77) rested on his compositions as well as his poetry, and, like Du Fay or Ockeghem a century later, he was on good terms with his patrons. In 1487, Ercole d'Este requested the chapter of the Church of St Donatian's in Bruges to give its choirmaster, Jacob Obrecht, permission to visit his court, citing his particular admiration for the composer's music. Nearly twenty years later, Ercole succeeded in appointing first Josquin, then finally Obrecht, as his choirmaster: in both cases it is their skill at composing that attracted him. These appointments are roughly contemporary with the first known instance of a composer being paid a salary to compose (1496), that of Henricus Isaac at the Imperial Court at Innsbruck.[16] Around the same time (1503), Isaac's patron, Maximilian I, paid Obrecht for a 'Missa Regina celi' (almost certainly the Mass that survives under the name *Sub tuum presidium*). This last case is just as remarkable because the document implies that this was a commission and actually names the work, which is extremely rare. It is no accident that these 'firsts', clustered around the turn of the sixteenth century, should coincide with the launch of printed polyphony, which established composed polyphony and the names of famous composers as marketable commodities.

A final point concerning fifteenth-century singer-composers is their place of origin. It is striking how many came from a narrow geographical area comprising what is now northern France, Belgium, and the Netherlands. Though the reasons for this are still debated, a number of related social conditions must have played a part – notably a concentration of thriving urban economies in which taxation, gifts, and endowments supported large ecclesiastical institutions with a tradition of training choirboys in polyphony. In Italy they were known as *oltremontani* ('those from beyond the mountains', i.e. the Alps) or, more specifically, *I fiamminghi* ('the Flemings'). As with most terms designating foreigners in this period, these labels are approximate: a fair proportion of our singer-composers were not Flemish but francophone. The modern term 'Franco-Flemish' comes closest to describing the group as a whole. In any case, these terms (or their equivalents in other languages) designate a group that crisscrossed Europe for several generations. The first one of note, Johannes Ciconia (c.1370–1412), born in Liège, was in Italy by 1400, and the last wave of *oltremontani* to achieve a significant impact was the generation of Orlande de Lassus (c.1532–94) and his colleague Philippe de Monte (c.1520–1603). Both found early employment in Italy but ended their careers in prestigious posts, Lassus at Munich and de Monte at the Imperial Court (Vienna and Prague). Until relatively recently, scholarship has tended to view the music of the *oltremontani* as embodying a dominant, 'central' (i.e. 'Franco-Flemish') tradition at the expense of 'lateral' (i.e. local) ones. This obscures the fact that England, Spain, Italy, Czech, and German-speaking lands (to mention just these) had traditions of oral and notated polyphony whose distinctive features are still identifiable today. The so-called Speciálník

Codex, copied near Prague at the turn of the sixteenth century, is a fascinating document, in which international 'hits' by Josquin and his contemporaries rub shoulders with music that seems conservative in comparison but which retained a strong local currency. Any perception of local traits was balanced by exceptional fluidity of stylistic exchange, as singers and their music circulated with surprising facility. But makers of polyphony from 'beyond the Alps' were consistently celebrated for their ability to extemporize, which may have been the key to their collective reputation. Naturally that esteem extended to their compositions: the music that circulated most widely in the fifteenth and early sixteenth century was the polyphony of the *oltremontani*.

Isaac's appointment as imperial *Hofkomponist* ('court composer') was a watershed in another respect: he was not a churchman but a married layman. Over the course of the sixteenth century the status and career profile of the most sought-after makers of polyphony would diversify considerably: from near-exclusively male singers (and usually clerics), they increasingly included laymen; well-paid, salaried, instrumentalists whose renown was increasingly comparable to their singer colleagues; women, both in holy orders and at the courts of the nobility; and entrepreneurs, actively disseminating their music and accepting commissions from multiple patrons. Finally, whereas the most prominent composers around 1500 were singer-clerics, by 1600 most were instrumentalists.

Composers in the age of print

When Petrucci began his printing enterprise, the generation of composers born around 1450 was fully established. This was a remarkable period: for the first time in recorded history, the pre-eminent composers of a single generation can no longer be counted on the fingers of one hand. In 1502, Petrucci issued the first print devoted to a single composer, a volume of Masses by Josquin. So successful was it that he reprinted it not once but twice, and eventually he followed it up with two other Josquin Mass volumes. In the meantime, Petrucci issued nearly a dozen single-authored Mass collections by other composers, none of whom can have been born much earlier than 1450: Isaac, Obrecht, La Rue, Brumel, Agricola, Weerbeke (also known as Gaspar), Mouton, de Orto, and Ghiselin, who are sometimes reductively lumped together under the soubriquet of the 'Josquin generation' (a volume was also devoted to the rather younger Antoine de Févin). More recent writing on these composers tends to recognize them as personalities in their own right. Unlike the volumes devoted to Josquin, none of them appears to have been reprinted, and none was followed up with a second instalment; but their production suggests that the popularity of polyphony now extended to an interest in the works of individuals.

With the onset of single-impression type, single-author collections were issued in greater numbers, though typically in the more popular secular genres. Jacob Arcadelt's (1507–68) first book of madrigals was issued in 1539 by Gardano in Venice and was reprinted nearly fifty times over a half-century; three further volumes followed in the same year. This illustrates the reach and impact of the new medium, but in its early years there is no evidence that composers were directly involved in disseminating their work. Gradually they assumed a more prominent role, but surviving letters from composers to printers and patrons, complaining about delays and increased costs, suggest that printers did not usually pay composers whose music they printed. During the 1530s Elzéar Genet (*alias* Carpentras, c.1470–1548), former master of the papal chapel under Leo X, amassed sufficient wealth to finance the first 'complete works' edition of a living composer. More often, patronage played a part: where composers themselves took the initiative, the printer's costs were often subsidized by a third party in exchange for dedication of the volume by the composer in an introductory letter. (These prefaces can provide valuable information about composers and their working environment.) Another form of patronage was the granting by the ruler of a 'privilege' for a given period, which prevented others from printing the composer's work without authorization. Dedicatory letters also reveal the extent of patronage on which the better-connected composers drew: patrons were no longer exclusively nobles and high-ranking clergy but wealthy merchants, court officials, and diplomats. For their part, composers were no longer exclusively dependent on a single salary but could draw on a number of sources. Nor were they necessarily bound to the church. During the fifteenth century, lay singers had often been recruited to make up the numbers in ecclesiastical choirs, a practice that carried on throughout the Renaissance.[17] This was the case even in Rome, where in 1555 Pope Paul IV expelled the lay members of the Cappella Giulia, a measure that was quietly allowed to lapse (one of the laymen concerned being Palestrina, who eventually re-joined as chapel-master in 1571). But whereas in the earlier period chapel-masters were typically appointed from the ranks of the singer-clerics, by the later Renaissance several of the most famous composers and choirmasters were laymen: besides

Palestrina there was Lassus in Munich, de Monte at the Imperial Court, Cipriano De Rore in Ferrara, and Willaert and Giovanni Gabrieli at St Mark's in Venice. The subsequent pattern of Palestrina's activity is best described as freelancing. One of his regular patrons, the Duke of Mantua, even sent the composer music of his own for evaluation. In those areas where the Reformation took hold, musicians were laypeople as a matter of course.

Undoubtedly, print culture transformed the perception of composing as an activity. With their works far more widely available over a broader demographic, composers could achieve renown beyond the world of specialists and patrons, connoisseurs, and professional musicians: the notion of composers as singular creative personalities with their own styles became an accepted mode of discourse among commentators on music. The classic case is the last chapter of the highly influential treatise *Dodekachordon* by the Swiss theorist Heinrich Glarean (d.1563), published in 1547. This is a detailed appraisal of the musical personalities of 'the generation formerly known as Josquin'. Around the same time (1538), the Nuremberg printer Hieronymus Formschneider issued the print *Trium vocum carmina* without attributions (by then an unusual decision), giving the reason that the unnamed composers 'each have their own notable characteristics, by which trained musicians may easily recognize them'. Whether this was meant tongue-in-cheek or as a way of concealing his ignorance of the repertory's provenance, Formschneider presupposes an awareness of personal musical style that might not have been taken for granted a generation earlier. A composer who made the most of this change in attitude was Lassus, whose career took him from his native Mons in modern-day Belgium to Rome, Naples, and finally Munich, with visits to Italy, France, and further afield in Germany. Through his travels he established contacts with printers throughout Europe, who disseminated his work enthusiastically, and cultivated royal, imperial, and papal patrons along the way. In a curious reversal, print culture brought about a change in the notion of musical ownership: soon after Lassus' arrival at the Bavarian court, his new patron, Duke Albrecht V (r.1550–79), commissioned a number of works, including a cycle of settings of the seven Penitential Psalms, which he had copied in a series of choirbooks of exceptional size and splendour. Lassus was expressly forbidden to print them during Albrecht's lifetime: reserved for his exclusive use, they were heard only by members of his court and honoured guests.

By comparison with Lassus, the fame of Victoria, Byrd, or even Palestrina was comparatively circumscribed. The latter's reputation eclipsed that of Lassus only after their deaths. The poet Ronsard (several of whose poems Lassus set to music) called him 'the more than divine Orlande', putting him on equal footing with leading literary figures of the day, and at his death his sons published a retrospective survey of his output, intended to be as complete as possible. All this speaks to the perception of the composer as 'author' in the modern sense. But print culture has also allowed a far greater proportion of music by lesser- or little-known composers to survive than had previously been the case. During Lassus' lifetime, the sons of another adoptive Bavarian, Leonhard Paminger (d.1567), planned a similar posthumous collection in ten volumes of their father's compositions (only four of which were issued). Although Paminger is virtually unknown today, his productivity and technical range shows the fluency of which 'minor' Renaissance composers were capable.

Instrumental ensembles and soloists

Over the course of the Renaissance information about instrumentalists as makers of polyphony becomes increasingly plentiful.[18] The two decades before 1500 saw several decisive shifts. The first concerns the rigid distinction between loud and soft instruments (in the French of the time, 'haut' and 'bas'[19]), respectively associated with celebratory, outdoor music and more private entertainment. Loud instruments were winds (excluding the recorder) and brass (excluding the trumpet family, always a special case and never used in polyphony); soft instruments were strings (plucked, bowed, and keyed). Crucially, it would seem that the two categories seldom if ever mixed, but within each one the mixing of timbres was possible, and there is evidence that ensembles were sometimes constituted in families of the same instrument in different sizes. Ensemble members often played several instruments; each individual specialized in a specific voice-type, switching to the appropriate instrument as required, ensuring the ensemble's versatility and stability. This leads to a second point: the polyphonic repertory of instrumental ensembles before c.1500 was predominantly extemporized. Already by the mid-fifteenth century, the contrapuntal practice of both high and low instruments conformed broadly to the rules acknowledged by singers, but much of it was taught by ear – especially among wind players. (A typical wind set-up involved a borrowed tune with a part above and one below – a scoring ideal for improvising parallel tenths around a cantus firmus, which is not only well attested by writers but a commonplace of written polyphony during this period.) The borrowed material could be sacred, for sacred music did indeed form part of their repertory, but chansons and secular songs were more commonly the basis of extemporization. Both monophonic and polyphonic soft instruments appeared as soloists, but never loud instruments. It seems that performers on soft instruments were more generally musically literate than their 'loud' colleagues, judging by the substantial body of keyboard music of the Faenza Codex (c.1420) and the Buxheimer Orgelbuch (c.1470). By the same token, they also accompanied solo singers in the performance of songs; as in later periods, the voice was regarded as the ideal to which instrumental performers aspired. All of which leads to the third point, arguably the most crucial as regards polyphony: with the exception of the organ, instruments and vocal ensembles never performed together.

Within a couple of decades either side of 1500, these long-standing conventions were suddenly overturned. The distinction between high and low disintegrated, creating new combinations: the cornet (first documented in these years) displaced the shawm in the habitual combination with sackbuts. Alongside the cornet, several other instruments appeared for the first time, whose sounds are now closely associated with Renaissance music: the viol, the crumhorn, and a little later the violin. Paradoxically, as the distinction between high and low instruments broke down, the earlier tendency to group ensembles into families of the same type increased: a set of viols was commissioned by Isabella d'Este, Duchess of Mantua and daughter of Ercole I in the 1490s. (The creation of violin ensembles encompassing all members of the family happened later, there being little solid evidence for their existence before the second half of the sixteenth century.) It is likely that these new ensembles would have played composed polyphony, dissolving the earlier distinction to do with repertory; the case of the wind ensemble performing written polyphony in Venice with added voices (discussed in the previous chapter) shows that such ensembles were considered in no way deficient compared to those of their singing colleagues. Simultaneously, reports and visual representations of vocal and instrumental ensembles performing together make their first, sudden appearance. In 1502–3, the much-travelled cornettist Augustein Schubinger performed with the Imperial Chapel at Innsbruck, making a profound impression (presumably alongside falsettists; he had previously played the sackbut, but it is with the new instrument that he achieved international renown). Precisely during these years, a new musical repertory arises that gives the impression of having been intended for instruments. Though the musical and source evidence is ambiguous (since instruments are never specified, and the music is notated and presented in the same way as explicitly vocal music), the emergence of this repertory alongside the exponential increase in evidence for single-instrument consorts (both at court and through the prints aimed at city-dwelling amateurs) can hardly be a coincidence. Other evidence points to a degree of social hierarchy among instruments. The popularity of lutes and viols with the aristocracy is reflected in the manuscript (rather than print) transmission of the English viol consort repertory; conversely, printed music was commonly advertised as being equally appropriate for voices or instruments of all sorts. Certain winds (e.g. recorders, flutes, and crumhorns) were cheaper to produce and easier to learn, and thus especially popular with amateur musicians.

The participation of instruments in sacred music will be considered more fully in Chapter 14, but a few points stand out. First, after 1500 instrumentalists could and did perform both sacred and secular vocal music, even in church. While a cappella performance remained the norm in certain areas and mandatory in some institutions, after 1500 instruments were incorporated into choral performances. The widely attested use of the *bajón* (or dulcian, the forerunner of the bassoon) as reinforcement of the bass part in otherwise all-vocal performances of Spanish polyphony is a familiar feature on recent recordings, as is the playing of motets during Mass by wind ensembles in the same period. The Venetian example just cited does not mention where the performance took place, but the writer hints at a sizeable audience ('all Venice wishes to hear nothing else'). A painting by Gentile Bellini of a wind band participating in an outdoor procession on the Piazza San Marco, painted in the same decade, might almost have provided a postcard for his report home.[20] (It is reproduced on the cover of this book.) In short, the situation was very fluid; performance traditions were most often determined by local custom and circumstance. In the larger towns, the term 'local' could apply to individual institutions, provided they were sufficiently important, but truly special occasions would have mobilized a sizeable proportion of a town's resources. The forty-part motet *Ecce beatam lucem* and the Mass based on it (composed by Alessandro Striggio the Elder (1536/7–92)) were performed in several places in 1567/8 under the direction of the composer: this tour took in Munich (for the splendid wedding celebrations of the future Duke of Bavaria), Paris, Vienna, and London. The wedding of the Grand Duke of Tuscany in Florence some twenty years later in 1589 was the occasion for the 'Intermedii' of the play *La Pellegrina*. A record of the event survives, and although it does not specify how many musicians were involved in any given piece, the scale of the event was on a par with Striggio's Mass. While the sound of the court orchestra was not far off, the notion of the formally constituted orchestra was yet to come.

Soloist performers of polyphony played either keyboards or strings; an intermediary category between soloist and ensemble was the duo of like or matched instruments, which might include plucked and/or bowed strings. Less is known of their early training than that of their singing colleagues, but a strikingly common trait is visual impairment. The extent of this is unknowable in individual cases since it was covered by the one catchall term ('blind'), but musical pedagogy encompassed their education to the highest level. The most highly regarded were organists and lutenists, the former because of the connection with the church and the latter by virtue of the lute's status as the aristocratic male's instrument of choice (keyboard instruments being deemed more appropriate for women). Keith Polk has suggested that the organ and lute may have been natural instruments for the visually impaired because mobility (which would have been usual in processions) was not required of them.[21] Though sometimes contracted to a single institution, organists frequently held several posts simultaneously, also hiring out their services to nobles and aristocrats: like their singing colleagues, they benefited from the fluid exchange between church and court. The reactive nature of their craft (extemporizing for an extended but unpredictable duration, stopping suddenly as the liturgical situation required, and adapting to the pitch-standard of others) required great skill in improvising. Judging by the audition exercises they underwent, the level of proficiency expected of them was comparable with a chapelmaster's. The fame of Nuremberg-born Conrad Paumann (c.1410–73), court organist at Munich, compared favourably with that of the greatest singers.

Lutenists and keyboardists in a courtly setting likewise tailored their performances not only to circumstance but also to the mood of their listeners. Their ability to affect the audience is plentifully and admiringly documented: contemporary descriptions stress not only dexterity or the ability to extemporize but also the manner of the performance. Whereas it was fashionable for amateur noblemen to play well but without undue display or visible effort (a quality called 'sprezzatura', a nonchalant virtuosity), the Ferrarese lutenist Pietrobono (d.1497) was renowned for performances of furious inspiration. (A similar quality reputedly informed the impromptu recitations of the Neoplatonist philosopher and priest Marsilio Ficino (d.1499), who accompanied himself on a stringed instrument: in both cases the link between musical inspiration and the magical realm is strongly implied.)[22] In the pattern established in the medieval period, instrumentalists benefited from aristocratic and civic patronage. For the best performers this entailed a salary (as laypeople they were technically ineligible for benefices), but like singers this stable income was often supplemented by one-off payments and gifts in kind. Notwithstanding a courtly stipend and his wide renown, Pietrobono also taught private individuals. This is typical of the fifteenth century, where the boundaries between court and town were less rigid than they later became, but formal contractual arrangements with noble or princely patrons continued in the next century. Many of the most famous Renaissance lutenists were either Italian or found employment there; Alberto da Ripa (d.1551, better known as Albert de Rippe), followed Francis I of France on his travels and performed for kings and popes.

Whether organist or lutenist, the soloist's art was essentially grounded in improvisation – in fact the greatest of them seem to have written down very little, let alone seen it into print. Nothing survives of Pietrobono's work; what we have by Vincenzo Capirola or Alberto da Ripa was collected by others either in their lifetime or posthumously (a tendency that persisted into the eighteenth century). More generally, what found its way into print was intended not as finished works but as models or examples of their manner or style of performance; in that sense, most of the surviving repertory is rooted in improvised practice. This is particularly true of the genre where improvisation and written polyphony become closely entwined: alongside freely invented pieces, lutenists also published 'intabulations' of existing polyphony, in which the music was not only transcribed for the instrument but ornamented and embellished idiomatically. Francesco Spinacino's two books of lute music, both published by Petrucci in 1507, contain the first examples of this. They range from more or less literal transcription to elaborate re-workings. The popularity of these intabulations may be judged from the number of lutenists who committed them to paper or print. At their weirdest (those of the Hungarian virtuoso Valentin Bakfark (d.1576), for example), the original work is stretched and altered beyond recognition. Intabulations are the most extreme but also literal illustration of the basic point that most instrumental music of the Renaissance derives from vocal polyphony.

Women and polyphony: cloth and court

That Renaissance women participated in polyphony alongside men both as performers and composers is certain, but, as with so much else in early modern society, documentation is patchier and what survives tended to be ignored by music historians until very recently.[23] The social gulf between the ruling class and commoners is typical, and most available information concerns the former. Nevertheless, there is evidence that urban girls in the fifteenth century were taught music (including extemporized polyphony) and even performed in public, from which aristocratic children would have been discouraged.[24] While it would have been exceedingly rare for such training to be carried over into adulthood in a professional context, it is touching to think of children of both sexes being trained together in polyphony.

Practically no evidence survives of composition by early Renaissance women, and for most of the next century there are only a few named individuals, sometimes represented by just a single song or motet. The first woman to have had music printed was Maddalena Casulana (c.1544–?), whose three books of madrigals (a respectable number by any standard) were published between 1568 and 1583. A celebrated lutenist and singer, she participated in the 1568 wedding festivities at the Bavarian court, to which she also contributed music. The dedications of her prints reveal a strong personality, fully aware of her skill and forthright in her claim for the equality of women in the compositional sphere. From the 1590s single-authored prints appear more regularly, many of them composed by cloistered nuns. Women in holy orders often came from well-to-do or aristocratic families, bringing a substantial 'dowry' as financial contribution to their new community. A convent's requirement to be self-sufficient allowed its members to exercise their abilities in ways that were seldom possible outside it, and in convents, as elsewhere, music at services was an integral part of community life. Certain convents developed a strong reputation for music, such as San Vito in Ferrara, where Vittoria Aleotti (c.1575–after 1620) was admitted at a young age, later taking the name Rafaella upon taking holy orders. Vittoria seems to have been the first woman to publish sacred music (Venice, 1593), and she issued a book of madrigals in the same year. That a nun should have written madrigals as well as motets was less surprising to contemporaries than it seems to us.[25]

If women's compositional aptitudes were only beginning to be recognized, their skills as performers were widely admired. In matters of musical literacy and connoisseurship, women of the high nobility and aristocracy had no reason to envy their brothers and husbands, but practical skill was only for show, and the tendency to flattery at court makes it hard to identify genuine proficiency (though the same is true of the men). In the early Renaissance, records of one-off payments to unnamed female performers are not unknown, especially when a court was on the move (perhaps they were the young town girls mentioned earlier). But the Renaissance's most famous female performers were the women of Ferrara who in the 1580s and 90s formed the so-called 'concerto delle dame', Laura Peverara, Anna Guarini, Livia d'Arco, and Tarquinia Molza (the latter apparently a guiding spirit rather than an active member).[26] Of aristocratic upbringing, they excelled both as singers and instrumentalists and had music written for them by Luzzaschi, Marenzio, and possibly Monteverdi. Here were singers who were recognized as equal to their male colleagues, not just individually but as an ensemble. It is already unusual that specific pieces can plausibly be associated with them, and still more remarkable that their fame inspired similar ensembles elsewhere in Italy and music by composers who may not have worked with them directly: one might say that they created a new genre. But they were not immune from the sorts of rumours that attached to successful women operating in the sexually charged atmosphere of a Renaissance court (or to female performers more generally). Tarquinia Molza was dismissed from the Ferrarese court in 1589 following the revelation of her affair with the composer Giaches de Wert (1535–96). Tragically, the *concerto delle dame* was formally dissolved in 1598, when Anna Guarini (daughter of the great Renaissance poet, Giovanni Battista Guarini) was murdered by her husband and her brother for supposed adultery. All too often, the perception of female musicians in the Renaissance conforms to the depressing stereotype: either virgins or 'whores'.

Chapter 4 | Pitch: an overview

Although this book is not primarily concerned with music theory, an understanding of the basic principles is a necessary starting point. The following chapters focus on polyphony's essential building blocks – in this chapter, those that relate to pitch. But this initial step is no easy task, for several reasons. The first is the considerable distance that exists (as in most historical periods) between theory and practice. Contemporary musicians and theorists (whom we really ought to call 'teachers', since their purpose was primarily pedagogical) disagreed as to the relative importance of this or that aspect of their systems, and today writers also differ in their interpretation of concepts, their practical application, and their relevance. And as with everything else that concerns Renaissance music, our understanding of the gap between theory and practice is dependent on the sources that happen to survive. A second difficulty is that many of these principles can appear contradictory, especially those pertaining to pitch – unsurprisingly, since they were developed over hundreds of years across a wide geographical area, and devised not with polyphony in mind but plainchant. The move from a single line to several simultaneous ones was a paradigm shift that teachers struggled to accommodate. The beginning of this chapter introduces these theoretical constructs as they developed before the Renaissance, independently of polyphony; the second part sketches their co-existence with polyphony and contrapuntal practice. The individual concepts covered in the following chapters (including the gamut, the species, modes, counterpoint, and mensural theory) have generated a vast literature and, in many cases, considerable controversy. My treatment of them is not intended either to be exhaustive or necessarily impartial. The main focus is on their relevance to musical style and compositional practice.

The gamut: measuring musical space

The conception of a metaphorical musical 'space' marked out by steps measured in tones and semitones appears to have had its origins in ancient

Γ A B C D E F G a b♭ b♮ c d e f g aa bb♭ bb♮ cc dd ee

In this diagram, the letter names are those of the medieval system: 'c' is equivalent to middle C.

Figure 4.1 The gamut

Greece, but its earliest influential formulation is that of Boethius, who sketched a two-octave modal system (with written A as the lowest pitch) in abstract terms, with names borrowed from Greek.[1] Around 1000 CE, the letter-names A–G were assigned to the steps of Boethius' system, the same letter being used for pitches an octave apart. Around the same time, Boethius' two-octave compass was being expanded in both directions. The lowest note, a tone below Boethius' lowest pitch A, was named after the Greek letter Gamma, and by the time of the great teacher Guido of Arezzo (d. after 1033) it extended upwards by a fourth, to which he added a further pitch above this (Figure 4.1). Guido was instrumental in the adoption of stave notation. He assigned a red line to the pitch f and a yellow one to c' a fifth above it. These two lines were especially important, since they showed the location of the semitones e–f and b–c' – all other steps, of course, being tones. Eventually, clefs (from *claves*, the Latin for 'keys') were assigned to the two pitches' position on the stave, replacing the colours – so called because they 'unlocked' the reading of the stave. Guido is also credited with another innovation whose consequences resonate deeply within the Renaissance (though ironically, it neither appears nor is even described in his surviving writings). This is the Hand (Illustration 4.1), a mnemonic device aimed at helping singers find their way through the gamut and navigate its interval structures, the better to understand the chant repertory. Its individual articulations represented the degrees of the gamut (known as 'loca', or 'places'). In the post-Guidonian era, a typical Hand featured both the A–G letters and the six syllables *ut re mi fa sol la* (more on which below). The former unequivocally indicated the diatonic intervals, or the steps of musical space that corresponded to positions on the stave, while the latter helped budding singers intone those intervals correctly.

At this point one should observe that within the gamut the letter-name B can be read either as flat or as natural, as shown in Figure 4.1. (Note that on the Hand, the two readings are assigned the same 'loca'.) This has its origins in plainchant, in which B was often flattened (by means of a sign placed before it), usually to smooth over the tritone dissonance that

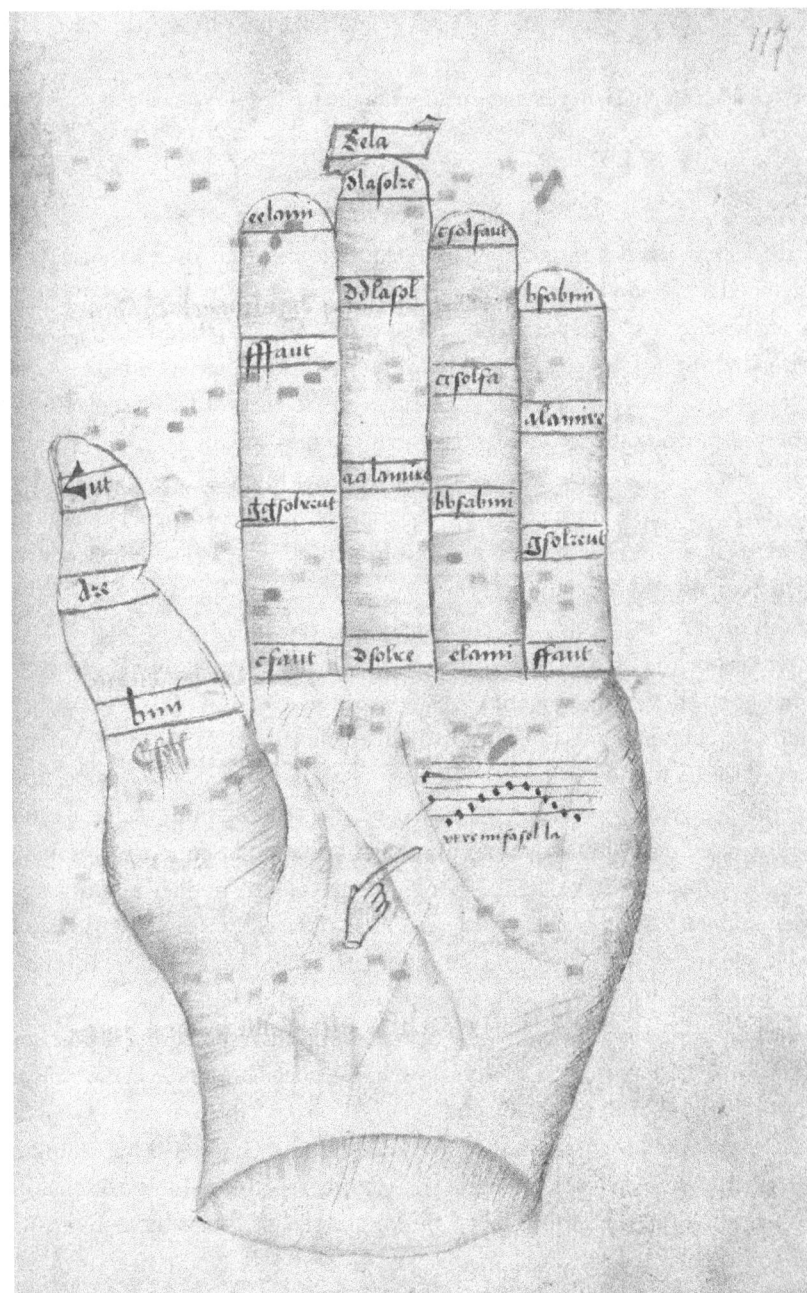

Illustration 4.1 Guidonian hand
Brussels, Koninklijke Bibliotheek/Bibliothèque Royale, Ms. 1758, f. 117ʳ (reproduced with permission)

otherwise resulted from its conjunction with the pitch F. Depending on the reading of B, writers recognized two possible pairs of semitones within the octave, either E–F and B♮–C or E–F and A–B♭. From a modern perspective, this inclusion of a 'black-note' pitch within the diatonic system is one of the most surprising aspects of modal theory. But it is crucial, because the location of the semitones within the octave is essential to ordering musical space in terms of recurrent interval structures.

The earliest of these structures (also inherited from ancient Greece) were the 'tetrachords' (four-note collections), of which at first only one kind was recognized (S T T, counting upwards); the other two possible configurations (T S T and T T S) were admitted later, and five-note collections ('pentachords') were formed by adding a tone above or below.

Species and modes

These theoretical concerns took place against a backdrop of monody, namely, the body of plainchant used in the liturgy of the Christian church. As the chant repertory grew in volume and complexity, it became necessary to order it for the purposes of copying and classification, and for training novices (young boys) in the monasteries to memorize and sing it.[2] (Here again, the link between what we call 'theory' and pedagogy is crucial; writers on music were monks, for whom the singing, teaching, and learning of chant were daily activities.) By the ninth century at the latest, the Byzantine classification of eight modes was being adapted for this purpose, and by Guido's time, the link between the eight modes and the 'species' (as the collection of tetrachords and pentachords came to be called) was established. Each mode is constituted of a species of fourth and a species of fifth, which together made up the modal octave (see Figure 4.2). The eight modes are grouped into pairs named after the Greek numbers from one to four. The first pair ('Protus') consists of the so-called first species of fourth and fifth, with the semitone in second position; the second ('Deuterus') has the second species of fourth and fifth, with the semitone in first position; and in the third pair ('Tritus', with the third species of fourth and fifth) the semitone is in final position. The fourth pair ('Tetrardus') has the last available species of fifth, with the semitone in third position; the available species of fourth having been exhausted, it reverts to the first species. The two modes of each pair have a different modal octave, determined by the position of the species relative to each other: in the 'authentic' (odd-numbered) modes the species of fourth is on

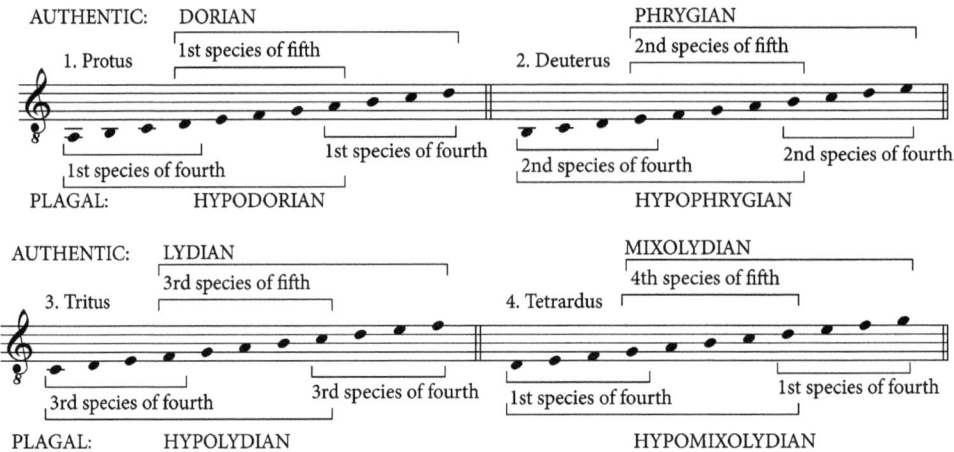

Figure 4.2 The eight church modes and the species of fourth and fifth

top, and in the 'plagal' (even-numbered) modes it is on the bottom. The modes are assigned individual names according to their 'finals', the pitch on which the plainchant normally comes to rest. The prefix 'hypo' (for 'lower') distinguishes the plagal form from its authentic counterpart: hence, 'Dorian' and 'Hypodorian' for the Protus pair with a final on D, 'Phrygian' and 'Hypophrygian' for the Deuterus pair (final: E), 'Lydian' and 'Hypolydian' for the Tritus pair (final: F), and 'Mixolydian' and 'Hypomixolydian' for the Tetrardus pair (final: G).

But modes are more than a set of abstract pitch collections or scales. In most authentic modes, the final may be approached from above or below, and the ranges of many chants typically include the pitch below the final.[3] Each mode has a different set of melodic formulae and behaviours peculiar to it. In plainchant, this is seen in the chanting of psalms and responsories, which typically involve a stable pitch called 'reciting tone' (or 'tenor') and a set of formulae associated with the beginning, middle, and ending of phrases. Due to their rootedness in plainchant they were part of the mental landscape of any Renaissance singer, and references to them in polyphony are legion.[4] But in polyphony too, modes may emphasize pitches other than the final (thus in Phrygian pieces, C often functions as an alternative pitch-centre). In this respect at least, modes resemble the 'keys' of tonality, each having its own characteristic properties, which are further inflected in the practice of individual composers.

As was mentioned at the start, the co-existence of modal theory and polyphony was not without its problems; but even in plainchant, modal classification of pieces was not always straightforward. Pieces were

Example 4.1 Anon., *L'Homme armé* (in Dorian and Mixolydian) with solmization syllables. Translation: The armed man, one must fear the armed man. Everywhere the cry goes up that each must arm himself with a coat of chain mail.

described as being modally 'mixed' or 'commixed' when they included passages in different modes. In matters of melodic design, species of fourth and fifth are often more tangible than the modes themselves. A useful demonstration piece is the famous fifteenth-century tune *L'Homme armé*. As shown in Example 4.1, it circulated in two versions, the one in transposed Dorian (with signature flat), the other in Mixolydian (without signature flat). Its neat ABA form clearly articulates the two types of species. The relative position of the species (here, with the fourth uppermost) identifies the mode as authentic. Both phrases 'A' and 'B' are contained within a perfect fifth, but whereas phrase 'A' lies entirely within the species of fifth, the top note of phrase 'B' exceeds the compass of the octave, and – crucially – lies outside the species of fourth. This explains why it is perceived differently from the top note of phrase 'A': its arrival is the highpoint of the tune, not just literally but also affectively. (Notice how in phrase 'B', the top note of the species of fourth is stated repeatedly from the start so that the arrival on the fifth gives a sense of breakthrough or climax.) This stepping outside the species is a common melodic gesture in monophony and polyphony, and very often a carrier of expression. Note also that in both versions phrase 'B' is identical, since the

Dorian and Mixolydian modes are both constituted with the first species of fourth (T S T). The earliest polyphonic settings of *L'Homme armé* use both versions, sometimes in the same work.

Measuring musical space with syllables: the hexachord

Another theoretical construct with which Guido is credited derives from an observation made almost in passing (ironically, given its later consequences). He noticed that pitches separated by a fifth have a similar position relative to the pitches on either side of them (to use his term, there is 'affinity' between pitches a fifth apart because the ordering of tones and semitones around them is identical). Since the pitches from G to e and from C to a (and those at the octave above) share the same interval structure (T T S T T), he proposed that these equivalent degrees be given a common name, assigning to them the syllables *ut re mi fa sol la*. Unlike the species of fourth and fifth, in which the position of the semitone among the tones is moveable, the placement of the semitone in this ordering is fixed (always between *mi* and *fa*). But it is crucial to understand that Guido intended this device as a pedagogical tool, not an alternative 'system' to the seven letter-names (nowhere does the term 'hexachord' appear in his work.) His conception is perhaps best viewed as a moveable, virtual grid, mentally superimposed by the singer on the seven letters in order to navigate the gamut more efficiently. As Stefano Mengozzi has argued, the primary interval of the hexachordal system is not the sixth, but the fifth, since it is at the fifth that the hexachord syllables are replicated; in fact, Guido explicitly stated that the interval with the most perfect affinity was the octave.

Nonetheless, later writers (particularly from the thirteenth century onwards) adapted and developed Guido's ideas in directions that he could hardly have foreseen. Soon after his death, a third set of 'deductions' (the contemporary term) from F to D (reading upwards) was proposed in order to accommodate both readings of the pitch B. Deductions beginning on C became known as 'natural', those on G as 'hard' (Latin 'durus'), and those on F as 'flat' (Latin 'mollis') – there being seven individual deductions within the gamut (Figure 4.3). In time, the individual degrees were given names that combined the original letter-name with the hexachord syllable or syllables on which they could be sung. Thus, the lowest pitch was called 'Gamma ut' (hence the name 'gamut', which by extension was applied to the medieval diatonic system as a whole). Certain pitches had no fewer than

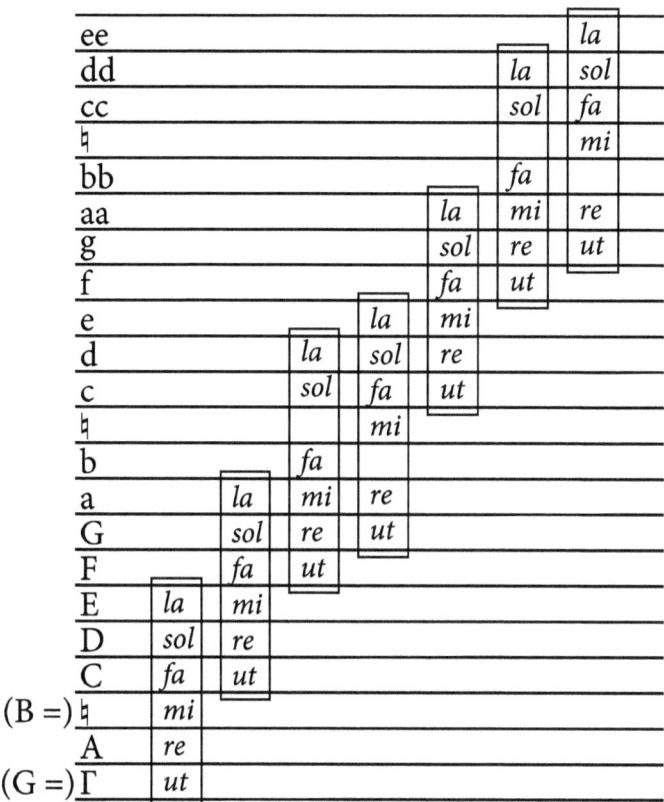

Figure 4.3 The gamut and the hexachords

three syllable names associated with them: our middle C (c'), for instance, was 'c sol fa ut', since it could be read as any of these syllables depending on the deduction in which it was sung (reading from the lowest deduction to the highest: refer again to Illustration 4.1 and Figure 4.3).

The next point to consider is a practical one. When 'solmizing' the *L'Homme armé* tune in its Mixolydian version (omitting the signature flat in Example 4.1), the first phrase is sung entirely in the hard hexachord (as I call it from now on), so that its first note (g) is *ut*, and the second phrase is sung in the natural hexachord, in which the first note, g', is *sol* and the top note is *la*. When singing *L'Homme armé* in its Dorian version (with a signature flat), the first phrase is sung in the soft hexachord (beginning on g as *re*), and the second in the natural hexachord. But in Renaissance polyphony (and a good deal of plainchant) vocal ranges frequently exceed the octave and do not come packaged (like *L'Homme armé*) in hexachord-friendly phrases. How then does one move stepwise from *la* to the note just above, or conversely from *ut* to the note below? This is done by exchanging a pitch's solmization syllable, in effect transferring it from one hexachord to another – a procedure known as 'mutation'. Usually, mutation involved a different pair of hexachords, depending on whether or not a flat was present in the key signature: if there was a flat in the key signature, the natural and soft hexachords were used, and if not, the hard and the natural. In a rising phrase the point of mutation was towards *re* of the next hexachord (with the previous degree being either *la* or *sol* of the hexachord below), and in a descending phrase towards *la* (with the previous degree being either *mi* or *re* of the hexachord above).[5]

In Mengozzi's words, '[by] *c.* 1300 at the latest, the hexachordal system had acquired the form and the conceptual apparatus that were bequeathed to the Renaissance'.[6] But the near-universal acceptance of the term 'hexachord' to indicate Guido's 'deductions' was a Renaissance phenomenon: Mengozzi specifically locates it within the last quarter of the fifteenth century. This is confirmed by the quite sudden mushrooming of compositions that make explicit reference to the hexachord and its syllables (discussed in Chapter 13), which also coincides with the vigorous promotion of the hexachordal system by the most influential theorist of the generation after Tinctoris, Franchinus Gaffurius (*c.*1451–1522). References to the hexachord within composed music, musical practice in general, and music-related iconography from this point onwards are virtually innumerable, to the point that in Senfl's *Lust hab' ich g'habt zur musica* (discussed in Chapter 10) it is used to denote music itself. But even during the hexachord's heyday some theorists held out against it, notably Bartolomeo Ramos de Pareja in the fifteenth century, and Nicola Vicentino (1511–*c.*1576) in the next.

Contrapuntal practice: polyphony and modal classification

More or less from the origins of composed polyphony, teachers began to set rules governing the succession of different types of interval (that is, perfect and imperfect consonances, and dissonances) when a free voice was added to a pre-existing one derived from plainchant. Additional voices were composed first in relation to the plainchant-derived voice, then taking account of any others. In other words, no matter the number of voices involved, the theoretical framework regulating them was essentially dyadic, note against note – '*punctus contra punctum*', whence the term 'counterpoint'. Contrapuntal rules were thus largely independent of modal considerations, since when dealing with notated music rather than abstract representations of musical space, modal theory was concerned only with monody.

But it would be an oversimplification to say that modal theory and polyphony were in conflict.[7] Few teachers explicitly considered them to be so. On the one hand, the modal classification of polyphony was advocated as far back as the thirteenth century. Masses and other liturgical forms (such as Magnificats) were frequently designated by mode where no other descriptor was available (e.g. '*Missa quarti toni*'), and grouping according to mode remained the standard way of organizing music collections throughout the Renaissance. On the other hand, the opinion that mode and polyphony had little to do with one another was nearly as old, and was expressed as late as 1540 by Sebald Heyden (1499–1561) in the final chapter of his treatise *De arte canendi*. A similar contradiction occurs in the descriptions of modal character by Renaissance writers, who often do no more than parrot the opinions of classical authorities.[8] Thus, the connection between Phrygian polyphony and texts connected with penitence and mourning is seldom mentioned, because the view of classical teachers (who wrote from an exclusively monodic perspective) was very different. A significant exception was the Swiss theorist Heinrich Glarean (1488–1563), who in his *Dodekachordon* ('On the twelve modes', published in 1547) proposed re-ordering the modal system to align modal theory with current polyphonic practice.

But even writers who regarded the modal classification of polyphony as self-evident struggled with it in practice. For one thing (as noted earlier), the voice-ranges of polyphonic pieces routinely exceed the modal octave. Teachers explained this by invoking the principles of modal mixture or commixture. Similarly, the different voices of a piece are usually in different modes because of their ranges, some lying in the authentic modal range and others in the plagal. A much-quoted passage from Tinctoris (from Chapter 24 of his *Book on the Nature and Properties of the Modes*), intended to illustrate this feature, inadvertently shows up the problems that arise:

[If] anyone were to say to me, 'Tinctoris, I ask you, of what tone is the song [*carmen*] "Le Serviteur"?', I would reply 'in general, of an irregular first tone [c Protus authentic, because the song's key signature has three flats], because the tenor, the principal part of the song, is of such a tone'. If however he were to ask in particular, of what tone the superius or contratenor might be, I would reply in particular, [that] the one and the other were of the second tone, also irregular [c Protus plagal].

Figure 4.4 Voice-ranges of Du Fay, *Le Serviteur*, showing the constitutive species of fourth and fifth

In the first place, Tinctoris' classification of the individual voices of Du Fay's song is incorrect because the contratenor is in the same range as the tenor (that is, authentic Protus), and because all their ranges exceed the octave (see Figure 4.4). Tinctoris' attempt to classify the song as a whole is similarly problematic: he can only do so by stating that one of the voices has priority over the others. This conforms to the orthodox view (expressed in the sentence preceding the quotation) that the tenor is the 'foundation' of the polyphony, but fails to take account of the relationships of the other voices. In fact, modal classification of polyphony according to the eight modes (or even twelve) is sometimes impossible. Du Fay's song *Se la face ay pale* is entirely centred on C, which has no status as a final in the eight-mode system (the song pre-dates Glarean's re-instatement of the Ionian mode by about 150 years); and in the cantus firmus Mass that Du Fay based on it, the pitch of the song's tenor is maintained but the other voices cadence on F. Nor is Du Fay's *Missa Se la face ay pale* alone in pitting voices in different modes against each other. The setting of *Regina celi* by Pierre de La Rue (c.1460–1518) has the Lydian plainchant in the tenor, but the other voices consistently cadence on E. Small wonder that some modern writers bypass mode altogether and refer to pieces by their finals. Given all this, the persistence of modal theory throughout the Renaissance may appear strange, until one remembers the centrality of plainchant in the lives of church musicians: Du Fay was not only consulted on a matter of modal classification of chant but also commissioned to compose it.[9] The fact that modal commixture was common in plainchant makes it easier to explain the foregoing examples, however much they play havoc with Tinctoris' definition. Renaissance composers plainly enjoyed exploiting the ambiguities of the theoretical systems they inherited.

The cadence (*clausula*)

From the beginnings of notated polyphony, the fundamental syntactical unit was the '*clausula*' or cadence. This was defined as the arrival by a pair

Example 4.2 Two-voice cadential motion

Example 4.3 Cadential ornaments

of voices on the octave or unison (the most perfect consonances), proceeding stepwise in contrary motion from the nearest imperfect consonance (the major sixth or the minor third). Example 4.2 shows the cadence in its simplest form. In octave cadences (Example 4.2a) the lower voice, called 'tenor', descends, and the upper voice, called 'discantus' (one of several possible names), rises. These positions are reversed when the cadence is at the unison (Example 4.2b; voice-names are considered at length in Chapter 5). The principal difference between this dyadic form of cadence and the cadence of tonal music is that it is complete in itself and requires no other voices. But the similarities are greater than may first appear: like a tonal cadence, the dyadic cadence is predicated on the principle of contrary motion, and on tension and resolution; and, as in tonality, cadences may occur on other pitches than the final or tonic.

Another similarity between the two-voice (dyadic) and triadic cadence is that although the basic structure remains in place for centuries, changes in local contrapuntal detail become indicators of style (Example 4.3: note that in all these cadential forms the voices may be inverted). By the fifteenth century, cadences were usually inflected by delaying the arrival on the major sixth via a suspension in the ascending voice (Example 4.3a), and further ornamented or embellished with 'inessential' notes (i.e. notes that do not affect cadential function). Throughout the fifteenth century, the under-third cadence (sometimes known as 'Landini cadence') was the most common type of embellishment and took many forms (Examples 4.3b–d). By about 1520 it had been replaced by simpler ones (Examples 4.3a and

4.3h). The descending voice's approach to the final was the more standardized of the two, but the penultimate pitch (above the final) could also be prepared in several ways: in practice, most of the descending cadential patterns in Example 4.3 are interchangeable. Certain cadential forms were localized not only in time but also in place: English polyphony was distinguished by its idiosyncratic cadential usage. Examples 4.3e, 4.3f, and 4.3g are typical of fifteenth-century England, where the suspension so common elsewhere was generally avoided. In the early Renaissance, forbidden consecutive octaves could be offset if just one pitch intervenes between them (Example 4.3g). Later, these blunt forms of displacement were less frequent. In general, 'forbidden' consecutive intervals (usually the octave or fifth) were more readily tolerated in the fifteenth and early sixteenth centuries, when they occur reasonably often.

Cadence and mode

I chose the pitch F for the cadences in Example 4.3 because it is the most straightforward of the four modal finals on which to cadence. The upper stave of Example 4.4 shows two-voice cadences on each modal final. Although the cadence on E (Example 4.4b) satisfies the definition given above, it alone places the semitone in the descending voice rather than the ascending one. However, the cadence's 'gravitational pull' resides in this semitone motion, just as it does in the Lydian. In the two remaining modes, Dorian and Mixolydian (Examples 4.4a and 4.4d), the discantus' penultimate pitch must be sharpened (hence the editorial accidental placed above it). Of all the unwritten inflections applied when reading from original notation, this is the most important.

Example 4.4 Three-voice cadences on modal finals, (a) Dorian, (b) Phrygian, (c) Lydian, (d) Mixolydian

The cadences on the upper stave of Example 4.4 are the first indication that the rules of counterpoint have priority over notions of modal 'purity'. This is even more evident when voices are added to the basic two-voice framework. In three-voice cadences, the most common strategy is for the added voice (on the middle stave of Example 4.4) to supply the fifth below the cadential preparation in the descending voice (Example 4.4a). The resulting leap up a fourth to the final is one of several options (the others are shown in black notes). But this solution is impossible for the Phrygian cadence, since the fifth below the cadential preparation is diminished – a forbidden dissonance (Example 4.4b). The only available option is for the added voice to leap above the descending cadential voice (as shown in the lowest stave of Example 4.4). This type of voice-crossing is very common in the mid-fifteenth century, since it works for the other modes as well – except the Lydian (Example 4.4c), in which the leap of a fourth in the added voice results in the forbidden interval of a tritone (from f to b).

Example 4.4 demonstrates that the Phrygian mode behaves differently from the others, but it also highlights the problem with the dissonant interval F–B in the Dorian and Lydian modes (since it is not possible to have a fifth below the final in the Lydian mode, for the same reason). To get round this, most pieces with finals on D, and virtually all those with a final on F, have a B♭ key signature. Strictly speaking, Dorian on D with a flat is *not* Dorian, any more than Lydian on F with a flat is actually Lydian, but they were still classed as such. (A very rare instance of 'pure' Lydian polyphony, requiring no signature flats in any voice, is the four-voice motet *Stella celi* by the late fifteenth-century Englishman Walter Lambe (*fl.* 1490).) In the *Dodekachordon*, Glarean attempted to address this ambiguity by expanding the number of modes from eight to twelve: his two added finals on C and A (Ionian and Aeolian) may have been intended to restore Dorian and Lydian to their unflattened state. But as with so many innovations arising from conflicts between pitch theory and contrapuntal practice, his proposals were not universally adopted (though one eventual adherent was the equally influential theorist of the following generation, Gioseffo Zarlino (1517–90)).

So far, only three-voice cadences have been shown because they are the most standardized and demonstrate cadential functions most clearly. Because the disposition of cadences for four and more voices is closely related to the question of voice-ranges and functions – the subject of the next chapter – they will be considered there.

A short note on *musica ficta*

The issue of classification lays bare the tension between polyphony and mode, both as regards melodic design and contrapuntal fabric. On the local contrapuntal level also, the relationship is not without its problems. The same is true of hexachord theory, albeit to a lesser degree; some of the rules concerning dissonance treatment were formulated in hexachordal terms.[10] The best-known prohibition concerns the sounding of a pitch solmized *mi* against one solmized *fa* in another, leading to a tritone or diminished fifth. In such situations, musicians would tacitly correct these intervals by altering either pitch. Teachers of the time disagreed about how to do this; tellingly, they distinguished between situations that required correction ('causa necessitatis') from those that were a matter of preference or taste ('causa pulchritudinis') – a distinction suggestive of possible ambiguity. Changes in practice can be detected throughout the period: Karol Berger has suggested that in the early Renaissance flattening was preferred to sharpening, but that by the end of the fifteenth century the latter was increasingly accepted. Another prohibition was the melodic leap of a tritone or augmented fourth, though this was relaxed if a sufficient number of notes, or a rest, were introduced between the two pitches. It was generally agreed that if forced to choose between a harmonic and a linear tritone, the latter was considered the lesser evil. Often, the performers' tacit corrections introduced pitches that lay 'outside the Hand'. Teachers designated the pitches contained within the gamut with the term '*musica recta* or *vera*' (roughly translated as 'correct music', in the sense of 'orthodox') and those that lay outside it as '*musica falsa*' or '*ficta*' (literally 'false', or more exactly, 'feigned').[11]

This is our first encounter with a contentious aspect of Renaissance pitch treatment, and before continuing it is worth clearing up a common misconception. Anyone who sings medieval or Renaissance music from modern editions is familiar with accidentals placed over the stave, inflecting the pitches directly beneath them. This distinguishes them from accidentals notated in the original source or sources, which are placed next to the pitch to which they apply. Pitches above the stave are properly called 'editorial accidentals', meaning that the modern editor takes on the role of the Renaissance performer reading from original notation, supplying accidentals with reference to the contrapuntal rules just mentioned; in a form of shorthand, modern-day singers commonly refer to these editorial interventions as '*musica ficta*', or even just '*ficta*'. Not only is the misnomer misleading, but it also introduces subtler ambiguities: for one thing, not all 'black notes' lie outside the Hand; for another, applying contrapuntal rules does not always result in notes outside the Hand. Finally, it misrepresents the editor's role, since 'adding in ficta' (another shorthand) is not done on a whim but makes explicit an alteration that is either implicit in the original notation (in the editor's judgement) or called for by the melodic or contrapuntal context. The point about judgement is important, because the rules by which these alterations take place frequently come into conflict. This is not to discourage performers from questioning an editor's decisions (since different editors of the same piece will propose different solutions) but to stress the need to do so from as informed a perspective as possible.

Signature flats and expanded hexachords ('*conjunctae*')

The practice of signature flats over and beyond *B-fa* arose – at least in part – from the need to provide consonances (specifically, perfect fifths) on as many pitches as possible. It also enabled the transposition of modes onto other degrees so that the same clefs were used for different modes, as with the two notated versions of *L'Homme armé* shown earlier (thus, pieces using the tune's Dorian version are all notated on G with a signature flat). But adding a flat signature to all the voices merely displaces the problem noted earlier by a fifth, since the third and sixth degrees of the mode (now B♭ and E) make an augmented fourth. The solution to this difficulty is one of the more unfamiliar features of early Renaissance polyphony, sometimes referred to as 'mixed signatures', whereby some or all of the lower voices carry one more signature flat than the higher ones. Example 4.5 gives three examples from three-voice pieces, one for (transposed) Dorian (Example 4.5a), the others for Lydian. In the first Lydian example (Example 4.5b), the upper voice has no flat and both lower voices have one; in the second (Example 4.5c), the two cadential voices have a flat and the added voice has two. Unfamiliar as they seem today, these mixed signatures are very common, albeit haphazardly applied, in manuscript sources (they may be present in one copy of the same piece but not another, this being a case of individual scribal choice). Their use declined after 1500, coinciding with the advent of music printing, which contributed to the growing standardization of notational practice.

The presence of signatures with multiple flats fits within a wider historical context. By the thirteenth century at the latest, it was clear

Example 4.5 (a) Delahaye, *Mort, j'appelle de ta rigueur* (excerpt); (b) Du Fay, *Bien veignés vous, amoureuse lyesse* (beginning); (c) Ockeghem, *Missa Quinti toni*, 'Kyrie II' (beginning)

that every whole tone could be split into semitones. One late fourteenth-century writer, perhaps identifiable with the composer Goscalcus, describes a process of 'mental transposition' (*intellectualis transposicio*) of Guido's deductions as a means of navigating such situations, which is strikingly reminiscent of the 'silent transposition' of improvised polyphony known as 'sighting'.[12] (This formulation, incidentally, supports the notion that hexachords were basically superimposed on the letter-system in the act of singing.) But placing hexachords on pitches other than the seven usual 'places' (the practice known as *conjunctae*) is mentioned only by very few teachers, and present-day writers debate the extent of its applicability; yet more proof of the difficulty of adapting these pre-existing constructs to composed polyphony. By 1500 the use in polyphony of pitches below the gamut was commonplace: F and E are routinely the lowest notated pitches in Lydian and Phrygian pieces, respectively. Though encountered more rarely, pitches beneath these were not unheard of, down to B, and even A,. Certain pieces of the Eton Choirbook (copied just after 1500) extend the notated compass in the opposite direction (up to two octaves above middle C), but the two extremes did not co-exist until the end of the Renaissance.

Enhanced chromaticisms

A related area of expansion concerned the pitches within *musica ficta* and their enharmonic spellings. The first indications of enharmonic keyboards with split or raised keys date from the early fifteenth century, but they seem geared to facilitate just intonation rather than expand the range of possible tuning systems.[13] This is roughly contemporary with the tail-end of the *ars subtilior* style (with which Goscalcus was associated), which produced that early experiment in radical chromaticism, Solage's *Fumeux fume par fumée* (which has notated accidentals on both sharp and flat sides, including the enharmonic relationships (F♯ and G♭, C♯ and D♭, G♯ and A♭)). (For what it's worth, Goscalcus' proposals regarding 'expanded hexachords' were made in the context of plainchant, not polyphony, and it is hard to see how useful they would have been in negotiating *Fumeux fume* and other hyper-chromatic pieces.) As far as is known, such explicit chromatic experimentation did not re-enter the musical mainstream until the sixteenth century. By then, an interest in expanded tunings was very much in evidence, hence the survival of several instruments with split keys (none of them, alas, in working order) and detailed descriptions of others of which no physical record survives. The intention behind these split keys is disputed even by contemporary writers, but they include possible distinctions between B♯ and C and between E♯ and F, and raised keys split not two but three ways. Vicentino, here as in much else a radical who put his ideas into practice, not only constructed an 'archicembalo' capable of the very finest enharmonic distinctions but also wrote quarter-tones into his music.[14]

But unlike the situation 150 years earlier, the practical expansion of chromatic space was not only theoretical or seemingly confined to the odd experiment or showpiece (though there were some: Cipriano's *Calami sonum ferentes* is notated in low clefs, like *Fumeux fume*.) Unsurprisingly, it was a habitual resource of later Renaissance keyboard music. In the work of the extraordinary Giovanni de Macque (*c*.1548–1614), chromaticism goes hand in hand with wildly extrovert and unexpected gestures and extreme contrapuntal licence, and the madrigal repertory from Willaert and Cipriano onwards cannot be envisaged without it. De Macque's presence at the court of Carlo Gesualdo (1567–1613) is significant, since Naples and the surrounding area (which included the family seat at Venosa) was fertile ground for chromatic practice; but Gesualdo also had close personal ties with the Este court at Ferrara, which enjoyed a similar reputation and innovated in other ways. Until recently, the historical significance of Gesualdo's heightened chromaticism could be misrepresented, because of the tendency to gloss over the context from which it sprang. Nonetheless, it is illuminating as regards musical style. First, it illustrates the general point that intense concentration on a given musical parameter (here, chromaticism) is often counteracted by a stepping-down in the importance of other ones: thus, Gesualdo's daring in matters of pitch contrasts with a conventional attitude to form (his madrigals are overwhelmingly in two sections with internal repeats). Second, it shows emphatically that heightened chromaticism is not only a Baroque phenomenon but is fully of the Renaissance. Its expansion of the possibilities of pitch treatment corresponds with similar explorations taking place at the same time in registral space and scoring, considered in Chapter 11.

An even shorter note on dissonance treatment

The first systematic study of dissonance treatment in modern times was Knud Jeppesen's influential *The Style of Palestrina and the Dissonance* (1925). Palestrina was an ideal model because, with few exceptions, dissonances in his music are covered by a half-dozen rules, making his style relatively easy to codify. (His approach to fashioning points of imitation is similarly economical, as Peter Schubert has demonstrated.[15]) Palestrina's most prominent contemporaries (notably Lassus, Victoria, or Byrd) are more flexible in this regard, and, in general, the further one goes back in time, the greater the variety of dissonance encountered. Peter Schubert's teaching manual, *Modal Counterpoint, Renaissance Style*, focuses primarily on sixteenth-century counterpoint and includes examples from earlier composers such as Francisco Guerrero but does not venture much earlier than 1530. Dissonance treatment earlier in the Renaissance is considerably more varied, and several fundamental rules of Palestrina's style do not apply in the fifteenth century: consecutive fifths are common enough in Josquin (though under certain conditions), and unprepared, unresolved, and accented dissonances are frequent in the previous generation. (Jeppesen frequently cites Obrecht's music in support of these differences; significantly, Obrecht was the only early Renaissance composer whose entire known output was thought to have been published by that point.) Their sound world can appear quite alien to those more familiar with sixteenth-century music, which tends towards ever-increasing uniformity in most of the stylistic categories discussed in this book.

Chapter 5 | Voice-names, ranges, and functions

The review of theoretical pitch-constructs in Chapter 4 introduced concepts whose Renaissance meanings differ significantly from their modern ones. This familiar experience for students of Renaissance music continues as we investigate the concepts named in the title of this chapter. What do the names and ranges of the voices in polyphony have to tell about how it works?

Figure 5.1a shows the typical nomenclature and ranges of a standard modern 'SATB' choir, with the voice-ranges next to the clefs (and notional extremes of range in brackets). Each name designates a range that is fixed both in terms of 'absolute' pitch (fixed between a'=440 and 448) and relative pitch (i.e. the position of the four ranges in respect of each other is unchanging: notwithstanding some overlap, the soprano is higher than the alto, the alto higher than the tenor, and so on). But the names also denote a *type* of voice, as do other names of voices that lie between the four principal ones (e.g. mezzo-soprano, baritone, or countertenor). Like the voices with which they are associated, clefs also have a fixed meaning: they denote both relative and absolute pitch (hence the modern use of a treble clef with an octave sign below to indicate the tenor range). But there is no correlation between clef and voice part: for example, the soprano and alto share the same clef even though this entails using ledger lines for the alto part. Similarly, there is no consistent relationship between the names of clefs and the voices to which they are assigned: the 'bass clef' applies to the bass voice, but the alto uses the 'treble clef', from which the clef used for the tenor is adapted.

This situation is comparatively recent. Figure 5.1b shows how the same voices, with roughly the same ranges, were notated a century or so ago (and still are in some pedagogical contexts). The two inner voices have their own clef, each of which locates the pitch c′ on a different line. Apart from logical consistency, this has the practical advantage that ledger lines are rarely needed; but there is a qualitative advantage as well, for the voices' actual ranges coincide with those of the stave. In this configuration, the clefs still denote fixed, absolute ranges, but their relation to their respective voices is clearer. (In fact, they are still referred to as 'alto' and 'tenor' clefs even

Voice-names, ranges, and functions

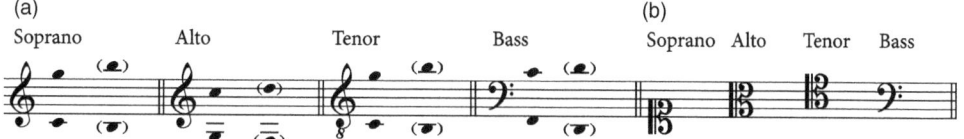

Figure 5.1 (a) Modern SATB clefs and voice-ranges; (b) Old-style SATB clefs

though they have been largely superseded in vocal and choral music.) Thus, clefs once played a more significant role in the notation of voice parts than they do today. In fact, Figure 5.1b is a survival of medieval and Renaissance practice, in which the role of clefs is essential.

What clefs mean (and what they don't)

From the earliest stave notation, the number of lines was less important than the location of the semitones. Originally, this was the sole function of clefs, the most common of which indicated the position of the pitch C, and therefore the semitone between it and the B below it. The stave, meanwhile, denoted the voice's overall range. Since plainchants rarely exceed the octave, four lines were usually sufficient, and if a few extra notes were needed, the position of the clef could be shifted temporarily. But just as important as the clef's meaning is what it didn't mean: the clef indicated relative pitch (that is, the voice's relation to other voices) but not absolute pitch. In a monophonic framework, there was of course no need to indicate absolute pitch: the pitch-level was selected to accommodate the available voices. Of all the clef types, the one on c' was the most prevalent, followed by that a fifth below it (the modern bass clef). Both of these could be located on any line of the stave, but the usual position of the f was on the second highest. (The treble clef locating g' only became common currency towards the turn of the fifteenth century. In its earliest usage, it often carried a signature flat on the top line, which marked the placement of the *mi–fa* semitone.) A more rarely used clef, named 'Gamma' after the lowest note of the gamut, was used for very low pitches lying up to a seventh 'outside the Hand'. The essential point is that in polyphony, clefs indicate the voices' *relative* ranges. There is no evidence of absolute pitch in the Renaissance, any more than for other types of measurement: as with currency, weight, or distance, pitch-standards were a matter of local custom.

Cadential function and the principal voice-types

In the earliest composed polyphony, the voice bearing the plainchant assumed the descending cadential function, and cadences marked off a piece's internal sections and the final close. The plainchant-bearing voice was called 'tenor' (from the Latin verb *tenere*, 'to hold'), perhaps because it carried the plainchant, which itself carried the divine Word; hence its status as the 'foundation' of polyphony, to use Tinctoris' expression. The tendency in plainchant is for stepwise motion, with leaps no larger than a fifth. By the time Tinctoris was writing in the 1470s, tenor lines were not always borrowed from plainchant and could also be freely composed, but the voice still retained its defining function as the lower of the two cadential voices. The voice whose function was to cadence with the tenor had several names, which are interchangeable and almost never designated in manuscript sources: 'discantus' (later shortened to 'cantus'), 'superius', or 'supremus' (the last two terms indicating that it was the highest voice). That the voices were defined by their function is demonstrated by the terms denoting their cadential motions, respectively, '*cantizans clausula*' and '*tenorizans clausula*' ('the cadence that behaves as the cantus/tenor').

A concise illustration of these functions is Du Fay's three-voice rondeau, *Je requier a tous amoureux*, composed not long before 1430 (Example 5.1). Each of the text's four lines is of roughly the same length and ends with a clear-cut cadence: the first (b. 4) and the last phrase cadences on the final, and the two middle ones (bb. 9, 14) on other degrees. The discantus and tenor alternate contrary and parallel motion, with prominent consecutive sixths at cadential approaches. The cadential ornaments in the discantus are a touch more emphatic at the close of each half of the song. *Je requier* also shows the division of the modal octave in both voices: the discantus' first phrase outlines the species of fourth, with the leap to g' taking the voice outside it before the cadence, while the tenor outlines the species of fifth. (Note that the only pitches that lie outside the discantus' octave are those of the cadential ornament in b. 8.) The top notes of each voice, which are only heard once, are worth noting: the tenor's d' (which is approached and quitted by step) lies just outside the octave, a gesture whose expressive purpose was mentioned in the last chapter in connection with the *L'Homme armé* melody; and the discantus' c" marks the song's melodic climax by reaching the top of the modal octave (and the song's highest pitch) in the final phrase, which quickly takes both voices through their respective ranges as a concluding gesture.

Example 5.1 Du Fay, *Je requier a tous amoureux* (complete). Translation: I take as witnesses all lovers who judge by their good breeding: those who dare not say 'my [woman] friend', are truly happy in love.

If the tenor is the 'foundation' voice of polyphony, the discantus–tenor pair constitutes its essential framework. In polyphony, duos are contrapuntally self-sufficient, but by the 1440s they were almost exclusively reserved for reduced sections within larger-scale pieces, with three- and four-voice scoring as the norm. The names, ranges, and functions of the added voices changed significantly over the course of the Renaissance. The most durable of these additional voice-types was the 'contratenor'. Today, the term in its anglicized form 'countertenor' designates a voice-type, but in its earliest occurrence (in the mid-fourteenth century) it denoted a voice lying in the same range as the tenor and complementing the discantus–tenor cadential framework. In other words, what distinguished the added voice was not its range but its role in relation to ('contra' in the sense of written 'against') the tenor. In Du Fay's *Je requier*, the tenor moves predominantly by step, but the contratenor consists mostly of leaps. It fills out the sonority by crossing constantly either side of the tenor. The cadences demonstrate this complementary function: in the first of the song's two internal cadences (b. 9), it is sandwiched between the parallel sixths of the cadential voices, and in the second (b. 14) it supports the tenor at the fifth below. In the song's first and last cadences, it leaps up the octave, finishing between the discantus and tenor. The cadences of *Je requier* exemplify the main patterns of contratenor behaviour before *c.*1440 and for some time thereafter. These differences of function may have had practical implications. Though located in the same range, contratenor and tenor parts may have required singers with different skills, timbre, or vocal production (for the tenor, the ability to hold long notes, and for the contratenor, greater vocal agility).

Registral tiers: the English *Caput* Mass and the contratenor bassus

The contratenor function seen in *Je requier* was already in place in the most famous work of the medieval period, Machaut's *Messe de Nostre-Dame* (*c.*1360). However different they may be in other ways, both share the same registral layout, with two distinct ranges a fifth apart (see Table 5.1). In four-voice music, a further voice was added to the upper registral tier, lying roughly in the same range as the discantus. This fourth voice was called 'triplum' (the name from which derives the modern 'treble') and doubled the discantus at the fifth at cadences: this is the distinctive double leading-note cadence so typical of late medieval music (see Figure 5.2). The decisive stylistic change that took place about 1440, ushered in by the English *Caput* Mass and its companions, was the addition of a third registral tier with a contratenor lying a fifth below the tenor. This new scoring soon superseded the two-tier layout in four-voice

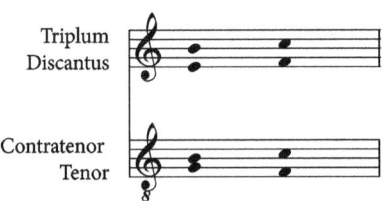

Figure 5.2 Four-part cadence, two-tier texture (pre-1400)

Table 5.1 Voice-names and functions in the Renaissance

	c. 1440 [4vv.] c. 1460 [3vv.]	c. 1500	c. 1540	
			chiavi naturali	chiavette
[Triplum] Discantus	Discantus	Discantus	Cantus	
Tenor, Contratenor	Tenor Contratenor altus	Altus	Altus	
		Tenor	Tenor	
	Contratenor bassus	Bassus	Bassus	

music: the triplum disappeared, leaving the discantus on its own at the top of the texture.

Although we do not know precisely what attracted composers to the new texture, its practical consequences were momentous. Previously, the handling of sonority was conditioned by the pitches of the tenor (especially at cadences), but now the options were considerably expanded, since the new voice could supply a number of consonances beneath it (Example 5.2). This passage also shows an increase in the voices' overall range compared to *Je requier*, encompassing the whole gamut: the gap between the tenor and the lower contratenor could be as much as an octave, resulting in new textural possibilities. The new range also changed the lower contratenor's melodic profile: with the tenor no longer treading on its toes, it was free to move in the more fluid, stepwise manner hitherto reserved for the discantus and tenor. The 'filler' quality previously associated with it was now left to the voice that lay in the same range as the tenor. With the contratenor function effectively split between them, they were labelled 'contratenor altus' and 'contratenor bassus' ('higher' and 'lower'). Eventually the word 'contratenor' was dropped, leaving only the Latin forms of 'alto' and 'bass'.

Example 5.2 Anon., *Missa Caput*, Sanctus (first tenor entry)

As far as is known (given that dating manuscript sources, and therefore musical works before the age of print, is no precise science), the transition from two to three tiers occurred more gradually in three-voice music than in four. In the chanson repertory, three-voice scoring remained in place longer than in sacred music (perhaps because the introduction of the '*Caput* texture' was specifically associated with four-voice music), and the two types of texture co-existed for a time. The tenor and contratenor continued to occupy the same range in some songs into the 1450s, though often with a less angular, more melodic style of contratenor (as in Ockeghem's virelai *Ma bouche rit*, discussed in Chapter 10). Although the tenor retains its key function at major cadential points, elsewhere it is not so easily distinguished from the contratenor as in *Je requier*, for example). By the 1460s, the three-tier texture was the norm in both three- and four-voice music, though it was not uncommon for a contratenor bassus to be disjunct one moment and melodic the next, as in Example 5.3, from a rondeau by Busnoys. Here the discantus and tenor imitate each other frequently, while the contratenor does so more

Example 5.3 Busnoys, *Quant ce viendra*, second part (beginning). Translation: From you my faithful consideration, which none can deflect.

sporadically. The functional importance of the discantus–tenor pair does not mean that the voices always had equal melodic importance, however. In *Je requier* the interest is centred firmly on the top line, and even after the three-tier texture had taken hold, such discantus-based pieces are still common.

The 'invention' of the contratenor bassus is arguably the most fundamental stylistic innovation before the basso continuo at the turn of the seventeenth century. It may explain Tinctoris' comment that his contemporaries considered music more than forty years old hardly worth listening to; if so, there is a certain irony in his continued reference to the tenor as the 'foundation' of polyphony (which dates from the same period), since this was actually less true than it would have been forty years earlier. The advent of the *Caput* texture meant that the other voices no longer had to have the same final as the tenor: either contratenor could take the tenor's place, cadencing with the discantus at certain points. Du Fay's *Missa Se la face ay pale*, was one of the earliest continental Masses to have been composed in the wake of the *Missa Caput*. That some of the more far-reaching implications of the new texture should have been exploited so early on is testament to the conceptual boldness of early Renaissance composers. The stylistic changes precipitated by the *Caput* texture go beyond vocal scoring, but this first step in the tenor's displacement as the functional centre of gravity may be viewed as the real paradigm shift. That is not to say that what followed was inevitable but that without it Renaissance music would have been very different.

Table 5.1 also shows the three critical junctures within the period 1440–1600 (the first of them being the shift to *Caput* texture). The clef combinations associated with them are indicative rather than absolute: first, because two sources of a piece may use clefs notated a third apart for the same voice, or the same clef may be used for two different voices having narrow but distinct ranges (in other words, a seemingly normative clef combination may conceal a registrally unusual piece, and vice-versa); second, because these shifts were gradual, and not all pieces fall straightforwardly within these norms; third, because composers sometimes experimented with vocal scorings that lay outside these norms; and finally, because polyphony in England developed along very different lines post-*Caput* (these last two points will be considered in Chapter 11).

From four voice-ranges to *chiavette*

A practical consequence of the *Caput* texture was the recognition of the bass as a distinct voice-type. (According to his contemporary Tinctoris, Ockeghem was not only one of the pre-eminent composers of his generation but an outstanding bass singer.) During the later fifteenth century, disjunct contratenors gradually fell out of use, but the one in the same range as the tenor tended to work around the other voices in the interests of the overall sonority: it was the least essential voice from a syntactical point of view. This is why when three-voice pieces have an added voice in some sources (as is the case with *Quant ce viendra*), that voice is almost invariably an altus.

As five-voice writing became more common after 1500, the three-tier texture itself began to split. At first, the fifth voice had no fixed designation because it had no fixed position; it was sometimes called '*quinta vox*' ('fifth voice'), sometimes the more evocative '*vagans*' ('wanderer'). After 1500 its position stabilized, occupying the same range as the tenor (and therefore creating two higher contratenors, one lying just slightly higher) and having its own clef, midway between that of the discantus and tenor. This split is noticeable from the last quarter of the fifteenth century. In Example 5.4, from a very early example of this type of scoring by Gaspar van Weerbeke (*c*.1450–*c*.1517), the contratenor altus is consistently higher than the tenor, but in some sources they have different clefs (c3 [that is, a clef with c on the

Example 5.4 Gaspar, *O salutaris hostia* (complete). Translation: O saving sacrifice, who opens the gates of heaven, our foes make war on us: give strength and succour.

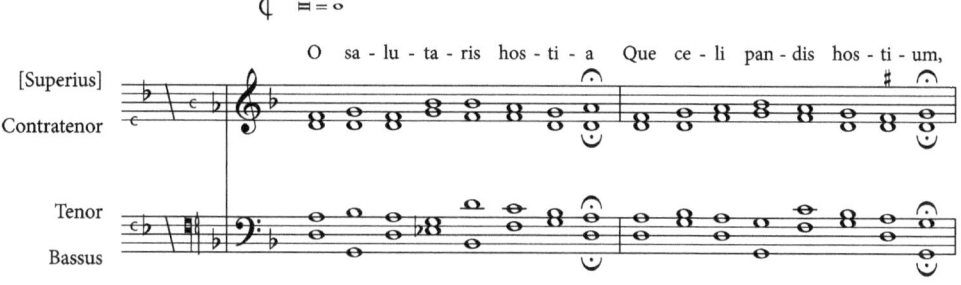

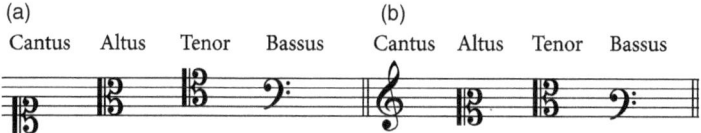

Figure 5.3 (a) *Chiavi naturali*; (b) *Chiavette*

third line] or c4) and in others the same one (c3). In Example 5.5, from a motet by Willaert (c.1490–1563) composed some fifty years later, the two have different clefs (c3, c4) and distinct ranges, as indicated by their imitative entries.

During the sixteenth century the number of voices in a composition was dependent on any number of factors: the solemnity of the occasion, the mood of the text, even the symbolic significance of the number of voices to the liturgical destination or the text's subject matter. However, the principle of four stable ranges (regardless of the number of sounding voices) was well established by the 1520s, as shown in Example 5.6, from a six-voice motet by Nicolas Gombert (c.1495–1560). In practice, there were two common clef configurations with clefs a third apart (Figure 5.3). The twist is that pieces

Example 5.5 Willaert, *Saluto te, sancta virgo Maria* (beginning). Translation: I salute you, holy virgin Mary, queen of heaven...

notated in the so-called 'high clefs' (called '*chiavette*', Italian for 'little clefs') sounded at the same pitch as those notated in 'low clefs' ('*chiavi naturali*'), meaning that the same singers could sing both. The practice, which is attested by many contemporary teachers, should not be regarded as 'transposition', since no absolute pitch-standard existed; rather, the two clef combinations entailed different pitch-levels. A particularly interesting case is that of Lassus' *Lagrime di San Pietro* (pub. 1595) in which the two configurations appear in different pieces. While it had been standard practice for prints to be organized in terms of mode (ever since Cipriano's first book of madrigals, 1542), the madrigals of the *Lagrime* form a continuous narrative, meaning that Lassus must have regarded continuous performance as at least possible – in which case the two clef configurations would have had to

Example 5.6 Gombert, *Media vita in morte sumus* (beginning). Translation: In the midst of life [we are in death]...

follow one another, directly posing the problem of their respective pitch-levels (we will return to this in Chapter 14).

The difference in pitch-level between the *chiavi naturali* and the *chiavette* (anything from a minor third to a perfect fourth) depended on the piece's mode. Both Phrygian and Hypophrygian pieces typically used low clefs with no flat in the signature (the absence of flats designated by the term '*cantus durus*'), whereas the clefs used for Lydian (high) and Hypolydian (low) were different, albeit that a flat signature (termed '*cantus mollis*') was used for both. On the other hand, Dorian pieces could be notated using either combination, with either a D final or G with a signature flat. The correlation between final and clef combination became so standardized that modern-day theorists have developed a system of classification according to these two parameters (either high or low clefs with or without signature flat – four combinations in all).[1] Pieces of the same 'tonal type' tend to share similar characteristics, as would later be the case with keys in tonality; certain tonal types were more commonly used than others and were favoured differently by individual composers. In practice, the distance between certain tonal types and the corresponding keys in tonality is so small as to be practically negligible (say, pieces with an A final in *cantus durus* on the one hand and pieces in A minor on the other). The logical consequence of this is Vicentino's proposal that the bass should be regarded as the fundamental voice in polyphony, not the tenor.

Finally, it is worth observing that the *chiavette* system differs from earlier practice only in being more systematic (a symptom, perhaps, of the tendency to standardization observed in the age of print). The written ranges of Du Fay's *Missa Ecce ancilla/Beata es, Maria* and his *Missa Ave regina celorum* are a fourth apart and have different clefs, but their relative ranges are practically identical. The difference is a matter of their respective finals, F and C. Both can (and probably ought to) be performed in the same sounding range and with the same types of singers on each part.

Another look at cadence

Although the finer points of contrapuntal practice are beyond the scope of this book, the handling of cadence shows these changes of vocal scoring in action and is an indicator of style in its own right.

As explained in Chapter 4, there are two types of contratenor motion at three-voice cadences in the two-tier system (pre-*Caput*). In the first (the middle stave of Example 4.4 above, p. 58), the contratenor is sandwiched between the cadential voices, while in the second (the lower stave of Example 4.4) the contratenor is below the tenor at the cadential preparation. In the latter configuration, the contratenor lies below the tenor at the preparation, typically finishing with an octave leap upwards. In the later three-tier texture (with each voice in its own range), cadences are overwhelmingly of this second type, except that the contratenor avoids the octave leap, finishing either at the unison with the tenor or at the octave below. When a fourth voice is added in the older two-tier texture, the added voice is the triplum, whereas in the three-tier texture it is the contratenor altus (Example 5.7). At its simplest, this voice need only hold a single pitch, except in Phrygian cadences, where it results in several forbidden intervals (Example 5.7b). For this reason, three-tier Phrygian cadences adopt the earlier 'sandwich' set-up, which sounds particularly exotic to modern ears (Example 5.8). In Example 5.8a, the added voice is the lowest, leaping above the tenor to take the third at the final sonority.

Example 5.7 Four-voice cadences on modal finals, (a) Dorian, (b) Phrygian, (c) Lydian, (d) Mixolydian

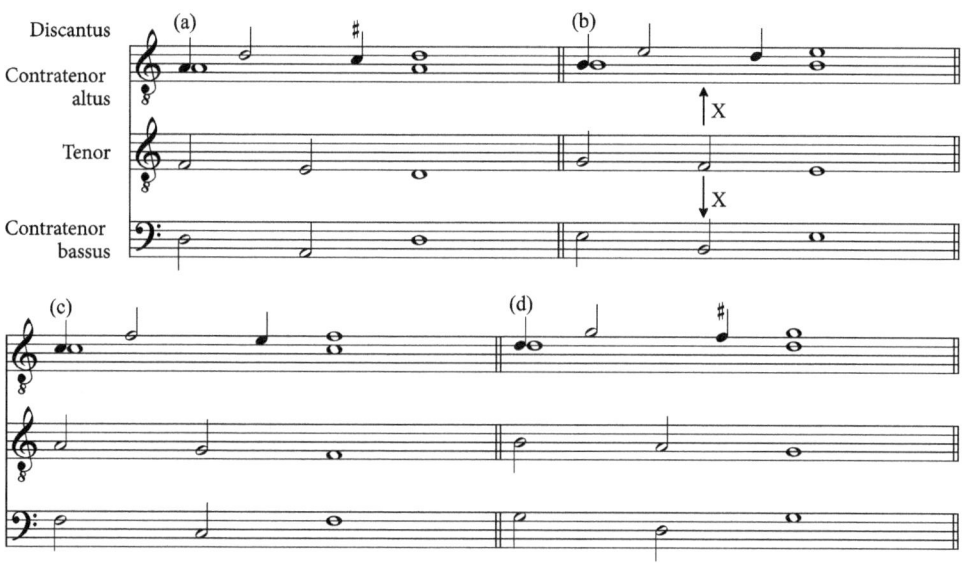

Example 5.8 Phrygian cadences

Example 5.9 'Fermata' cadence

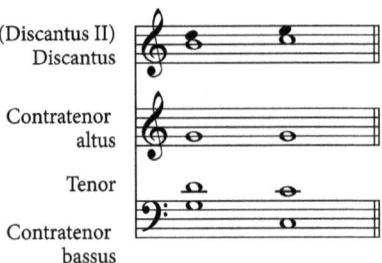

Examples 5.8b and 5.8c are typical of the Hypophrygian mode, because the lowest voice takes the fifth below the tenor either in the final sonority (Example 5.8b) or at the preparation (Example 5.8c). In the latter case, the free voices continue beyond the cadence in the discantus and tenor (remembering that in terms of contrapuntal theory it is the movement of the discantus and tenor that constitutes the cadence in Examples 5.8b and 5.8c, not the motion in the bass). Another stylistic marker is the presence of the third at final cadences: before 1500, when three- and four-voice music was the norm, it is rare (except in England, where it sometimes takes the place of the fifth). Example 5.9 shows a typical four-voice cadence of the 'fermata' variety, often used in sacred music to set the final 'Amen'. This type of cadence dispenses with the suspension; a third may be added by doubling the discantus in five voices (in black notes). It is most frequent in five-voice cadences, but over the course of the sixteenth century it extended to all types of scoring.

After 1500, an increase in the number of voices leads to more exotic cadences, as more voices have to be accommodated within the same vocal compass (cf. Example 5.10). In Example 5.10a, the 'Quinta vox' sounds the third below the bassus just before its appearance in sharpened form in the discantus. Though very common with Gombert and his generation, this cadential false relation was given the derogatory label '*Satzfehler*' ('part-writing error') by scholars in the mid-twentieth century who held an unfavourable view of the period between Josquin and Palestrina.[2] The *Satzfehler* is closely related to the so-called 'English' cadence (Example 5.10b), which exists in several forms, the most famous (not to say notorious) of which has the distinctive gesture in the voice labelled 'medius' ('mean' being the common designation for the second-highest voice), with the two types of third still closer together or even simultaneously. This sonority endured until the time of Purcell, more than a

Example 5.10 (a) 'Satzfehler' cadence; (b) 'English' cadence

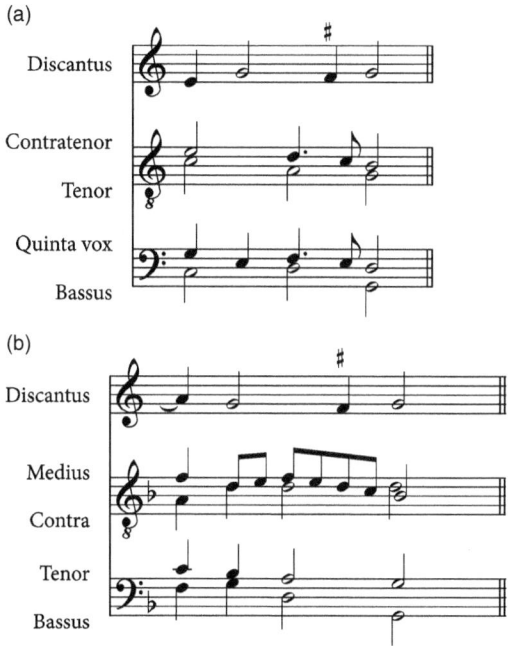

Example 5.11 Arcadelt, *Il bianco e dolce cigno* (conclusion)

century after its first appearance. With composers of the late Renaissance, these more exotic types of cadence types are abandoned in favour of simpler layouts. One is a form of pedal point derived from the cadential extension shown in Example 5.8c. Such coda-like material occurs throughout the Renaissance, but, during the second quarter of the sixteenth century, it is common for the discantus to hold the final on its own, as in Example 5.11, the conclusion of Arcadelt's famous *Il bianco e dolce cigno*. Although the tenor initially cadences with the discantus, pedal points like this signal a further loosening of the tenor's role as the structural voice: whereas traditional Renaissance theory continued to uphold the discantus–tenor framework, in practice the motion of the bass assumed comparable importance even in four-voice music. By the time of Palestrina and Lassus, this pedal-point ending was one of the most common closing gestures, regardless of the number of voices involved.

Chapter 6 | Mensural notation, duration, and metre

Compared with modal theory and the constructs pertaining to pitch, Renaissance polyphony's rhythmic and metrical organization was a comparatively recent development.[1] While their general principles were as old as polyphony itself, their specific configuration was only codified in the early fourteenth century, with the emergence of the framework known as the 'four prolations'. Among the mensural system's most fascinating attributes is the capacity of individual signs to have different meanings and functions, just as the syllable *ut* may express several modern pitch classes. This marks it out from common practice, in which the meaning of most signs is fixed (i.e. a breve is always equal to two semibreves, a semibreve to two minims, and so on). Much Renaissance notation plays on the fact that 'what you get' depends on different ways of reading 'what you see'; especially before 1500, many pieces cannot be fully appreciated without some understanding of their notational subtleties, which are as much part of their conception as the sounding result.[2] It is not necessary to know the mensural system in all its complexity to grasp these; what follows is not a crash-course but a demonstration of the essential features as they relate to style and concept. Equally, it should be borne in mind that after *c.*1510 most of them had ceased to apply in practice. Practically speaking, mensural usage after that date is essentially equivalent to common-practice notation.

The four prolations

From its inception, '*musica mensurata*' (mensural music) was a means of parsing time into units and coordinating voices (Figure 6.1). The earliest notated examples chiefly employed the two values 'longa' and 'brevis' (hereafter 'long' and 'breve'; note that these names denote relation rather than absolute quantity), which could be parsed into groups of two (binary division) or three (ternary division). A third value, the 'maxima' (at the top of Figure 6.1), greater than the long, was soon joined by a fourth, the 'semibreve', shorter than the breve, and later still, the minim (the lowest

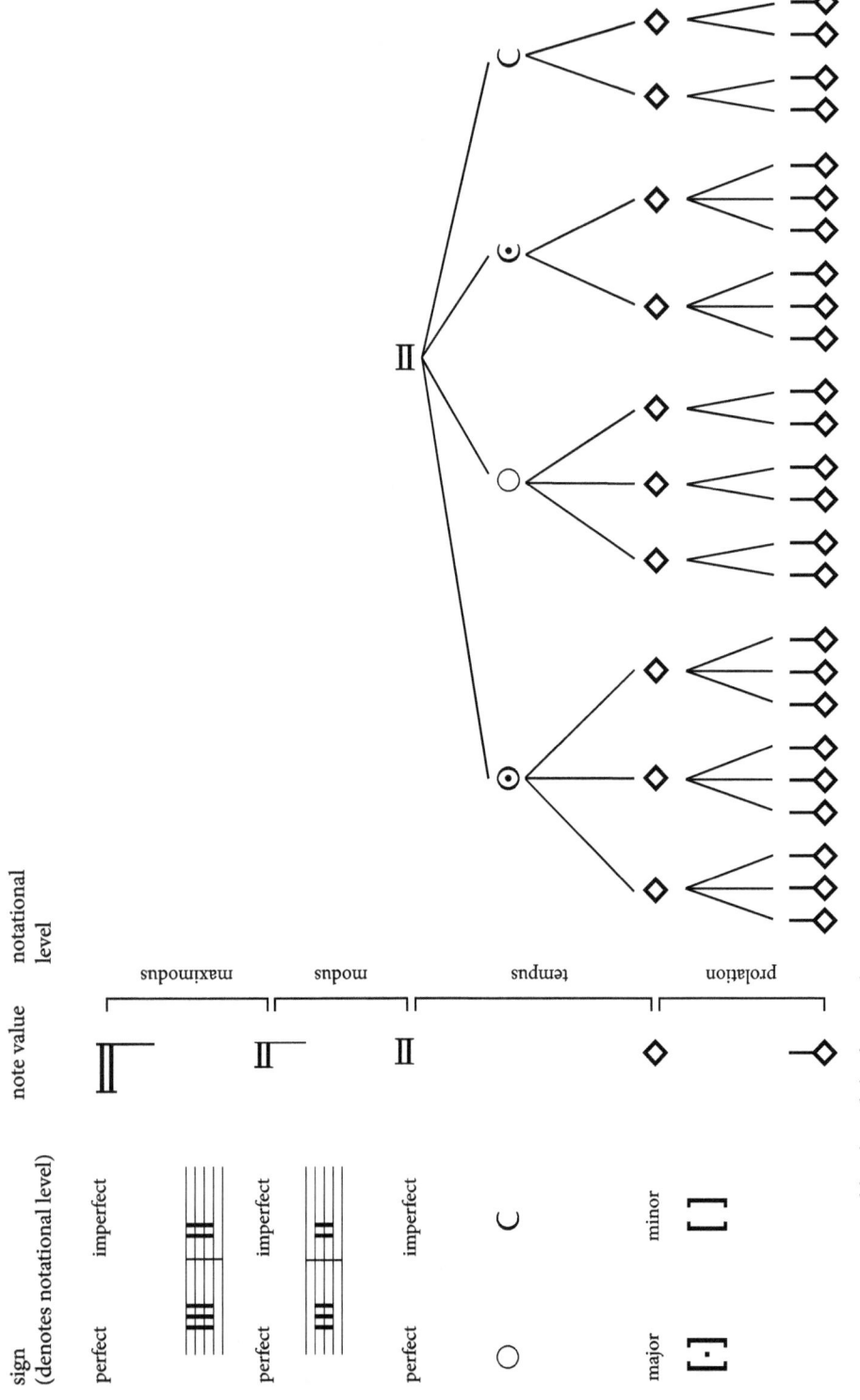

Figure 6.1 Mensural levels and the four prolations

value in Figure 6.1). Over the centuries shorter note-values were introduced with ever more fanciful names (in order, semiminim, fusa, and semifusa). By the early fourteenth century, the principle of binary or ternary division applied on several levels from maxima to minim, with each level designated by a term. Because the most common note-values were the breve, semibreve, and minim, the most common levels of division were those of 'tempus' (the relation of the breve to the semibreve) and 'prolation' (semibreve to minim), prolation being the lowest level at which both binary and ternary divisions applied. Figure 6.1 also shows the four combinations of binary and ternary division on the level of tempus and prolation – the 'four prolations', each designated by its own sign. A perfect circle indicated ternary division on the level of tempus (the perfect, self-containing nature of the circle being associated with the Holy Trinity), while an incomplete or 'imperfect' circle (resembling the letter 'c') designated binary division. On the level of prolation, division was either major (that is, 'greater', i.e. ternary) or minor ('lesser', i.e. binary), indicated by the presence or absence of a dot within the perfect or imperfect circle. Division of the long into breves and of the maxima into longs (known, respectively, as modus and maximodus) was indicated by notating rests in groups of two or three, as shown in the left-hand column of Figure 6.1. The total number of possible combinations of binary and ternary groupings on all four available levels is sixteen. (The mid-fifteenth-century *Missa Dixerunt discipuli* by Eloy d'Amerval cycles through all of them.) The resulting groupings designate not only the relationship between rhythmic levels but also their internal organization. By 1440, modus and maximodus were less tangible presences than they once had been, but the persistent habit of grouping long and maxima rests into groups of two or three (to denote binary or ternary division, as shown in Figure 6.1) suggests that they were not simply theoretical. Whether they had any palpable, experiential pertinence for Renaissance musicians is a moot point (and in any case they soon disappeared from standard notational practice), but it is significant that the development of the mensural system in the thirteenth century is roughly contemporary with the first Western examples of that quintessential instrument for measuring time, the mechanical clock.

Modern editorial practice tends to render the four prolations as time signatures with equivalent levels of metrical organization. During much of the twentieth century (when quartered note-values were the norm), they were transcribed as 2/4 (or 4/4 if barring according to the original long), 3/4 (or 6/4), 6/8, and 9/8. If transcribing according to halved note-values the denominator is doubled, and, when using original

Example 6.1 Original notation (upper stave) transcribed according to C (middle stave) and O (lower stave)

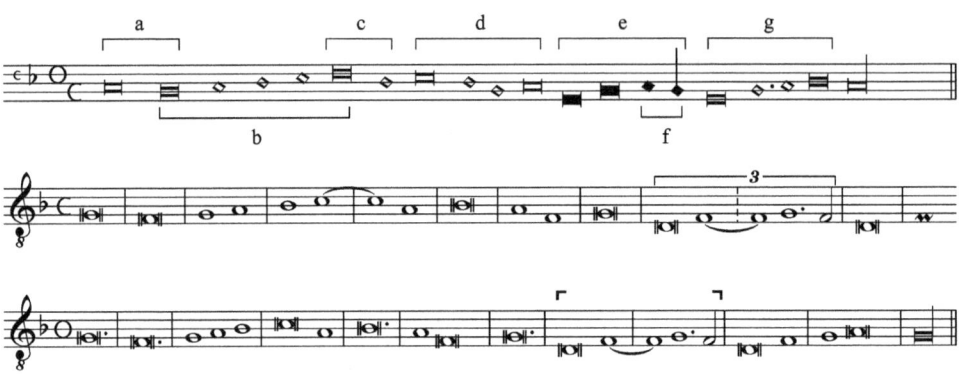

note-values, editors often indicate the original mensural sign instead of a time signature. Figure 6.1 also shows that a value – say, the breve – can have different durations depending on the sign under which it is read. Under ☉, where ternary subdivision applies on the level of both tempus and prolation, it may be worth up to nine minims; under ℂ and O, up to six; and under C, just four. But even under the same mensuration, the durations of note-values are not fixed, but contextual. Example 6.1 gives a flavour of these rules and their practical implications. The same notated passage (upper stave) is transcribed in original note-values in C (middle stave) and O (lower stave). With the exception of the passage bracketed under 'g', it can be straightforwardly transcribed under C, since both tempus and prolation are binary, whereas under O its durations are reckoned differently. In reading what follows, it helps to remember that the usual effect of these rules is to parse the notation of perfect tempus (and/or major prolation, as the case may be) in groups of three.

If a breve is immediately followed by another breve (a), the first remains perfect, and the value of the second depends on the context. The group of three semibreves (b) that follows also makes up a ternary group, so that they, in turn, make the preceding breve perfect as well. In group (c), the semibreve is said to 'imperfect' the breve that comes before it (making it worth two semibreves), which forms another group of three: the breve that follows group (c) is the beginning of a new group. (In major prolation a breve can also be imperfected by a minim so that it is worth *five* minims, which rarely happens under O.) All these cases demonstrate the **rule of perfection**, whereby breves in O (and semibreves in ℭ and ☉) are perfect unless followed by a single note of lower value. Again, the end result is to create groups of three.

The next most important rule is **alteration**: when two breves under ☉ occur either side of a pair of semibreves (d), the first breve is perfect, and the second semibreve is said to be 'altered' by doubling its value, making up a ternary grouping with the first. (Alteration is an essential component of the system, since it would not otherwise be possible to notate a 'short–long' group in major prolation or perfect tempus.) Alteration itself triggers another impossibility, the notation of the hemiola (⋈ o | o ⋈), that is, the temporary shift from two groups of three semibreves within a two-bar group to three groups of two semibreves. To override the rule of alteration, a **dot of division** is placed between the two semibreves (g). It functions like a modern bar-line, indicating that the previous semibreve is grouped with the preceding breve (which it imperfects), and the one after is grouped with the following breve. The dot of division is visually identical to the **dot of addition**, which adds half its value to the preceding note and survives in common-practice notation, but is usually distinguishable from it because of the different contexts in which it occurs: the position of the dot of addition on the stave is always aligned with the note to which it applies, whereas the dot of division is often placed above the notes that it separates.

The notation of larger groups of hemiola accounts for the phenomenon known as **coloration**, where note-shapes are filled in or blackened (usually indicated in modern editions by square hooks showing where coloured note groups begin and end). In principle, coloured notes lose a third of their value: thus, a string of breves that would be perfect under ☉ are worth only two semibreves when coloured (e). Such groups tend towards the formation of perfections or groups of perfections on the next-highest level; e.g. two groups of three imperfect semibreves may be replaced by a single group of three imperfect breves. When applied to imperfect values or binary mensurations, coloration results in triplet formations in modern terms (as with (e) in the middle stave of Example 6.1). The semibreve–minim pattern (f) commonly known today as 'minor color' likewise loses a third of its value, having a combined value of an uncoloured semibreve. Scribes often changed the coloured semibreve to an uncoloured dotted minim, thereby re-interpreting the coloured minim as a semiminim (the two are visually identical: again, it is only context that distinguishes them).

These precepts are best understood as rules of thumb: ambiguities are always possible, especially when the rules come into conflict. But in the overwhelming majority of cases, the correct solution can be deduced from the context and would have been second nature to performers. A final notational category concerns **ligatures**, which combine several durations in one symbol. Derived from plainchant neumes, their practical significance for Renaissance polyphony is uncertain: as with minor color, groups of pitches found under ligature in one source are written separately or grouped differently in another. (Ligature groups are indicated in modern editions by brackets over the relevant pitches.) Since they have no known relevance to musical style, I pass over the rules governing them here. In the mid-sixteenth century, some teachers state that pitches under one ligature are sung to the same syllable, but the evidence that this rule applied much earlier is mixed.

It remains to introduce another sign, the stroke, which can be placed through any of the four prolations. In its original meaning it usually signalled **diminution.** This is best understood by observing the placement of dissonances and suspensions: in uncut mensurations, suspensions are typically placed over a semibreve and last a minim; in cut mensurations they are placed over a breve and last a semibreve. In other words, the unit being beaten is transferred to the next-highest level, i.e. the breve instead of the semibreve. But the stroke can denote that the resulting beat is subdivided, with each subdivision functioning in some respects like a full beat. The stroke is most commonly associated with the sign C and signals the division of the breve into two parts, an upbeat and a downbeat (each being worth a semibreve). By the later fifteenth century, the sign signalled a faster-than-usual tempo with the beat on the semibreve. The stroke is related to other signs, known as **proportions**, which inflect the four principal mensural signs. Since they relate to tempo relationships as well as metrical organization, I will consider these separately.

Mensural usage and musical style

As with the voice-ranges and functions examined in the previous chapter, mensural usage during the Renaissance underwent several changes (see Table 6.1). Prior to 1440, pieces in major prolation outnumber those in

Table 6.1 Normative mensural usage in the Renaissance

before c.1430	c.1440–1500	c.1490/1500–
C, O	O/¢	¢, C

Example 6.2 Anon., *Confort d'amours* (beginning). Translation: [this opening melisma carries no text] The comforts of love humbly...

minor prolation, with ⊙ by far the most common mensural sign – so much so that scribes did not always indicate it. The compound rhythms of major prolation are its most distinctive feature, but one can usually distinguish major from minor prolation with reference to the notation: in major prolation the most common note-values are semibreves and minims, which may be coloured. This results in hemiola at the level of prolation (within the bar, in modern transcription). The push and pull of these cross-rhythms, due to the presence or absence of coloration in different voices simultaneously, is another audible stylistic marker (Example 6.2). The prevalence of major prolation coincides fairly exactly with the two-tier texture mentioned in the previous chapter; pieces exhibiting the two features together can be dated before c.1440 with a fair degree of confidence.

The date is significant because it is about then that the anonymous *Caput* Mass began to circulate in continental sources. In addition to the change from two- to three-tier texture, the new style precipitated a change in mensural usage: major prolation was replaced with minor prolation, with O as the most common sign. (In audible terms, this means the abandonment of compound rhythm.) In minor prolation, breves are much more common than under major prolation, and the cross-rhythms and hemiola (coloration) so typical of major prolation rather less so. (All this is seen in the examples of music in O from previous chapters.) As shown in Example 6.3, when hemiola is present, it is transferred to the level of tempus rather than prolation, that is, across two bars of modern transcription. (Unlike the other examples in this chapter, Example 6.3 is transcribed in halved note-values because in this particular context the mensural sign O2 prescribes that notated longs are read as breves, and breves as semibreves, as will be explained in the next section.) Rhythmic tension in O typically resides in the alternation of groups of one- or two-bar groups (e.g. bb. 1–2 and 4–5 as against b. 3). In some two-bar groups (e.g. bb. 4–5), the beginning of the second bar does not count as a 'strong' beat (in other words, hemiola may occur independently of coloration). As in all forms of hemiola the ambiguity is intentional, but it is easily obscured in modern editions by the presence of bar-lines. Although it takes on a different guise in O compared to ₵ (since under C two-bar groups are subdivided into triplets), hemiola is an essential stylistic component of both. The potential for metrical ambiguity, dissolving any sense of mensural groupings or even downbeats, is typical of the mid-fifteenth century: perfect breves can even be placed on 'weak' beats and ternary groupings occur in ₵. Some composers exploit these possibilities more than others (for example, Ockeghem more than Du Fay).

The predominance of O after *c.*1440 was not as pronounced as that of C in the earlier period: many single-section pieces after *c.*1440 are in ₵, particularly rondeaus. Because the two-tier texture endured longer in three-voice music than in four-voice music and because three voices was the standard scoring for chansons until the turn of the sixteenth century, many chansons of the 1450s in O or ₵ retain the 'older' two-tier texture, with the tenor and contratenor in the same range. Although it is usually the case that stylistic changes do not involve just one musical parameter but several at once (as with the changes of both scoring and mensural usage *c.*1440), such changes were probably not as clear-cut as they seem to us; besides, our knowledge is based on manuscript sources whose dates are overwhelmingly a matter of conjecture.

Example 6.3 Busnoys, *Noel, noel* (beginning). Translation: 'Rejoice, rejoice'

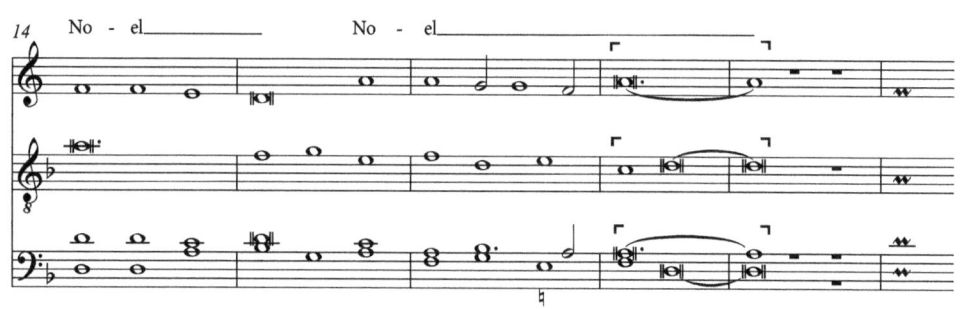

The influence of the *Caput* texture (or rather, the new style which it introduced) went beyond scoring to include matters of mensural practice. Just as important as the move from major to minor prolation was the alternation of mensural signs as a means of structuring large-scale works. Like other English Masses of its time, *Caput* has two main sections per movement, the first in O and the second in C, with the cantus firmus being stated once in each section (the duration of its notated values potentially changing, dependent on the sign under which it is read, as shown in Example 6.1). This alternation of ternary and binary mensurations is a deceptively subtle phenomenon. Essentially, the shift from O to C (the latter always expressed in continental sources as ₵) involves a speeding up on one level and a slowing down on another: in O the beat is on the semibreve, whereas in ₵ it is on the breve, and therefore slower; on the other hand, in ₵ the breve is subdivided, but the semibreve in O is not, so there is a perceptible distinction between the semibreves, which are faster in ₵ than in O. The tension between simultaneous 'slower' and 'faster' may well explain why continental composers were so taken with this feature. They adopted it in Mass music and large-scale motets, where it persisted until the last quarter of the fifteenth century. The shift from O to ₵ is especially perceptible in Busnoys' *In hydraulis* and Josquin's *Illibata Dei virgo nutrix*, whose cantus firmi consist of very short ostinatos whose progress is easy to follow. Both pieces conclude with a return to triple time, in which the tenor material accelerates yet again by way of a concluding flourish (indicated either by coloration or by a proportional sign inflecting the ₵ rather than returning to O). The use of ternary subdivisions as a concluding gesture endured well into the sixteenth century, by which time the O/₵ framework had been superseded.

A second great mensural shift began during the final quarter of the fifteenth century, with ₵ gradually displacing O as the standard mensural sign. As with the previous shift forty years earlier, this was roughly contemporary with a corresponding change in the standard scoring from three tiers to four. After c.1510, O began to disappear altogether, triple time being most often signalled by a proportional sign. Soon, C was the only one of the four prolations left standing; the notational subtleties associated with the others fell by the wayside, effectively paving the way for common-practice notation (Examples 6.4 and 6.5). By 1550, the visual appearance of notation had changed noticeably, with semibreves, minims, and semiminims predominating, breves being rarer, and longs, coloration, and ligatures rarer still. This is a clear indication (among a few others) of a gradual slowing of the notated pulse after that date: comparing Examples 6.4 (pub. 1547) and Example 6.5 (pub. 1595) shows that by 1600 the notated beat had practically shifted from the semibreve to the minim: the semibreve of Example 6.5 is noticeably slower than in Example 6.4.

These changes in mensural practice are subject to the same caveats as those concerning voice-ranges and functions in Chapter 5. 'Older' and 'newer' features could and did overlap: in Example 6.2, which combines

Example 6.4 Janequin, *Toutes les nuictz* (beginning). Translation: Every night you are present to me/In sweet and pleasant dreams...

Example 6.5 Lassus, *Lagrime di San Pietro*, no. 16, 'O vita troppo rea' (beginning). Translation: O life, too cruel, too deceitful...

major prolation and the two-tier texture, the contratenor is consistently lower than the tenor. Taking textural and mensural usage together is a very reliable indicator of style in Renaissance polyphony.

Tempo and proportions

Inconveniently for us, the framework of the four prolations gives no intrinsic indications of tempo. In fact, the issue of absolute tempo is one of the most uncertain in Renaissance performance practice. What contemporary writers say about it is ambiguous, even when describing that most fundamental concept, the 'tactus' (beat): it is not always clear to which notational level the tactus should apply or how it should be subdivided. Modern-day theorists disagree about the interpretation of individual signs (as did their Renaissance counterparts), but here again, their meaning is not fixed but contextually dependent, changing from period to period, region to region, and composer to composer (or even within the practice of the same composer). The performance implications of this situation will be further explored in the final chapter, but a few essential points can be made straightaway.

As with most other notational features discussed previously, the meaning of mensural signs with respect to tempo was not absolute but relative and contextually determined. The most common situation in the early Renaissance was the one just observed, the change from O to ₵ in multi-sectional pieces. The semibreve was somewhat faster under ₵ than under O, although contemporary writers differ as to precisely by how much (most statements put it somewhere between 3:2 and 4:3). Where the sign C was followed by ₵, the same principle applied, although the ratio could be anything from 'somewhat faster' (as before) to notionally 'twice as fast' (though for the latter only rarely). Mensural signs were also inflected by the use of proportions, usually expressed in terms of numbers. Thus, in a section under ₵, adding the figure '3' denoted that three semibreves should take the place of two (although this did not necessarily imply a strict 'metronomic' ratio). Proportional signs could also signal that the beat was transferred to the next-highest notational level, usually the breve instead of the semibreve. With the standardization of ₵ in the early sixteenth century, proportional signs became the standard way of indicating changes of metre, from binary to ternary or vice-versa. Finally, mensural signs could also occur simultaneously (that is, different voices in the same piece could carry different signs). In such cases, ratios were necessarily absolute. Most straightforwardly, a breve under ₵ was worth a semibreve under C. More complex relationships (such as 3:2, 4:3, and so on) could be expressed by juxtaposing different signs: a special case is the use in early Renaissance Masses of major prolation to signal augmentation (typically of a c.f.-bearing tenor line) against minor prolation in the other voices (see Example 12.3 on p. 179). Alongside this specialized notational practice, there existed a parallel one, whereby different mensural signs occurred simultaneously, but with the minim as the common denominator between the voices (thus, a notated breve might be worth nine minims in one voice, and six, four, or even fewer in others). It is worth bearing in mind that different interpretations of the mensural system, such as the two just described, could co-exist in the same period – even in the work of the same composer. What is more, these intricacies underpin some of the most impressive inventions of the c.f. Mass repertory. Pieces like Busnoys' *Missa L'Homme armé*, Josquin's *Missa L'Homme armé super voces musicales*, Ockeghem's *Missa Prolationum*, or Obrecht's cycles on *Malheur me bat* and *Maria zart* (to be examined in later chapters) stretch the mensural system to its conceptual limits. For all their surpassing aesthetic beauty (or perhaps because of it), it is understandable that later composers stepped back from such complexities: their potential had not only been fulfilled but perfectly expressed.

Later commentators (especially of the nineteenth and early twentieth century) often criticized the mensural system for its unnecessary complexity. But this point of view is easily reversed: one could say that compared to it, common-practice notation lacks flexibility (witness the recourse to tied notes, which are superfluous in mensural notation) and sacrifices a system of great elegance on the altar of efficiency.

Chapter 7 | Genre, texts, forms

Beyond the building blocks of syntax explored in the previous chapters, Renaissance polyphony is shaped by formal conventions, which in discussions of later periods typically go under the heading of genre. As applied to Renaissance music, however, genre is a problematic concept. Individual pieces are like a butterfly pinned to a cork, labelled according to a system of classification (called 'taxonomy') into species and subspecies. The label fixes the insect conceptually as rigidly as the pin does its body, but it didn't begin life as a butterfly. In an earlier stage of its development it is called 'caterpillar', similar to its later incarnation in some ways but in many others very different. And we typically use the term 'caterpillar' indifferently to designate all caterpillars, despite the fact that they evolve into many different types of butterfly … The point is that in later music (particularly in the Classical and Romantic periods) the notion of musical work is closely linked to genre, which is integral not only to its production (by the composer) but also to its subsequent reception (by performers and audience). Renaissance musicians saw things differently; although a conception of the musical work undoubtedly existed, it differs significantly from the post-Enlightenment view.[1] As we shall see, the re-purposing of polyphony outside its original context was common; in other words, the link between production and reception was far more fluid. Notwithstanding this, certain modern writers view the art of pre-modern periods, including music, as limited to (or constrained by) the social function it fulfils, but that view is also problematic, not least because it implicitly denies Renaissance composers' creative agency, to which their music bears ample witness.[2] The butterfly analogy is a helpful starting point to explore why notions of genre need careful handling in this period. In this chapter I address the slippery nature of genre in Renaissance music and its link with an equally complex issue, the relationship of text and music.

The genre problem

An underlying premise of genre theory is that 'form follows function'; the function of most Renaissance polyphony is determined by the words it sets.

In a famous passage from his *Dictionary of Musical Terms* (c.1475), Tinctoris described three types of polyphony: 'cantus magnus' ('great'), referring to the Mass; 'cantus parvus' ('small'), referring to songs; with 'cantus mediocris' ('middling'), namely motets, occupying an intermediary position. At first blush it may appear that Tinctoris was referring to size – songs are short ('parvus'), motets longer, and the Mass longest – and until recently this statement was interpreted as an early statement about genre. But some songs are longer than motets, and some motets are on a scale comparable to most Mass movements. In fact, Tinctoris' frame of reference was the classification of types of speech in Ciceronian oratory, which have to do with function.[3] Mass music was loftiest (another meaning of 'magnus') because of its place in the liturgy, secular music or songs ('carmina') the lowliest because they related to human affairs, and motet texts could be either secular or sacred. For Tinctoris, the Mass was the pre-eminent category not primarily because it gave composers greatest scope for invention but because of its function – nothing to do with form, let alone later notions of genre. Is that to say that his tripartite division is of no use in discussing polyphony? Not quite. For even if we think of them solely as categories of function, the three headings are distinguished by the sorts of texts being set, which is fundamental to Renaissance musical forms. In other words, the music's function is vested in the text, whose forms are reflected in the music. In discussing musical forms, therefore, Tinctoris' categories are at least plausible starting points.

Yet notions of genre in later periods typically transcend form. For Beethoven or Brahms, writing a string quartet was not the same as writing a symphony or a piano trio, even though the musical forms involved were essentially identical. (Thus, a transcription for piano trio by Beethoven of one of his own symphonies was not and could not be confused with one of his piano trios.) This conception of genre is strongly linked to that of the autonomous artwork – a viewpoint that dates from the late Classical and early Romantic periods, when it was thought that music had superseded its previous social functions (that is, its subordination to the requirements of religious worship and court life) and become an end in itself, along with other art-forms. Related to this 'autonomy aesthetic' is the view of the composers as freed from the obligation to cater to those social functions in their music; but, as we saw in Chapter 3, the concept of the composer was just gaining traction in the Renaissance, and the idea of the autonomous artwork was a long way off. In practice, the forms of polyphony remained linked to the function for which a given work was first conceived, which was inscribed in the text. When a piece is transmitted without a text, we can often infer its type by examining the musical form: a short fifteenth-century piece in two halves, with a clear cadence at the end of the first part and no change of mensuration, is highly likely to be a rondeau, like Du Fay's *Je requier*. Typically, then, a composer's first consideration was to respond to the form of the text being set; musical conventions tended to be mapped onto the textual form.

However, in most cases where the same music is transmitted in several sources, at least one will have a text; sometimes, different sources for the same piece have different texts, for example a sacred Latin text in one and a French text in another. Here again, the musical form is usually the key to establishing which text form the composer had in mind when writing. Supposing it corresponds to the rondeau form, then the Latin text is most probably a later substitution, for which there may have been any number of motivations. The Latin-texted version is called a 'contrafactum' (plural: contrafacta), meaning a piece with a text supplied in replacement of the original. (Such Latin-texted contrafacta of French chansons were especially common in German and central-European manuscript sources.) Traditionally, modern scholarship has tended to regard contrafacta as having less authority than the composer's presumed original. But this bias rests on assumptions rooted in the autonomy aesthetic, which prioritizes the role of the composer and the related concept of 'Urtext' (that is, a 'definitive' musical text deriving directly from the composer). Renaissance sources themselves give no indication of such a bias. From an emic perspective, the music's function was changed simply by changing the text. A well-known example is the motet *Ave regina celorum* (on a different text from the Marian antiphon) by the Englishman Walter Frye (*fl*. 1460), which survives in nearly forty sources and was reworked countless times, making it the most popular piece of the fifteenth century. (So famous was it that it features in several contemporary paintings of Mary surrounded by angels, who sing from what is plainly a chansonnier: the piece can be read straight from the paintings, which therefore count as musical sources.) Although the Latin text fits the music well enough, the musical form is plainly that of an English ballade (an analogue of the French virelai), and it is probable that the work originated in this form. The vanishingly small number of native mid-fifteenth-century song sources explains why the song's text has not survived, but it is still remarkable that the piece achieved fame not in its initial form but in its contrafacted one. A slightly later example is a piece by Isaac, reportedly composed over just two days in 1502 (according to one of Ercole d'Este's ambassadors; see Example 7.1).[4] The musical text is transmitted in several sources (Illustrations 2.2, 2.3, and 2.4 on pp. 14–17 above), the first as a textless secular piece with the name 'La mi la sol', the

Example 7.1 Isaac, *La mi la sol, la sol la mi* (beginning)

second as a motet with a sacred Latin text, 'Rogamus te, piissima virgo', and the third as a Mass section of the Credo (from the *Missa O praeclara*). Thus, the same music appears in contemporary sources under the guise of all three of Tinctoris' classifications. But there is nothing in the music to indicate which is the most likely 'original'. The ambassador's testimony suggests that Isaac composed it with the motet in mind but that the underlying idea (*'fantasia'*) behind the piece is intrinsically musical.[5] That said, the incorporation of the music within the Mass setting cannot have been undertaken by anyone but Isaac. Whatever the immediate performance situation he envisaged and however strongly it informed his conception, the piece's subsequent history was shaped not by its initial function but by the needs of subsequent users. The recycling of *La mi la sol* by Isaac himself suggests that at least some composers were quite accepting of this situation. A later example of such re-purposing is the English *In nomine*, a family of free-standing instrumental pieces which takes its name from a sub-section of the Sanctus from John Taverner's *Missa Gloria tibi trinitas*, whose plainchant (always in equal long notes) spawned countless instrumental re-workings up to the time of Purcell (and, after a hiatus of over 300 years, into the twenty-first century).

This fluidity of practice tallies with what was observed in Chapter 2 concerning added voices and changes of performance contexts. It sets Renaissance polyphony apart from later periods in which genre defines both the production (composer) and reception (performers and audiences) of composed music; in fact, the re-purposing of polyphony was very common. The change of text was crucial, but the change of function could also be signalled by a change of context: Isaac's *La mi la sol* appears as a motet in a print devoted to motets, as a Mass section in a volume of Masses, and as a textless work in a manuscript containing a cluster of similar pieces. In each context it is equally appropriate; the idea that the context for its composition meant that the 'original' version had primacy over the others would have had little pertinence to Isaac's contemporaries. That is why the notion of genre poses such problems in our period: many individual pieces, performance situations, or even entire repertories straddle the categories of Mass and motet, motet and chanson, or combine their different functions.

To return to a previous point, the composer's first decision was to respond to the formal conventions of the text (where they existed), and there were undoubtedly shared assumptions about how one set certain textual forms. But Tinctoris' classification indicates that the function of the text was also a matter of tone, and there were also shared assumptions about the implications of tone for musical style. Syllabic, chordal declamation in short note-values was typically associated with light-hearted or humorous texts or with popular song-forms, in which polyphonic writing was largely avoided (such as the Italian frottola and strambotto or the Spanish villancico), whereas the traditional topics of courtly love poetry called for more melismatic and expansive melodic writing. A subtle case is Ockeghem's rondeau *S'elle m'amera/Petite camusette* (Example 7.2), one of a number of so-called 'combinative' songs that features two or more texts. The rondeau text, '*S'elle m'amera*', portrays a courtly lover unsure whether to declare his feelings and agonizing over his predicament ('Whether she will love me I do not know but I must try to gain her favour somewhat ... '). It is sung by the top voice in the expansive style just described, complemented by a wide vocal range. The other text has a famous popular tune with a typically much narrower range, featuring the stock characters Robin and Marion, who go off into the woods to do what comes naturally. In polytextual pieces like this, the different texts typically comment on each other; here, the contrast between aristocratic handwringing and the peasants' uncomplicated approach to love is reinforced by the juxtaposition of different musical styles. But there is a further twist, because the borrowed tune is worked in the three lower voices in strict imitation and long note-values, reminiscent of a cantus firmus. Ockeghem's courtly audience would undoubtedly have appreciated this ironic reversal, the sophisticated treatment of a melody associated with simple country folk. The mixing of social registers is not far removed from similar games

Example 7.2 Ockeghem, *S'elle m'amera/Petite camusette* (beginning). Translation:
Discantus: Whether she will love me, I know not/But I shall try/To gain her favour in some measure…
Lower voices: Little snub-nose, you are the death of me. Robin and Marion go off to the pretty wood…

played by Classical or Romantic composers, which recent musicology studies under the heading of 'topic theory'. But what conditions this aspect of *S'elle m'amera/Petite camusette* is not its form but its texts – in this case, the combination of different texts, each of which brings certain expectations to do with their setting, which Ockeghem cleverly subverts. The combinative approach to text and music inherited from previous generations persisted throughout the early Renaissance – not only in polytextual chansons but also in motets and Masses by Obrecht, Antoine Brumel (*c*.1450–*c*.1512/13), and their older contemporary, Johannes Regis (*c*.1430–1496), who was especially fond of it (examples from his output include all three of Tinctoris' categories). Arguably it is this principle that Ockeghem references in his setting, rather than anything to do with the rondeau form as such.

The play with different textual registers was so ingrained that even contrafacted texts could be used in a knowing way. A neat example comes from the time of the French Reformation, when risqué texts of well-known chansons were replaced with devotional ones. In an extreme example, the first line of

Clément Janequin's *Il estoit une fillette* ('there was a girl who wished to know the game of love') is modified so that the young woman of the tale morphs into the Virgin Mary: a graphic seduction scene becomes a retelling of the Christmas story. The trick of this contrafactum is that it sticks as closely as possible to the original. Of course, the very act of turning a smutty song to a higher purpose would inevitably have reminded listeners of the original lyric, but this would not seem to have troubled them particularly.[6] This type of slippage is observable not only on the level of the individual song but over an entire form: the Spanish villancico, which started out as a popular song-form with secular texts, was gradually turned to sacred purposes even though the literary form remained the same. It became common for single pieces to be supplied with two texts, one sacred and one secular, so the villancico's later absorption into church services happened quite naturally.

To sum up: notions of genre in Renaissance music are closely linked to textual forms, but form is only one of the conventions associated with text setting, and not always the most important when it comes to understanding individual pieces. Oftentimes it can be argued that a given category of compositional practice (such as musical borrowing, combinative situations, scoring and texture, and so on) has a greater role in shaping the character of a given work. Besides, the relationship of words and music in Renaissance polyphony is itself a thorny issue.

Words and music

Around the time when the anonymous *Missa Caput* was composed, a change is observable in the practice of music copyists: before that point they generally copied the words before the music, but after they did the opposite.[7] One of the consequences of this change is that the alignment of words and music can appear more haphazard than previously, giving the misleading impression that their co-ordination in performance was a matter of secondary importance. Precisely how singers negotiated that co-ordination is debatable, but the change in scribal practice underlines a more general point: the relationship of words and music is itself a matter of negotiation, of changing and competing priorities, and this holds true for composers, performers, and scribes of all periods.[8] How did music take account of the text being set? How precise was the co-ordination between them? How far were the words meant to be audible? Modern-day discussions of these questions are shaped by approaches to text setting from the Baroque onwards (the distinction between emic and etic is again useful): the notion that musical scansion should follow that of the words (that is, the placement of accented syllables on strong beats and longer note-values and conversely of unaccented syllables on weak beats and shorter durations); that music should reflect the mood of the text or illustrate the meaning of specific words ('word-painting' or 'madrigalism' as it is sometimes called with reference to the Renaissance); and that the intelligibility of the words is a priority, summed up in the well-known comment attributed to Monteverdi, that 'the speech should be the mistress of the harmony [i.e. the music], not the servant'.[9] These notions can be subsumed under the general heading of 'text sensitivity', a widespread but problematic concept (if only because it implies that composers whose music does not conform to those assumptions were somehow *in*sensitive to the texts they set). Undoubtedly, composers' habits changed considerably during the Renaissance; by the end of the period, several of these underlying assumptions had indeed begun to take root. But it would be quite wrong to view them as absolutes, let alone consider pieces that do not exhibit these priorities as less 'progressive' than those that do.

The relation of music and language exercised Renaissance thinkers of all stripes because the status of language itself was a fundamental concern. As mentioned in Chapter 3, the Reformation challenged the universality of Latin, proposing that divine worship should be conducted in a language that everyone could understand. At the very same time, gatherings of intellectuals throughout Europe sought to promote their respective vernaculars, for example by proposing them as worthy successors to the learned languages of antiquity, Latin and Greek. This was partly to do with the Humanist impulse that runs throughout the Renaissance,[10] but it was politically motivated as well, since language and geopolitical identity were closely aligned. These different agenda found musical expression, most concretely in the religious sphere: new music was needed for the new forms of worship. But there was also a growing sense that musical settings in each language had their distinct identity. Where French had been acknowledged for centuries as the international courtly language (hence the European vogue of French poetry and its musical settings in the fourteenth and fifteenth centuries), the Italian madrigal began to gain wide currency throughout Europe, alongside newer strophic forms of French chanson. Conversely, in Italy the term 'canzona alla Francese' came to describe, paradoxically, an instrumental piece beginning with a dactylic rhythm (long, short short) because so many French chansons of the time began that way. Although the secular music of other regions (for example Iberian, Dutch-, or German-speaking lands) was not so widely disseminated, print culture ensured its healthy distribution.

Despite their differing, not to say competing, motivations, religious leaders and secular thinkers of the mid-sixteenth century were united in the conviction that music should enhance the intelligibility of the text. The most famous case of this is the recommendation to that effect issued by the Catholic Church, with Palestrina's *Missa Papae Marcelli* held up as a quasi-mythical model. But during the same period, metrical psalms were being sung at the French court in translations by the poet Clément Marot, and the circle around the composer Claude Le Jeune devised the *vers mesurés à l'antique* (see Example 13.11 on p. 207), which worked along very similar lines, with a system of accentual patterns comprised of long and short values and minimal use of melisma. An unmistakable echo of it can be heard in Lassus' early *Prophetiae Sybillarum* of c.1560 (Example 7.3), whose texts were thought to derive from antiquity. This was no accident, for the 're-birth' of Graeco-Roman culture was the Renaissance's defining project. But all these pieces date from the very middle of the century, and recent research has questioned how far the aesthetic ideals that inform them can be backdated. Josquin's music is often held up as a watershed of text sensitivity, but the music of Gombert, who began composing at the end of Josquin's life, was widely praised by his contemporaries even though his approach to scansion can be described as inconsistent and his dense imitative textures suggest that textual audibility was not a priority for him. Nevertheless, there is no suggestion that Gombert's style was regarded

Example 7.3 Lassus, *Prophetiae Sybillarum*, 'Sybilla Cimmeria' (excerpt). Translation: [Through the agency of the host] everlasting, a holy virgin will suckle a king, in whom the hearts of all will rejoice greatly…

as anything other than 'modern'; the view of his approach to text setting as a throwback to 'pre-Josquinian' attitudes is a much later construction. The same recent research questions whether the impact of Humanist ideals on Renaissance music was as widespread as is often assumed.[11] The sung recitations of Marsilio Ficino a century earlier have already been mentioned, and settings of Horatian odes and classicizing texts by Petrus Tritonius were published (1507, with reprints over the following half-century) in a similar syllabic vein; but the drive towards intelligible text setting was equally informed by other considerations.

In reality, even before the Renaissance, composers knew perfectly well how to ensure that key words could be heard when they chose, how to reflect the mood of a text, or illustrate the meaning of specific words. (Lassus is rightly held up as a supreme example of text sensitivity in a wide range of genres and forms, including motets and chansons.) But there is plenty of music in which the matching of words and music speaks to different priorities: in combinative pieces like Ockeghem's *S'elle m'amera/Petite camusette*, the interplay between texts is at least as important as the texts themselves. Polytextual situations in sacred music (for example in Masses by Du Fay and his younger contemporaries Regis, Pierre de La Rue, and Obrecht) could be interpreted in another way: in Catholic worship, the essential liturgical action was that of the priest who intoned or spoke the words of the Mass. Because the musical settings of these words were only an adornment of the liturgy (that is, liturgically non-essential) it did not matter that the words were obscured by multiple cantus firmi, for example. For the same reason, composers and singers felt free to omit certain phrases of the lengthy Credo text: as long as the priest pronounced the right words in the right order, the Mass was valid. (Only later, as a result of the challenge posed by the Reformation, was it proposed that the words as sung should be audible to the congregation.) It has been pointed out that the layout of polytextual motets in choirbook format mirrors the appearance of the books of glosses, in which commentaries on biblical texts appeared alongside the sacred text itself, often using different fonts or scripts to distinguish them: in this analogy, the c.f.-bearing voice is like the biblical text, picked out in breves and semibreves, and the faster-moving texts and music of the other voices the commentary.[12] Another strategy relating to audibility is even more radical, that of flirting with outright incomprehensibility: in the character-pieces of Clément Janequin or Mateo Flecha (described in Chapter 10), a multitude of text fragments and onomatopoeia call and respond to each other in a riotous jumble.

The precise relationship of words and music was thus dependent on factors that varied from work to work, even within the output of an individual composer. As in later periods, music could reflect a mood, for example through the choice of mode. The association of the Phrygian mode with mourning has already been mentioned; then again, Binchois' ballade *Dueil angoisseux*, a Lydian setting of the poet Christine de Pisan's lament on the death of her husband, shows that he understood as well as Mozart that sadness can be expressed in a 'major' key. Likewise, the illustrative response to specific words ('madrigalism') predates the genre with whose name it is commonly associated. Ironically, one of the criticisms that led to the rise of monody was the over-use of such literal illustrations in polyphony – downward phrases at the words 'descendit de celis' and rising ones for 'Et ascendit in celum' – which had become so clichéd as to excite ridicule (in the *Dialogo della musica antica et della moderna*, published in 1581 by Vincenzo Galilei (c.1530–91)). Like so many of the resources available to Renaissance composers, text setting was subject to competing priorities, negotiating between the requirements of the text and the many possible responses to it. A teleological view of Renaissance music (in this case, as a progression from an 'abstract' to a 'sensitive' approach to text setting) misrepresents the range of those responses. The fact that fifteenth-century chansons tend towards a prescribed formula for syllable counting doesn't preclude depth of expression. Not so long ago, literary scholars derided the poetic texts of this repertory as crabbed, mechanical, and overly restricted in their expressive range, in contrast to the supposedly freer rhythms and sentiments of the sixteenth-century poets. That view has been superseded: the ability to say something fresh within strict stylistic and technical constraints is one of the special qualities of *forme fixe* poetry, and the same can be said of the music. A century later, Giaches de Wert (1535–96) demonstrates the impact of the madrigal aesthetic on the telling of biblical stories. Though justly famous, his *Vox in Rama* (which depicts the Old Testament figure Rachel lamenting her dead children) is a relatively conventional portrayal of grief. Wert sounds a more individual note in *Ascendente Jesu in naviculam*, which recounts Christ's calming of the waters when at sea with his disciples (Example 7.4). As the oncoming storm unleashes extreme syncopations (Example 7.4a), the disciples' cries for help and Christ's admonishment of them are wittily rendered: his rebuke ('O ye of little faith!') is expressed as a string of sounding (but not written) consecutive fifths (Example 7.4b). A truly magical effect comes when the sea falls still at Christ's command, ushering in wave after placid wave of longer note-values (Example 7.4c). 'Madrigalism' or not, there is nothing clichéd in these sonic representations.

Genre, texts, forms 107

Example 7.4 Wert, *Ascendente Jesu in naviculam*, (a) first part (excerpt); (b) second part (excerpt); (c) second part (excerpt).
7.4a Translation: And behold a great storm shook the sea and the boat…

7.4b Translation: And Jesus said unto them, 'Why are you fearful, o ye of little faith!'…

7.4c Translation: And there was a great calm…

The following chapters address Tinctoris' three broad categories: Mass, motet, and secular music. Accounting for even the principal forms and types of polyphony in a book this size would be like crowding angels on the head of a pin. Rather than attempt the impossible, I aim to give some idea of the breadth of practice that was possible in all three, while keeping in play the potential for slippage between them.

Chapter 8 | 'Cantus magnus': music for the Mass

The experience of Mass was a central focus of life in the Renaissance until the Reformation (and beyond, in those areas where Catholicism continued to hold sway). The feasts of the liturgical year were classed according to their degree of solemnity, from 'ferial' (daily) and 'low' Masses (which the priest spoke quickly and quietly) to the highpoints of the calendar, whether universal (e.g. Christmas, Easter, the principal Marian feasts and those of major saints), local (a city's patron saint's day), or occasional (the accession, wedding, or death of a ruler). The more solemn or significant the feast or occasion, the more elaborate the music composed for it (a distinction that also applied to extemporized polyphony). Alongside these 'official' occasions in the calendar were Masses endowed by private individuals, which might be accompanied by chant or polyphony, as in the case of Du Fay in Chapter 3. This explains why polyphonic Masses vary in length from less than quarter of an hour to nearly an hour. The title of Lassus' *Missa Jäger* ('Hunter's Mass') refers obliquely to a continuous tradition of shorter Masses known as 'Missa brevis'. It was meant to accommodate his ducal patron's wish for polyphony at Mass *and* a full day's hunting. Regardless of the occasion, the climax of the liturgy was the elevation, when the priest raised aloft the consecrated host, making it visible to the congregation.[1] Tinctoris' definition of the 'Mass' specifically names the five movements of the Ordinary, but for our purposes it includes other music that had a formal place in the Mass and the broader liturgy.

The Mass cycle

Arguably the most significant musical development of the fifteenth century was the setting of the Ordinary as a unit.[2] The oldest by a named composer, Machaut's *Messe de Nostre-Dame* (c.1360), appears not to have been followed up by composers of the following generations: its sections employ different compositional techniques, with audible links between some sections but not all. Composers of the early fifteenth century began relating sections of the Ordinary more explicitly. The earliest known examples concerned paired sections – most often Glorias and Credos (whose texts are far longer than those of the other movements), and more rarely the Sanctus and Agnus dei. Typically, the pairs were linked by a common mode and texture, and by the re-use across both sections of similar or identical musical ideas. The most audible unifying device was the 'head-motif', heard at the beginning of both sections and sometimes at the start of sub-sections. In some cases the shared material was drawn from a pre-existent polyphonic song, a principle which Du Fay carried over across all five sections of the Ordinary in his *Missa sine nomine*, composed in Italy during the 1420s and plainly building on the example of contemporary Italian Mass pairs. (It has many elements in common with his ballade *Resveillés vous* and sometimes appears under that name). Du Fay is closely associated with another experiment from the same period, the so-called 'Plenary' cycle, which sets not only the five Ordinary movements but also the Propers (that is, the parts of the Mass liturgy whose texts, unlike those of the Ordinary, change according to the feast being celebrated, as shown in Table 8.1). In the few Plenary cycles that survive, the two groups are clearly distinguished in that those of the Proper are not unified on the basis of mode, being based on the plainchants corresponding to the texts of the individual items. In Du Fay's earliest surviving Plenary cycle, the *Missa Sancti Jacobi*, the Gloria–Credo pair is scored for four voices and the Sanctus–Agnus pair for just three (thus integrating the principle of paired

Table 8.1 The Ordinary and Propers of the Mass

Proper cycle	Ordinary cycle
Introit	
	Kyrie
	Gloria*
Gradual	
Alleluia*	
Tract	
Sequence (very rarely set)	
	Credo*
Offertory	
	Sanctus-Benedictus
	Agnus dei
Communion	
Post-communion	
(occasionally in Requiem Masses)	

(*) denotes movements not prescribed in Requiem Masses

movements within the Plenary concept); in the much later and widely circulated *Missa Sancti Anthonii de Padua*, the mode and the scoring of the five Ordinary sections are identical. Judging by the little that has come down to us, the vogue of the Plenary cycle was very short-lived but had far-reaching consequences.

The early fifteenth century was exceptionally fertile for the development of the Mass cycle. Although these experiments predate our period, they help explain the impact of the *Missa Caput* and its stablemates: with the exception of borrowing from pre-existing secular pieces (an idea whose time would come), these most recent English Masses combined several of the individual elements just discussed in a particularly focused way: unity of mode and a head-motif encompassing all five Ordinary sections, which were further linked by shared material to an extent not previously attempted, and through a technique that was likewise new in Mass music: a recurrent plainchant cantus firmus in long notes stated twice in each of the five sections, once under O and then under C. The very earliest settings were for three voices rather than the four of *Caput* and *Veterem hominem*, and their Kyries were troped following English custom. Continental composers very soon adapted the details of the basic plan in a number of ways (most obviously in the plan of the Kyrie, whose troped forms were not in use on the continent), but the fundamental principles of the c.f. Mass endured well into the sixteenth century.

Composed c.1460, Du Fay's *Missa L'Homme armé* is one of his most extended and complex statements, showing these fundamentals in play alongside newer developments (Example 8.1).[3] The most obvious is that the c.f. is not plainchant but a monophonic song (refer back to Example 4.1, p. 51). The principle of paired Mass sections is still evident in the Gloria and Credo, which adhere to the 'double statement' principle in O and ₵. The Sanctus also distributes two statements among its five sub-sections: in the 'Pleni sunt caeli' and 'Benedictus' the tenor is silent (the former is a trio, the latter a duo), which allows for freely composed episodes with no reference to the song. The phrase 'Hosanna in excelsis' is repeated after the 'Benedictus', but whereas many continental Masses simply repeat the same music, a significant number have different music for each statement (including all four tenor c.f. Masses securely ascribed to Du Fay). This is usually reflected in the layout of the c.f.: here, the second Hosanna has the second statement (in ₵) all to itself. The other movements maintain the broad two-part division into O and ₵ but distribute the tune's statements differently. The Kyrie allocates a separate phrase to each sub-section ('Kyrie I'/'Christe'/'Kyrie II') with the mensurations O/₵/O.

Though reflecting the tune's structure, this straightforwardly expository function (with just one c.f. statement) is typical of continental Kyries. But, in general, it is the design of the Agnus dei that diverges most from English usage: the tripartite design harks back mensurally to the Kyrie. The first sub-section has a complete setting of the tune in O; the 'Agnus II' is treated as a reduced section in a contrasting mensuration, ¢ (the typical approach in continental Masses), but the tune features there as well, albeit more loosely than in the fully scored sections (it is shared between the two lower voices). At the beginning of the Agnus III the tenor has the tune in retrograde and long note-values (in O), and, when this has run its course, *L'Homme armé* is heard the right way round and at twice the speed, bringing the Mass to a close. Keeping a trick up one's sleeve for the final Agnus dei became a staple of Renaissance Masses up to the time of Palestrina; Du Fay's retrograde statement of the c.f. here is one of the very first.[4]

Just as Du Fay is freer than most of his English predecessors in his approach to the c.f. Mass's structural plan, he is also more flexible in handling the c.f. itself. The two-voice head-motif (shown boxed in Example 8.1a: compare with Examples 8.1b and 8.1c) is extended to three in the Kyrie. Filling out the sonority makes the Mass's opening bars more imposing, but the added voice also introduces a descending motif (circled) that is heard countless times through the work. This is one of several features that can be understood in terms of long-term structural design. Where English c.f. Masses typically maintain a similar or identical rhythmic cast for the c.f. across the five sections, Du Fay varies its rhythmic shape with each statement, ornamenting it with passing notes and cadential figures (a technique known by the modern term 'isomelism') and inserting 'codas' after some statements. The final bars of the 'Kyrie II' and of the 'Agnus dei III' (Example 8.1d), corresponding to the tune's last phrase, are identical in all four voices. It has been suggested that they were added to the Kyrie as an afterthought, since its statement is complete without it. This literal quotation, linking the first and last of the five main sections, is one of the long-term structural features just mentioned, a pendant to the head-motif (a 'tail-motif', so to speak). An increasingly inventive approach to the treatment of the model and the deepening of connections across sections characterizes the subsequent development of the Mass cycle. Thus, the borrowed material is at times disguised (as in its very first entry at Example 8.1a, where it is masked by the previous note in the lowest voice) and at others plainly heard (Example 8.1e). The two approaches are juxtaposed in

Example 8.1 Du Fay, *Missa L'Homme armé*, (a) Kyrie (beginning); (b) 'Et in terra' and 'Patrem' (beginning); (c) Sanctus and Agnus dei (beginning); (d) 'Kyrie II' (conclusion); (e) 'Christe' (excerpt); (f) 'Agnus dei III' (excerpt)

the Agnus III, when the tune reappears after its deliciously disorienting retrograde statement (Example 8.1f).

The formal layout of Du Fay's Mass is typical of Renaissance cycles subsequently.[5] Most stable is the tripartite division of the Kyrie, albeit with a reduced-voiced 'Christe'; most variable are the Gloria and especially the Credo, which typically have between two and four sub-sections; that said, the

Example 8.1 (Cont.)

structural midpoint of each is fairly stable (respectively, the first 'Qui tollis' invocation and the 'Et incarnatus', each at the approximate textual midpoint). The broad two-part scheme can also accommodate a move into triple time near the end. Until about 1520 the Agnus dei has a similar design to the Kyrie, but later it may consist of just two sections (as in many of Palestrina's settings) or only one, with the other invocations sung in chant or with the single setting repeated. Finally, the five-fold cast of the Sanctus is fairly constant, though in England and in shorter ferial Masses, the 'Hosanna' statements often follow the 'Pleni' and 'Benedictus' without a break. The 'Benedictus' corresponds to the moment of the elevation, to which composers often respond with a significant gesture: in Du Fay's Mass the second 'Hosanna' is the first complete statement of *L'Homme armé* with its original rhythms, a moment of revelation paralleling the host's in the liturgy.

These basic formal schemes vary according to regional liturgical custom (as the different approaches to the Agnus dei make clear). In the Bohemian Speciálník Codex, for instance, the Agnus dei is routinely omitted in copies of Mass cycles that survive with all five movements elsewhere, and, by the turn of the sixteenth century, English troped Kyries were replaced by plainchant or free-standing settings based on chants known as 'squares'. Another local practice was the so-called 'alternatim' settings (notably by Isaac and his pupil Ludwig Senfl (*c*.1490–1546) for the court of Maximilian I), in which only every other verse was set polyphonically (and the others improvised, for example by Maximilian's renowned court organist, Paul Hofhaimer). More widespread was the tradition of free-standing Credos, most often based on plainchant but sometimes on pre-existing polyphony; the latter frequently included references to phrases of the best-known plainchant setting, Credo I, which makes cameo appearances in complete cycles alongside the named borrowed material.

The second decade of the sixteenth century inaugurated a new approach to the Mass cycle: instead of locating borrowed material principally in a single voice of a model, composers quoted from different passages using all the voices as they sound together. This soon displaced the c.f. as the principal technique of Mass composition. Often referred to in contemporary sources as Masses 'in imitation' of their models – '*ad imitationem Susanne un jour*' for example – the practice acquired the label 'parody' only in the twentieth century (this Greek-derived term is known only from a single contemporary source, Jacob Paix's *Missa parodia* of 1587). Latterly, the term has been criticized because of its negative associations. The alternative term 'imitation Mass' that has recently been proposed is not without its own ambiguities (the potential confusion with the contrapuntal technique known by the same name), but it has gained a measure of acceptance. Imitation Masses broadly adhere to the formal conventions just discussed, but not all Renaissance Masses display the strong interconnections typical of c.f. and imitation Masses. As seen in Chapter 12, some seem deliberately to problematize the notion of cycle, while others exhibit few audible links beyond a common mode, voice-ranges, or mensural usage. Published in the 1590s, Byrd's semi-clandestine settings adopt some old-fashioned traits (such as the use of the head-motif), but eschew parody; yet in their formal design (not least the setting of a Kyrie) they are nearer to continental practice than to the English tradition, which had lain dormant for a generation.

The affinity of the Mass cycle with that other multi-movement form, the symphony, explains its appeal to modern audiences, but it has had an unfortunate side-effect: where no model is named or can be identified, the label 'sine nomine' (like that other ubiquitous stand-in, 'anonymous') condemns the work to oblivion. That attitude shows signs of changing, but it explains why modern-day performers tend to overlook some of the other polyphonic forms explicitly connected with the Mass.

Propers, Requiem Masses, and other liturgical forms

Whereas polyphonic settings of the group of five Ordinary sections together were a recent development, the setting of Propers (Table 8.1) was as old as polyphony itself; the oldest known descriptions of polyphonic performance mention Propers chants as the starting point, as do the earliest notated sources.[6] As early as the eleventh-century Winchester Troper, a persistent feature of the repertoire (extending into the Renaissance period) is its tendency to be transmitted in bulk. This reflects its functional nature, since the number of feasts for which polyphony might be required was considerable. Many of the manuscript collections transmitted anonymously must have been collective projects or composites, but there is strong evidence that individual composers approached the setting of Propers not as separate individual cycles but as sets or even cycles of cycles. A group of more than a dozen is transmitted in the Trent Codices; six of them have been convincingly linked with a decree of Philip the Good, Duke of Burgundy, establishing a weekly cycle of Masses to be sung at the Sainte-Chapelle in Dijon.[7] This group has been conjecturally attributed to Du Fay, who may have written some of the others. A still more substantial undertaking was the chapter of Constance Cathedral's commission to Isaac in

1508 for a cycle of Propers for the major feasts of the liturgical calendar. To fulfil this, Isaac undoubtedly drew on previous projects (including cycles composed earlier for the Imperial Court), but died before he could complete it. This was eventually accomplished by Senfl, and, after further editorial interventions, the collection was published by Formschneider of Nuremberg in the 1550s under the title *Choralis Constantinus*. The publication of such a monumental enterprise so many years after Isaac's death testifies to its enduring utility, which is confirmed by later examples: Lassus included a selection of cycles for the major feasts within a more broadly based collection (the *Patrocinium musices*) in 1574; the following decade in Prague, the Slovenian composer Jacobus Gallus (also known as Handl) published a four-volume collection of Propers for the entire liturgical year with the title *Opus musicum*; and a substantial proportion of the posthumous Paminger edition (mentioned in Chapter 3) consisted of Propers settings. With over a hundred individual pieces, the encyclopedic aspirations of Byrd's *Gradualia* (two volumes, pub. 1605 and 1607) are all the more remarkable given English anti-Catholic sentiment at the time of the Gunpowder Plot (1605).

The forms of Propers sections involve the repetition of textual elements. Texts and chants are often specific to the individual feast, and polyphonic settings of the earlier Renaissance overwhelmingly have the plainchant in the top voice, where it is easily recognizable (incorporation of other borrowed material was rare). Because even the best-known chants varied from place to place, it is sometimes possible to identify the area, city, or even the institution for which a set of Propers was composed. The same is true of saints or feasts of only local significance, which existed in abundance before the reforms of the Council of Trent imposed a greater standardization. (A sign of changing times, perhaps, Byrd's *Gradualia* are freely composed.) The prevalence of plainchant within Propers settings underscores their functional nature, which may explain the perception of them nowadays as poor relations of the Ordinary; but this view passes over the quality of much of the repertory, from Du Fay to Byrd. Example 8.2 shows a particularly elaborate six-voice Introit by Isaac, with the chant in the Secundus Discantus (but even here, the verse is dispatched with remarkable economy; chant pitches are marked with a cross).

Their lesser visibility with modern audiences notwithstanding, Propers relate to a genre whose notoriety today rivals that of the Mass Ordinary. The Requiem Mass (also 'Mass for the Dead') was a relative latecomer to polyphony, which may have been deemed inappropriate to the sobriety and solemnity of mourning; by 1470 this attitude had changed, for in that year a

Example 8.2 Isaac, *Salve sancta parens* (beginning). Translation: Hail, blessed parent, who brought forth…

Requiem by Du Fay was copied at Cambrai, which the composer requested be sung at his memorial. The link with Du Fay is probably no accident, given his demonstrable interest in Plenary cycles, for liturgically speaking, a Requiem Mass is essentially a pared-down Plenary Mass (see Table 8.1). Du Fay's setting having been lost, the earliest surviving example is the incomplete one by Ockeghem. Although the Requiem's early history is unclear, its early popularity in Spain is well documented: the one by Pedro de Escobar was probably written by 1500. The Iberian peninsula accounts for some of the most striking settings before 1650, extending its 'Golden Age' of polyphony well beyond the time of Victoria.[8] Other early settings include those by La Rue, Brumel, and Antoine de Févin. They differ considerably as to which sections and texts are set. As with Propers more generally, the reforms of the Council of Trent in the mid-sixteenth century brought a degree of uniformity, but some latitude for local preference remained.

The expectations connected with the setting of Requiem texts are surprisingly contradictory. From Ockeghem's setting onwards there is a tension between the stark chordal style that one might expect and moments of rhythmic and formal complexity. The two tendencies are particularly finely balanced in Victoria's six-voice setting (1603), in which most of the voices are active throughout, creating a texture that is dense but uniform.[9] An earlier example by Jean Richafort (c.1480–c.1550) deploys a similar textural intricacy with a different aesthetic intention. Alongside the appropriate plainchants, Richafort has an additional one ('Circumdederunt me gemitus mortis' – 'the groans of the dead surround me') in canon at the upper fifth, and a phrase from a secular song, *Faulte d'argent, c'est douleur non pareille* ('Lack of money is a pain without equal'). Taking the phrase 'c'est douleur non pareille' out of context changes its humorous intention to a comment on the 'Circumdederunt' chant. Both citations refer to two of Josquin's secular pieces, *Nymphes nappés* (which has 'Circumdederunt' for a c.f.) and *Faulte d'argent*. Regardless of the official occasion for its composition (which is unknown), the references to the older composer are clear acts of homage, and the setting may also have been meant to commemorate him.[10] This is complexity of a different sort: dating from the midpoint of our period, Richafort's cycle shows how soon composers began treating Requiem Masses on a par with Ordinary cycles.

Liturgical polyphonic forms were not confined to the Mass. The liturgical hours that punctuated the daily lives of religious institutions gave rise to a host of polyphonic forms. They involved the singing of psalms, each of which was preceded by an antiphon. Antiphons were often brief introductions to psalms and canticles, but those for the highpoints of the liturgical calendar (particularly Marian feasts) could be very elaborate. Most liturgical forms involved either repeated structures or antiphonal exchanges between those sat on either side of the choir in monastic institutions (the sung recitation of psalms, for example), and verse forms were also prominent (e.g. in hymns and sequences). Today, the best known of these liturgical hours is Vespers, which took place around sunset and could be treated to very elaborate polyphony, making for lengthy services. Composers frequently excerpted texts from these liturgical hours from their original forms and contexts, setting them as free-standing pieces – in other words, motets. The boundary between Mass and motet, which in principle was very porous, was even more so in practice: depending on the period and local custom, the range of music considered admissible for performance during the liturgy went beyond the sacred to include secular music, including polyphonic songs and instrumental fantasias. The fluidity of this situation is reflected in the music itself, as will become apparent in the following chapter.

Chapter 9 | 'Cantus mediocris': the motet

From its earliest use in the thirteenth century, the term 'motet' (derived from the French for 'word', 'mot') designated settings of both sacred and secular texts, both Latin and vernacular, sometimes combining all of these in the same piece. In the Middle Ages motets could be composed for secular occasions (state, civic, or courtly) as well as sacred ones. By the start of our period, the motet was primarily associated with sacred topics in Latin, though its social and practical range remained considerable.[1] In a survival of its original meaning, the term was occasionally used in the looser sense well into the Renaissance: the collection of intabulations published in 1531 by Attaingnant under the title *Treze motets* includes the famous Italian song *Fortuna desperata*, which few would have regarded as anything other than a song. This versatility brought with it the potential for 'slippage' in the direction of either the Mass or any number of secular forms; whether during Mass or on public occasions, the performance of motets was ubiquitous.[2] A radical instance of such slippage is the so-called 'motetti missales' by Compère, Gaspar, and others, documented at the Milanese court in the late fifteenth century.[3] These are essentially motet cycles, unified in terms of mode and destination (e.g. 'Mass for Christmas', 'Mass for Our Lord'), but explicitly designed for performance during Mass in place of the customary Ordinary and Propers. From a liturgical perspective, there was nothing particularly problematic about this substitution, as we have seen, since the recitation of the Mass was the celebrant's responsibility. But the contemporary label ('motetti missales') indicates a more fluid approach to polyphonic usage than modern habits of classification allow. (Significantly, some of the cycles' individual components appear as motets in other sources.)

A more ambiguous case is that of *Si dedero* by Alexander Agricola (c.1456–1506), one of the most widely circulated pieces of the late fifteenth century (Example 9.1). Its three voices paraphrase a short passage of plainchant. No source gives any text other than the words corresponding to the chant, and many give just the first two. Further, matching them to the music is far from straightforward because the voices diverge considerably in their presentation of the plainchant's pitches (shown in the discantus

Example 9.1 Agricola, *Si dedero* (beginning). Translation: If I give sleep [to my eyes]…

with a cross above them): what words does the bassus sing beginning in b. 3 (or the discantus after b. 4)? Agricola's paraphrase treatment raises the question whether the words were meant to be sung. It has been said of this piece (and others like it) that it is not the words that he set, but the chant, in which case an instrumental destination ('like a fantasia') is not out of the question.[4] Hence, the precise function of *Si dedero* is impossible to determine; a reasonable conclusion is that the composer may have had no particular one in mind. But that is not to say that words were incidental; as a work's starting point, they remain integral to the musical design, whether they are explicitly foregrounded or remain only as a trace element, so to speak.

The textual form of individual *motetti missales* sections did not prevent their functioning explicitly as Mass music, any more than did *Si dedero*'s reference to the words of a plainchant necessarily imply a liturgical or even paraliturgical destination. Conversely, sacred music was routinely performed outside its original context, in some cases straddling what we would regard as the sacred and secular (a distinction that would have had little pertinence). The mid-fifteenth-century statutes of Eton College specified the daily singing of the Marian antiphon *Salve Regina* as a distinct communal action outside the liturgical hours, and public 'Salve services' were popular in Northern Europe: in Antwerp during the late fifteenth century the 'lof' (as it was known) was sung daily. That popularity is attested in polyphonic sources: more than two dozen Salves were copied together in the Eton Choirbook, and at least one surviving choirbook from the so-called Alamire manuscript complex is devoted exclusively to settings of the antiphon by Franco-Flemish composers. That there was often little practical distinction between liturgical and paraliturgical texts tallies with the motet's superabundant variety, scale, and technique.

A snapshot of the motet repertory: the Medici Codex

That diversity can be grasped very succinctly by focusing on a single collection. The Medici Codex was compiled at the court of one of the greatest Renaissance patrons, Pope Leo X, more or less dead centre of our period (1518), as a gift from the pope to a younger Medici relative on the occasion of his marriage into the French high nobility.[5] Its fifty-three pieces reflect the papal chapel's current repertory and its links with figures working at other courts, particularly that of the French king Francis I (at a time when diplomatic relations between the two courts were especially close). Its chronological sweep is contemporary rather than retrospective, taking in the older generation of Brumel and Josquin and the one just establishing itself, headed by Willaert. Willaert is the second-best represented composer in the manuscript, the first being his teacher Jean Mouton (the leading light at the French court, and much favoured by Leo), and the third, Josquin. But a fair proportion of pieces are by composers of whom practically nothing is known: the shadowy 'Elimot' (an anagram, possibly?), Johannes de la Fage, or Jean Le Santier. The choice of pieces is also remarkable for its breadth of coverage: hardly any destination or compositional technique goes unrepresented. Evidently it was intended not for liturgical use but as a showcase of the finest motets available, a snapshot of the current repertory; for our purposes it shows the range of the Renaissance motet in the round.

The motets of the Medici Codex range from the tiny (Mouton's *In omni tribulatione* and Brumel's *Sicut lilium** last little more than a minute) to the lengthy (Josquin's setting of the complete Psalm 50 (Vulgate), *Miserere mei, Deus*, lasts a good quarter of an hour). Marian antiphons are represented (settings by Festa and Willaert, and Le Santier's lovely canonic *Alma redemptoris mater*), along with psalm settings (Boyleau's *In principio erat verbum*), hymns (Willaert's *Veni sancte spiritus*), sequences (Therache's *Verbum bonum*), settings from the Song of Songs (de Silva's *Tota pulchra es*), motets in praise of royalty (Mouton's *Exalta regina Galliae*, addressed to Claude, Queen of France (r.1515–24) in celebration of her spouse's victory at Marignan in 1515), and even a singers' motet (Moulu's *Mater floreat, florescat**). The two French-texted pieces in the collection are both laments, Moulu's *Fiere Atropos/Anxiatus est** commemorating the previous French queen, Anne of Brittany (d.1514) and Josquin's *Nymphes des bois/Requiem*. By now, their presence in a motet collection comes as no surprise: both have a plainchant cantus firmus and neither is out of place in terms of texture or technique. In fact, their texts have more in common with occasional Latin motets than with typical chansons of the time.

Stylistic markers

Given its chronological focus (only Josquin's *Nymphes des bois* likely predates 1500), the Medici Codex's stylistic range is remarkable. Though composed just a few years after *Nymphes des bois* (at the request of Ercole d'Este in 1503/4), Josquin's monumental setting of Psalm 50, *Miserere mei, Deus*, would have been considered old-fashioned by 1520. Built on a descending and ascending plainchant tenor ostinato on its opening words, it is one of the few works of the collection in which the layout of the c.f. audibly shapes the musical form (the tenor remaining silent for long stretches between each statement). Its psalm text notwithstanding, it was evidently conceived as a free-standing work. (By contrast, Maistre Jan's *Lauda Jerusalem* was probably composed with an eye to liturgical function.) Two other Josquin motets belong to a newer category, which is well represented in the collection. In *Virgo salutiferi* and *Inviolata, integra et casta es* the plainchant is set out in long notes, like a c.f., but also as a two-voice canon. Both works are for five voices and in three sections, with the time-interval between the canonic voices decreasing with each new section: at three breves' distance in the first, two breves in the second, and a single breve in the last. In other ways the two motets are quite different, but their similar treatment of the plainchant suggests recognition of a fruitful procedure. It was certainly influential, for the canonic treatment of plainchant became a staple of motet composition. Eight other pieces in the collection feature the procedure, most of them placed near Josquin's settings (such 'thematic' groupings within a source are fairly common). The collection's most ambitious work technically, Mouton's famous eight-voice *Nesciens mater*, is made up of four pairs of canonic voices.

The early sixteenth century was the heyday of this type of canon, and the Medici Codex is one of several witnesses to its popularity (another is Antico's exactly contemporary print *Motetti novi e chanzoni franciose a quarto sopra doi* (1520), which consists entirely of canonic pieces by composers with close links to the French court). Also typical of its time is the transitional status of imitation, the procedure that defines Renaissance counterpoint more than any other. While it features prominently, imitative textures do not predominate to the extent that they will in the work of Gombert and his younger contemporaries: for the composers of the Medici Codex, imitation is still based on a two-voice framework that can be broadened to include the other voices as needed. Another telling sign of the stylistic times is the complete absence of *tempus perfectum*. Instead, ternary rhythms (expressed as a proportion) appear at or near the end of motets, a persistent collective memory of early Renaissance sacred repertories.

With this brief overview of the Medici Codex, we come to grips with style as a complex phenomenon, in that several distinct currents can be distinguished within the manuscript's repertoire; and we encounter two key techniques – canon and imitation – that are practically synonymous with Renaissance polyphony. Both are considered in detail in later chapters; meanwhile, the remainder of this chapter takes a closer look at specific types of motets, using pieces from the collection to illustrate the genre's expressive range. (In what follows, the names of pieces contained in the manuscript are in bold type.)

Motets for private and public devotion

The notion of private devotion and prayer gained in prominence during the fifteenth century: the popularity of small-scale 'books of hours', designed to accompany private individuals in their spiritual devotions, is the most concrete witness to this trend. A great number of short prayers arose in support of it, sometimes on the personal initiative of a pope or at the prompting of a specific or localized religious community (a well-documented instance is *Ave sanctissima Maria*, mentioned in Chapter 3). Musical settings of this type of prayer became extremely popular from about 1460. The Medici Codex contains several, such as Brumel's **Sicut lilium**. Its text derives from the Song of Songs, the Old Testament book relating a quasi-erotic dialogue between two lovers. Its subject matter was interpreted by Christian commentators as an allegorical dialogue between Christ and his spiritual 'bride', the church, but the passages spoken by the male lover could also be taken as praise of the Virgin Mary. The likening of Mary to 'a flower among thorns' is a commonplace of motet imagery: earlier examples include Du Fay's *Flos florum*, Pulloys' *Flos de spina*, and Frye's *Ave regina celorum*. While not all as short as *Sicut lilium*, such works are often cast as a single section, with the melodic interest centred on the top line. Apart from its opening point of imitation, *Sicut lilium* is hardly contrapuntal at all, the lower voices doing little more than support the discantus.

Though more varied than *Sicut lilium*, Mouton's **In omni tribulatione** (Example 9.2) also pares its contrapuntal resources to a minimum. After a chordal opening consistent with its devotional tone, it sets up a series of antiphonal exchanges between the high and low voices. The first two (bb. 4–7 and bb. 7–9) overlap, but each exchange has its own point of imitation. Another brief chordal episode is followed by another antiphonal exchange (bb. 12–14), though this time there is no imitation *within* each pair of voices: the replication is *between* the antiphonal pairs. The final phrase has the four voices succeeding each other at a beat's distance (bb. 15–17). In this motet it is not so much the individual sections that are remarkable – the imitative treatment of a descending figure is a commonplace of the years around 1500 – as the concentration of imitative gambits in a very short space.

Although devotional texts could be set more elaborately (Johannes Pulloys' bipartite *Flos de spina* (c.1460) has the familiar mensural layout of O and ₵, and Walter Lambe's *Nesciens mater* and *Stella celi* are only slightly less florid than the Eton Choirbook's large-scale works), a lack of contrapuntal ostentation was appropriate to the sentiment of humility when addressing Mary or Christ directly. The sense of wonder in the face of the divine presence is memorably expressed at the start of Victoria's *O quam gloriosum est regnum* (pub. 1585) with a series of chords on the opening syllable. That such chordal episodes were peculiarly suited to devotional texts is demonstrated by Victoria himself: his Mass based on *O quam gloriosum* explores the motet's imitative points to the full but omits any reference to those opening bars.

Closely related to the devotional motet in sentiment is the 'elevation motet', so called because of its place at this central point of the liturgy. But whereas the devotional motet focuses on the individual worshipper, the elevation is a public event, a collective experience, albeit one of inner contemplation. Recent research underlines that all manner of polyphony (including chansons) might be sung at that moment, in addition to or in place of the 'Benedictus', but Bruhier's **Ecce panis angelorum** is typical of motets conceived specifically for it: the text refers to the bread of the Eucharist (which had its own feast-day, Corpus Christi), its opening phrase is set with chords picked out by fermatas, and a general pause separates it from the simple counterpoint that follows. It is clearly modelled on the elevation motets of the *motetti missales*, composed nearly fifty years before

Example 9.2 Mouton, *In omni tribulatione* (complete). Translation: From all tribulation and worry, may the merciful virgin Mary rescue us.

the Medici Codex was copied; even the frequent toggling between triple and duple time is traceable to these early examples. Another object of contemplation and adoration was the instrument of Christ's Passion, the cross, addressed in vividly personal terms and giving rise to similar musical topics. The tension between private and communal devotion explains why some motets for the cross, such as Obrecht's five-voice *Salve crux* (see Example 11.5 on p. 150) are conceived as grand statements while others are on a more modest scale. That these works of adoration were closely linked in the minds of worshippers is confirmed by Petrucci's motet publication of

1503, whose title ('Motetti de Passione, de Cruce, de Sacramento... ') makes the connection explicit.

Penitential music

Josquin's **Miserere** refers back to the elaborate c.f. structures of the early Renaissance, but also to the more recent fashion for penitential music. By 1506 Petrucci had assembled enough material for two substantial prints devoted to the Lamentations of Jeremiah, but the scant survival of such music in manuscripts suggests a relatively new phenomenon. Thereafter, as with other texts associated with penitence and lamentation (notably the *Stabat mater*, the seven Penitential Psalms, or the texts of Old Testament figures such as Jeremiah, Job, David, or Rachel), such settings were extraordinarily popular. The list of significant contributors takes in the greatest figures of the age and the entire geographical area, including Iberian and English composers. Penitential music frequently brings out the best in lesser-known composers: two superb examples from around 1500 are the extended multi-sectional motet *Planxit autem David*, an extended work whose ascription to Josquin has recently been challenged in favour of one that gives it to Ninot le Petit (*fl. c.*1500–20), and the four-voice *De profundis*, also ascribed to Josquin but probably by Nicolas Champion (*c.*1475–1533).

Based on several related texts, **Super flumina Babylonis*** by Costanzo Festa (*c.*1490–1524, one of the collection's few Italian composers) is a powerful yet subtle expression of displacement and exile. Its opening point of imitation begins on A♭ and E♭, and most of its voices have two-flat signatures; but its c.f. is on G Dorian (with a single flat in the signature), and when it enters its first note is d', closely followed by a. This use of the 'mixed mode' phenomenon is extremely rare by this point and deliberately expressive in a way that the earlier examples mentioned in Chapter 4 are not. It persists throughout the motet, coming briefly to rest on an A♭ sonority two-thirds of the way through; nearer the end, a descending passage in self-consciously archaic fauxbourdon betrays the weariness of those who 'can hear no more', before concluding on the sonority of the plainchant's final, g. The effect is deliciously unsettling, like pulling on a sore tooth. It explains composers' predilection for texts that plumb the depths of human misery and the enduring popularity of such music with modern-day audiences.

Occasional motets

Laments could also commemorate rulers, a destination that had already gained traction by the time Moulu composed *Fiere Atropos/Anxiatus est*, a moving tribute to an outstanding patron who maintained a chapel separate from that of her royal spouses, Charles VIII (r.1483–98) and Louis XII (1498–1515). Technically, its text designates it as a chanson, but Moulu's style here is virtually indistinguishable from comparable settings of Latin texts; in this, he anticipates Gombert, whose motets and chansons can be hard to tell apart, but here this may be a reflection of the text. Moulu must have had in mind Josquin's **Nymphes des bois/Requiem** (especially its opening section), since a similarly sombre c.f. underpins both works; that said, use of the vernacular (rather than Latin) is unusual for the musical commemorations of a ruler. The Hypophrygian mode and the use of low clefs (with a bass extending to $A_{,,}$ a seventh below the gamut) are also typical of the topics of lament and mourning. In this case, the ambiguous 'motet-chanson' label (or should that be 'chanson-motet'?) makes eminent sense.

Another secular function of motets was connected with aspects of public and civic life. Ciconia wrote a number of such pieces during his residency in Padua (1401–13), and Du Fay's *Salve flos tuscae gentis* praises the city of Florence and its people. More often, public statements focused on the person of the ruler, praising him (or her) directly or indirectly: one of the Medici Codex's finest composers, Andreas de Silva, wrote a motet *Gaude felix Florentiae*, congratulating the city of Florence on Leo X's accession to the papacy (curiously, the motet is not in the Medici Codex). The work was probably meant for Leo's ears, on his first visit to his native city after his election. The occasional nature of such works confers special interest on their texts, which can admittedly be more significant than the music; valuable certainly as historical and social documents, they demonstrate the motet's versatility throughout the Renaissance.

Towards the motet of the later Renaissance

Several motets in the Medici Codex set biblical stories: Elimot's **Nuptiae factae sunt*** recounts the wedding at Cana (appropriately for a motet book intended as a wedding-gift); de Silva's **In illo tempore loquente Iesu*** and Brunet's **Ite in orbem** both set sayings of Christ; de Silva's **Omnis**

pulchritudo Domini* describes the Ascension; and in Festa's **Angelus ad pastores ait*** the angels announce Christ's nativity to the shepherds. Though new at the time, such subject matter proved a near-inexhaustible seam for later composers. All the pieces just mentioned use the word 'Alleluia' as a refrain, a strategy rooted in a liturgical form (the Responsory), but often found in motets with no explicit liturgical connection. The 'Alleluia' is stated in each motet at least twice, including at the very end, in which case the textual correspondence is often mirrored in the music. This happens in Brunet's two-part work (a genuine Responsory), in which the phrase immediately preceding the refrain is also duplicated. Festa's dactylic setting of 'Alleluia' (long, short short, long), set antiphonally between the upper and lower pair, is also found in another motet with 'Alleluia' refrain, de Silva's **Intonuit de celo***. This very attractive motet is a model of formal clarity. Its points of imitation always involve the two pairs of adjacent voices replicating each other's material, thanks to which the text is always audible. Each statement of the refrain builds upon the last, and, although the repetitions are not exact, their effect as a unifying device is identical. Perhaps because of its flexibility, the 'Alleluia' refrain proved an immensely popular formal device in the later Renaissance; other examples will be encountered later.

Although the Medici Codex showcases the motet's popularity and versatility at a time when the genre was in full expansion, many of its composers are barely known today. This is glaringly true of Willaert, whose profile is still bizarrely at odds with the veneration in which he was held in his lifetime; but it also applies to Festa, de Silva, and several other direct contemporaries and colleagues – notably Carpentras, the papal chapel-master at the time (though strangely unrepresented in the collection): all the more reason to shine a spotlight on its repertory, which deserves wider appreciation.

Chapter 10 | 'Cantus parvus': secular music

If the Renaissance motet resists description because of its versatility, secular music defies it by dint of sheer numbers. David Fallows' catalogue of polyphonic songs composed between 1415 and 1480 has just over 2,000 entries; the number of entries for the rest of the Renaissance would reach five figures and barely scratch the surface.[1] The number of madrigals published by Philippe de Monte alone (1,100) is not far off the total number of French chansons in Fallows' catalogue. In this chapter, I focus on a half-dozen pieces from across the period in terms of the type they represent and the broader trends they exemplify.

Most of the surviving songs composed before 1500 set poetry in the so-called *formes fixes*. During the Middle Ages, French had been the international courtly language (just as Latin was the language of learning). France's cultural dominance, nurtured by strong dynastic ties between ruling families, fuelled intensive artistic exchange. Although this was by no means one-way, its influence in literature and music was particularly marked and persisted into the fifteenth century. (Vernacular equivalents to the *formes fixes* existed in other languages, but their very forms reflected that influence.) The early sixteenth century saw a new focus on vernacular languages, leading composers to cultivate local poetic forms more intensively than before, a trend encouraged by the burgeoning print industry (since vernacular texts were more marketable). Alongside his polyphonic prints, Petrucci catered to these popular tastes with numerous publications of *frottole*. By c.1510, strophic forms had superseded the *formes fixes* that had dominated poetry for over two centuries. Of course, more popular poetic forms had always existed, but as participants in courtly culture, composers devoted their energies to those associated with it. (A notable exception is the Spanish villancico, whose poetic and musical form relates it to the fourteenth-century virelai but whose subject matter, initially at least, was secular.) Petrucci's prints also show the public taste for instrumental music, which ranged widely in style and destination.

Formes fixes: Ockeghem, *Ma bouche rit*

In the fifteenth century the three *formes fixes* commonly set to polyphony were the ballade, rondeau, and virelai (whose abbreviated fifteenth-century form is sometimes called 'bergerette'). The ballade, which was most clearly associated with aristocratic topics, had dominated the fourteenth century, but by 1440 its popularity was on the wane, along with that of its counterpart, the isorhythmic motet. The few surviving examples written after that date (including Ockeghem's lament for Binchois, *Mort tu as navré* of c.1460) allude to its aristocratic origins but have a slightly different musical design. Conversely, the virelai, which had experienced a temporary eclipse in terms of polyphonic settings earlier in the century, came back into favour around 1450. By then, the most popular form by far was the rondeau, which accounts for roughly 75 per cent of chansons in the period 1415–80. Because these poetic forms are intricate and sometimes misunderstood, it is worth pausing to consider them more closely.

In musical terms, the rondeau and virelai both have two sections, which map onto their texts differently. The pattern of the rondeau is typically expressed as ABaAabAB, where the two letters denote the two sections of text and music. 'AB' is the first text stanza, which is partially repeated ('A') midway through, and fully repeated at the end. The sections of text in lower case are different from the refrain, but follow the same rhyme scheme; in most fifteenth-century rondeaus the refrain has either four or five lines with either eight or ten syllables per line. (In Du Fay's *Je requier a tous amoureux*, discussed in Chapter 5, the midpoint comes with the cadence at b. 9.) The schema for the virelai is ABbaA, where the initial 'A' is a four- or five-line refrain and 'B' a two or three-line verse. In musical settings, the first statement of 'B' may have an 'open' ending, equivalent to a half-cadence, and the second a 'closed', full cadence. Typically, the two sections of a virelai are more self-contained than those of the rondeau, whose first part often concludes with a cadence other than on the final. This system of related musical and textual repeats poses challenges for poet and composer. In the rondeau, the returns of the refrain in the text can be set up by the text that immediately precedes them; this is especially true of the first, partial refrain ('a'). Du Fay's *Je requier* is an example of this, but the poet may go further still, so that what precedes the partial refrain is grammatically incomplete without it. The full stanza after the partial refrain ('ab') may take a different tack, before the full refrain closes the circle. In the virelai, the 'B' section often has a clear change of emphasis; it is a longer journey to the eventual return of the refrain ('A') at the end. In musical terms, the 'A' section of a virelai may be as long as the combined sections of an equivalently proportioned rondeau, and the beginning of the 'B' section is often signalled by a change of mensuration, texture, or vocal register. The compositional challenge of the rondeau is easier to grasp: put simply, the music must bear repeated listening, because it is heard again and again (five times in the case of the 'a' section), and the 'b' section must bring something different, first for variety, but also in order that the listener actively awaits its return. This is crucial to the aesthetic of the *formes fixes*, whose subject matter expresses the tension between frustration and hope in the face of unfulfilled desire. The repetitions of text and music accentuate that dynamic, given that the musical repeats are more frequent than the textual ones (the eventual return of 'b' standing for the possibility of fulfilment). The sense of closure at the end of a well-paced rondeau is one of the most satisfying experiences in Renaissance music.[2]

The popularity of *Ma bouche rit* is very likely associated with two key trends of the 1450s, the revival of the polyphonic virelai and the launch of polyphony in the Phrygian mode. The text's narrator is a forsaken lover who affects a joyful demeanour while being inwardly consumed with grief. Having contrasted his laughing mouth and smiling eye with his unhappy mind and rueful heart, at the 'B' section he addresses the heart of his beloved, which he holds responsible for his misfortune. The paradox with which the poem begins is a staple of the poetry of the time, and the change of addressee for the 'B' section is also typical. Ockeghem's setting has the tenor and contratenor in the same range, and although the contra does not participate in the other voices' imitative structures, it sometimes mimics their behaviour, alternatively following or anticipating it. But those imitative structures are loosely handled: after the opening phrase of each section, it is unclear (even in the discantus) how musical phrases map onto text phrases. The beginning of the tenor's third text phrase imitates the end of the previous phrase of the discantus, and the beginning of the final phrase of 'A' begins in the tenor without the rests that usually mark phrases out from each other. This unstable landscape may explain why Ockeghem avoids distinguishing the start of the 'B' section: on the contrary, its beginning recalls the very start, discantus and tenor following one another at the octave and at two breves' distance, except that this time it is the tenor that initiates things. Typically for Ockeghem, this new opening phrase gives the impression of being identical in both voices but is in fact subtly different, for they end up at a distance of one breve instead of the two with which they began.

There could hardly be a greater contrast with the style of Du Fay's *Je requier*, whose phrases are of roughly equal lengths and separated by clear cadences, reserving melismas to phrase endings. The strictness of these conventions is no impediment to Du Fay's directness of expression, and they quietly underpin Ockeghem's freer approach. In their differences the two songs demonstrate what is possible for composers working in the *formes fixes*.

Strophic song: Senfl, *Lust hab' ich g'habt zur Musica*

The onset of strophic forms at the turn of the sixteenth century broadly coincides with a turn away from the contrapuntal intricacy sometimes associated with *formes fixes* and towards a more melodic approach centred on a single line. (This is certainly the case with the frottola, the strambotto, and other more popular types of song; but as our look at the Medici Codex has shown, that observation holds for much early sixteenth-century sacred polyphony as well.) Like the *formes fixes* which they replaced, strophic forms involve repetition, but usually within, rather than between, stanzas. In the two most common strategies, the music for the opening pair of lines of text is exactly repeated for the next two (a well-known example is Pierre Sandrin's *Doulce mémoire*), or the music of the first or second line (or both) is repeated at the end (Sermisy's *Languir me fays*, Janequin's *Jouyssance vous donnerai*), with both the text and music of the last line repeated again. Some songs combine both (Sermisy's *Dont vient cela*) or aspects of them. Others are through-composed, with the same underlying structure for each strophe, in which case the recurring first line may serve as a refrain (as in Sermisy's drinking song *La la, maistre Pierre*). This general design holds for the sixteenth-century French chanson in particular (the epithet 'Parisian' chanson is misleading, given the importance of Lyon's printing presses in the dissemination of the genre), but its essential elements characterize strophic forms in later periods.

Ludwig Senfl's *Lust hab' ich g'habt zur musica* sets an autobiographical poem in which he pays particular tribute to his revered teacher, Isaac (therefore it cannot date from before 1517).[3] The first letters of its eleven stanzas spell out Senfl's name, but he encodes the first line of the text in musical terms as well: the pitches of the song's opening phrase are *la, sol* (representing his initials, LS) followed by an ascending hexachord (representing music). Like other German song settings of the period, *Lust hab ich g'habt* has the tenor as its principal voice, which proceeds in strict syllabic fashion and in long notes but with melismatic phrase endings. To that extent, it conforms to the general tendency of the period for a more direct and clearer melodic emphasis. But the other voices have more than a supporting role: having imitated the song's opening line, they amplify the tenor's upward hexachord with fast-moving statements in the opposite direction. Senfl fits these in everywhere he can; the placid texture suggested by the tenor becomes infinitely animated. The second pair of text lines is a musical repeat of the first. The middle section introduces a four-note dotted ostinato figure, which soon dominates the texture entirely in both ascending and descending forms. This pithy ostinato technique is a favourite with Senfl, but also of Isaac – hence its appropriateness here. In the last line, the tenor unbends from its syllabic approach and becomes just as florid as the other voices. Though not an exact repeat of line 2, the last line clearly recalls its shape; moreover, the two lines are the only ones that cover the tenor's entire range.

The contrast between the tenor and the activity of the other voices has encouraged the notion that these latter may have been conceived for instruments. While that view has been challenged in recent years, there is no denying that the German song repertory of this period sounds very well with a single voice accompanied by viols, which were just coming into fashion; less subjectively, this manner of performance draws these songs towards the sound world of the Elizabethan consort song.

Epigram: Lassus, *En un chateau*

The near (and badly behaved) relation of the strophic song is the epigram, usually a single-strophe narrative poem with a punchline. Most often the stories deal with the side of human behaviour usually covered by the epithet 'Rabelaisian': lustful monks, nuns (and women generally) of easy virtue, deceived husbands, country bumpkins, rustic shepherds and shepherdesses, and of course, pigs. The wordplay ranges from risqué to graphic obscenity, and unsurprisingly this type of chanson was just as popular as the more conventional love song. That popularity coincided with the vogue for the 'Parisian' chanson generally. With the significant exception of some combinative pieces, the *formes fixes* dealt in such subject matter far less often, and the *air de cour* (which came into vogue in the last decades of the sixteenth century) rarely ventured beyond risqué allusions. Due to the brevity of the text and the tone of the subject matter, epigrams tend to be very short and to apply strophic formal schemes loosely, if at all; some involve more than one strophe, in which case a refrain is common (a good example is Sermisy's *Je ne menge point de porc*, which dwells at length on pigs' propensity to eat … anything). Most of all they challenged the composer to match the wit of the writer with bustling counterpoint, sudden changes of texture, and word-painting for any situation – particularly at the last line, when the narrative typically reaches a climax (of whatever sort). As a subset of strophic forms, it might seem redundant to consider the epigram in a book like this one, but it usefully counteracts the perception of Renaissance polyphony as elevated, refined, and religious.

Selecting a representative piece for the epigram is as difficult as for other forms, particularly since some texts were set by more than one composer, and Janequin, Certon, and Sermisy all excelled at it. Lassus also was particularly fond of them, and the wit and elegance with which he responds to even the coarsest subject matter is, in the end, unrivalled.[4] (Contrast for example the through-composed refrain structure of the drinking song *Vignon, vignon, vignette* with Sermisy's *La, la, Maistre Pierre*, an identically conceived but far less sophisticated piece.) In *En un chateau*, a noblewoman has a stonemason make a statue of the ancient hero Hercules, but is dissatisfied only with its 'smallest member', which she judges to be deficient on such a well-proportioned body; to which the stonemason retorts, 'you're wrong, because back then those big holes of yours were small as well'. The opening point of imitation is combined with its retrograde; although this detail can be over-interpreted, it shows how lightly Lassus wears his contrapuntal skill. The top line grows expansive to evoke the sculpture's beauty ('beau le trouva'), but when its one deficiency is mentioned ('fors le petit membre') the ranges and rhythmic values suddenly shrink. Note that the syncopated rhythm that follows ('qu'elle a jugé') recurs in the last line: there, the lengthening of the beat contrasts the big ('vos grands trous') with the small ('petits'): this last word is repeated insistently. The mirroring between text lines of broad syncopation and repeated quavers subtly underlines the correspondence to which the stonemason so crudely draws attention. Essentially the punchline rests on the one word, 'petits', but the humour lies not only in its meaning but also in the sound of its repetition ('petits petits petits'). Lassus' unfailingly acute ear, and his ability to pack so much detail into so short a space, is marvellous.

Descriptive and narrative songs: Flecha, *La bomba*

The sound of the words is front and centre in the descriptive songs popularized by Clément Janequin, who published several in one volume in 1528.[5] Some were probably composed earlier: *La Guerre* most likely celebrates the victory of Francis I at Marignano in 1515 and conjures up the calls and cries of the soldiers, snatches of dialogue, and a series of onomatopoeia. Scenes are intercut with short passages in verse that comment on the action. Mimesis was not new in music (witness the evocations of birdsong from the late fourteenth century, to which Janequin also contributed with *Le Chant des oiseaux* and *Le Chant de l'alouette*), but, whereas previous examples were framed within poetic forms, here the music is freely invented, and long passages of text have neither rhyme nor metre, consisting only of onomatopoeia. Janequin made a speciality of these musical tableaus: others portray a royal hunting party (*La Chasse*), street cries (*Les Cris de Paris*), or a parley of gossiping housewives whose topics of conversation recall the world of the epigram (*Le Caquet des femmes*, published somewhat later). These pieces depict inherently noisy environments, in which individual words and phrases are tossed about at random. This derives from the musical genre known as 'fricassée' or stew, which contains similar jumbles of dialogue, allusions to well-known songs, street cries, and the like. In order for the texture not to disintegrate at these points, Janequin typically sets them to harmonic pedals; at the end of *La Chasse* this becomes part of the narrative, a chorus of hunting horns represented in long, unadorned repeated notes.

Janequin's pieces were widely copied (think of Orlando Gibbons' *Cries of London*, written nearly a century later). Of their many imitations, the ensaladas of his exact contemporary, the Spaniard Mateo Flecha (1481–1553) are of particular interest.[6] While acknowledging Janequin (most directly in *La guerra*), Flecha seems less concerned with a mimetic programme than with the genre's narrative and (shall we say) psychological potential. *La bomba* deals with a subject unique among these descriptive chansons, a near-shipwreck. (There are parallels with an episode in the *Quart Livre* (1552) of the French novelist and essayist, François Rabelais, which is roughly contemporary.) It begins with the storm in full swing, the sailors making ever more extravagant vows in exchange for their safety; the ship breaks in two, but the sailors are rescued by another ship before the storm dies down; the sailors give thanks to God with an appropriate plainchant respond, and a guitarist tunes up to accompany them in a song of praise; finally they set sail, the wind having turned favourable once again. The tableau ends curiously, with a moralizing Latin epigram cautioning that the perils posed by 'false brethren' are as dangerous as any shipwreck. The variety of the episodes is reminiscent of the fricassée, but each one is treated as a miniature scene, whereas Janequin sets a continuous narrative.

Also unlike Janequin's examples, the theatricality of the scenes is very self-conscious, the references to music especially so: Flecha's singers portray a situation in which their audience would have expected to find them (the intonation of the Respond), but here they do so within a narrative frame, which calls on them to portray themselves. Their voices' imitation of the guitar extends this idea, subverting Janequin's mimetic framework: it imitates neither nature nor noise but art music itself, further emphasizing *La bomba*'s theatricality; Flecha's ensaladas include other overt references to music (*La viuda* audibly cites *L'Homme armé*).

Instrumental music: Tye, *Sit fast* and *O lux*

As seen previously, the boundary between vocal and instrumental polyphony is by no means clear-cut, but by 1500 a sizeable body of textless pieces was in circulation. Much of it consists of cantus firmus settings drawn from the tenors of polyphonic songs, but some appears to be freely composed (that is, independent of pre-existing material). Agricola was a leading exponent of textless pieces; two of them, *Cecus non iudicat de coloribus* ('A blind man cannot tell colours') and *Pater meus Agricola est* ('My father is a farmer') are almost identically conceived: both are freely composed for three voices in two equal sections and sport enigmatic titles. That the earliest evidence for this repertory roughly coincides with the first records of aristocratic interest in the viol consort and the performance of composed polyphony by wind ensembles, is very suggestive. By mid-century, the documentary and source evidence for ensemble performance is far clearer and more plentiful, not least in the new genres to which it gives rise, some polyphonic in conception (the fantasia), some rooted in dance music, and others in variation form based on pre-existing songs, ground basses, or dance rhythms.

One of the earliest composers to leave a substantial quantity of instrumental music is the Englishman Christopher Tye (*c*.1500–72). Over twenty *In nomine* settings are ascribed to him, along with a few other plainchant settings and freely composed pieces. The three-voice *Sit fast* has much in common with the two Agricola pieces just mentioned. Scored for the same number of voices and in two equal sections, it consists of a series of through-composed episodes with ostinatos, syncopated and off-the-beat rhythms, and a gradual acceleration near the end of the two sections, offset by a final written-out 'rallentando'. Although Tye was born around the time of Agricola's death, the parallels suggest that Tye may have been familiar with *Cecus* and *Pater meus*.⁷ Like *Sit fast*, some of the titles given to them may have been directed at the performers: the In nomine 'Trust' gives each note of the c.f. a duration of five minims rather than a breve, implying a 5/4 metre (the title is perhaps an exhortation to the performers to steady their nerves). The five-voice plainchant setting *O lux* is one of Tye's finest: after an ear-catching dissonance at the start, its opening point of imitation is explored with singular purpose; mostly it proceeds at a leisurely pace, but, three-quarters of the way through, the outer voices launch into a string of dotted minims at a crotchet's distance, the remaining voices syncopating their lines more freely. By the end, dotted crotchets dominate the texture, though securely underpinned by dotted semibreves in the bass, echoing its earlier dotted minims. This carefully staged acceleration gives the impression of a later work than *Sit fast* even though its musical vocabulary is the same; the presence of a c.f. is incidental, in that the piece's musical argument is essentially independent of it.

Madrigal: Cipriano, *Da le belle contrade*

After its unassuming first appearance in print in the 1530s, the madrigal quickly became a vehicle for wide-ranging stylistic experimentation.⁸ The genre's first 'hit', Arcadelt's *Il bianco e dolce cigno* (1539), is close to the French chanson in its strophic form and emphasis on a memorable top line supported by effective but functional lower voices. While several prominent madrigalists of the first and second phase (Arcadelt and the slightly older Philippe Verdelot (c.1480–1532), then Willaert and Cipriano) were French or Flemish composers who spent most of their working lives in Italy, other notable early contributors were Italian (notably Costanzo Festa and his brother Sebastiano), and by the turn of the seventeenth century the more daring innovations associated with it were driven principally by native composers: Luca Marenzio (1553/4–99), Luzzasco Luzzaschi (1545–1607), and the emerging generation represented by Monteverdi (1567–1643) and Gesualdo (1566–1613). These innovations eventually encompassed most aspects of musical design: chromaticism and dissonance treatment, but also form and, eventually, obbligato instrumental parts. The madrigal established Italians as the trendsetters of the European musical scene, a status they retained until the eighteenth century. Even England, whose musical tradition stood as much apart from continental developments as it participated in them, domesticated the madrigal, to the extent of adopting the name. Finally, the madrigal was sufficiently well established by mid-century to allow for parody: some of the lighter types (such as the villanella or the canzonet – the latter being one of the models for the English style of madrigal) were a gently tongue-in-cheek reaction to a certain 'high style' established by the likes of Cipriano. The pastoral topics of these lighter genres were reinterpreted in their turn in a more complex way, encompassing psychological ambiguity and eroticism (as in Marenzio's notorious *Tirsi morir volea*). This gives some idea of the wealth of references and undercurrents to which the madrigal bears witness in its long history; in this respect it is unparalleled among Renaissance genres, with the possible exception of the Mass cycle (for very different reasons).

That high style was particularly associated with the sonnet, the form rediscovered (or better, re-appropriated) by sixteenth-century poets and composers. Their model was the scholar and poet Francesco Petrarca (1304–74), many of whose own sonnets were set to music in the Renaissance despite being 200 years old. The form consists of fourteen lines divided into two groups of four and two groups of three, with the rhyme scheme *abba abba cde cde* (though the rhymes scheme for the tercets may vary). Published posthumously in 1566, Cipriano's *Da le belle contrade* illustrates the high style at its most compelling. The male narrator of the anonymous poem relates the despair of his beloved, whom he leaves after a night spent together. The 'beauteous realms of the east' in the first line are those out of which the morning star appears; the couple's embraces are 'that pleasure which no human mind can fathom'.[9] The consistently allusive language is typical of the poetic style; also implicit is the outcome of the beloved's entreaties, which result in 'more entwinings than those of the ivy or acanthus'. So far, perhaps, so conventional, but the poem is deeply ordered. The first and last stanza are in the narrative voice (male, and addressing the listener), but the middle ones are in the female voice and addressed first to the narrator in the second stanza, then in the third to love itself, whose pleasures are 'uncertain and fleeting'. Thus, the poem's ordering is also deeply gendered (the female voice never addresses the listener directly). Cipriano's music clearly reflects that ordering but subtly undercuts its possible meaning. The narrator's material is solidly and consistently Lydian, and mostly fully scored (in the first stanza especially). His lover's material is initially signalled by a far greater textural instability, her beloved's cries of 'haimé' ('alas') are set to falling motifs, the discantus is left briefly on its own at 'sola'; but these almost predictable illustrative touches are triggered by an unravelling texture. Cipriano escalates this affect in the third stanza: as she addresses love itself, the security of Lydian is undermined by a series of sharp chromatic shifts, moving from C♮ to D♭ and back within a few bars (bb. 41–52). But, typical of Cipriano's use of the technique, this episode is controlled and contained: just as suddenly the music shifts back to F as the lover resumes his narrative. One can read the music conventionally, contrasting the male's sense of security and authority with the female's instability, lack of focus, and unreliability (*he* is the narrator, after all); on the other hand, the female's music is unquestionably the madrigal's affective core, the passage that would have struck the composer's contemporaries most forcibly. In comparison, the male's agreeable, self-satisfied Lydian episodes can be heard as framing devices. Finally, one could point out that the textural stability of the opening stanza is far less secure in the final one. In short, the woman has the more compelling music, and, by the end, it is her viewpoint and her will that prevail.

Chapter 11 | Scoring, texture, scale

Having established the text of a new piece and considered its broader implications for form and musical style, one of the composer's first concrete decisions was to determine its scoring – that is, the number of voices and their relative ranges. The significance of vocal ranges and functions was explored in Chapter 5, but mainly from a stylistic perspective; in this chapter I consider their practical application. This brings two related issues into play: texture (that is, the voices' interactions in terms of musical material) and scale. A few observations to begin with: in previous chapters the terms 'scoring' and 'texture' were more or less synonymous: thus, the so-called *Caput* texture is not only defined by its three registral layers (scoring) but also by the slower-moving cantus firmus in the middle layer (texture). But in the course of the Renaissance, the relation between the two changes considerably: the same composer wrote the largely homophonic *If ye love me* and the multiple canons of *Miserere nostri*. The sense of scale changes still more radically: the composer of the tiny *Sicut lilium* also wrote the twelve-voice *Missa Et ecce terre motus*, which lasts three-quarters of an hour. Such extremes are first encountered at the turn of the sixteenth century and are specifically a Renaissance development. Finally, not only do these three parameters condition how music functions, they fundamentally inform how we hear and experience it, and how it is grasped in real time. The examples from Tallis and Brumel show that the notion of 'scale' is not just a matter of duration. It is no coincidence that the new focus on scale discernible around 1500 is connected with a fundamentally different approach to scoring (the number of voices) and texture (the ways they are used and relate to each other). In this chapter, the three phenomena are treated in order, but as it unfolds they are increasingly considered together. With English polyphony, which until the reign of Elizabeth I developed quite distinctly from continental music, they are so inextricably linked that it is best considered separately.

Scoring: fifteenth-century experiments and beyond

By 1520, the presence of four distinct ranges was well established regardless of the actual number of voices, though this did not prevent the circulation of very popular pieces in the older three-tier scoring. All the same, within a few years the new arrangement had entirely superseded the old. By contrast, the fifteenth century had witnessed a succession of approaches to scoring: we have seen that, although the *Caput* texture was widely adopted in four-voice music soon after 1440, the previous two-tier arrangement persisted in three-voice chansons for at least another decade. The examples shown in Chapter 5 represent the most typical configurations, 'normative types' in analytical parlance; but in the second half of the century, composers experimented with a variety of different scorings for three, four, and five voices. Some are found in just one or two surviving pieces and were probably isolated experiments, while others are found in several widely circulated pieces, and one can plausibly relate that popularity to their scoring.

One of the better established of these exceptional scorings is the three-voice piece with a discantus and tenor in the same range. In these pieces, the function of the two voices is interchangeable or even invertible, leading scribes of the time and scholars today to disagree as to which was which. Ockeghem's *Fors seulement l'actente* and Busnoys' *Je ne puis vivre ainsi tousjours* count among their composers' finest creations: the former gave rise to countless re-workings by later composers, and the latter, written for Jacqueline de Hacqueville, is one of the most poignant expressions of longing in the chanson repertory. Related to this group is Du Fay's rondeau *Les Douleurs dont me sens tel somme*, whose top two voices are in canon at the unison and exchange their functions constantly. The scoring of this piece is doubly unusual because the canonic pair is supported by two contratenors in the same range an octave lower. Canonic pieces often have unusual textures: the discantus and tenor of Du Fay's *Puisque vous estiez campeur* are in canon at the octave, supported by a very wide-ranging contratenor, and Busnoys' ingenious rondeau *A que ville et habominable* (another song for Jacqueline, apparently recording their acrimonious breakup) gives the option to treat the top voice as a self-contained three-voice canon at the unison. Music for equal voices seems to have been of particular interest to Busnoys: the four-voice motet *Anthoni usque limina* has two equal discantus parts, one of which splits further into two in several places, and the rondeau *Bel accueil* is for three equal voices, each of which functions as discantus, tenor, or contratenor at different points.

Judging by these pieces' exceptional quality, composers found such unusual scorings especially stimulating. This sustained interest coincides with the arrival on the scene of the generation of Busnoys, Ockeghem, and Regis, and also Tinctoris, whose three-voice *Missa sine nomine* has a low contratenor notated in the Gamma-clef and extending a written fifth below the gamut. (The examples of unusual scorings in Du Fay's music are almost all associated with canon; it is reasonable to infer that he was not drawn to unusual scorings in and of themselves.) Ockeghem and Regis also cultivated five-voice writing, which was relatively uncommon in continental music before the 1490s. Because the sources for these mostly sacred pieces were compiled after their deaths, it isn't known when they were written, but they certainly predate the standardization of four-tier scoring. In each work, the placement of the extra voice is slightly different, with a general tendency to low notated ranges and an effective fourth range situated between the lowest voice and the tenor. Placing the fifth voice so close to the bass results in particularly dense textures, which must have seemed very new. While five-voice music was more common in the following generation, the newer approach was less bottom-heavy, with the added voice in the middle of the texture (e.g. Josquin's *Illibata Dei virgo nutrix*). The interest in low clefs carried on in parallel, not least in works associated with mourning (such as Pierre de La Rue's Requiem, the four-voice setting by Lassus, or Pierre Moulu's *Fiere Atropos/Anxiatus est*), and in several motets from Willaert's *Musica nova* (1559).[1]

A third substantial group consists of mostly three-voice pieces in which a c.f. (usually but not invariably plainchant) is placed in the lowest-sounding voice. The first known instance of this is probably Ockeghem's *Missa Caput* (c.1450), closely modelled on the anonymous English cycle but placing the chant in the lowest voice throughout. Placement of the borrowed material in a voice other than the tenor took on a life of its own within Mass cycles, but alongside it grew a parallel tradition of pieces with a low-lying c.f. functioning as a contratenor over a discantus–tenor pair. A coherent group of pieces emerges with Compère, Agricola, and Josquin, in which plainchant underpins a rondeau or virelai in the upper voices. The name 'motet-chanson' that is sometimes given to these pieces is unnecessarily confusing: essentially these are chansons that happen to incorporate plainchant. What unites them is a *musical* idea: the exploration of an unusual texture. The remarkable clarity Josquin achieves in *Que vous madame/In pace* (Example 11.1) is reinforced by the use of sequence in all three voices (requiring considerable embellishment of the chant);

Example 11.1 Josquin, *Que vous madame/In pace in idipsum* (beginning). Translation: Discantus; You alone, my lady, I swear, [will I serve]... Tenor: In peace [will I sleep]...

Example 11.2 Agricola, *Revenez tous regretz/Quis det* (beginning). Translation: Discantus: Arise again, regrets, I welcome you... Tenor: O that my request be granted...

Agricola's *Revenez tous regretz/Quis det* (Example 11.2) achieves the opposite effect by adding a fourth voice and having the overlapping middle voices shadow the plainchant at the third (recalling the five-voice works of Ockeghem and occasionally Regis). In these two examples, the same technique results in highly contrasted sound worlds.

Example 11.3 Ockeghem, *Missa Au travail suis*, 'Et resurrexit' (conclusion)

Alongside these collective efforts are individual pieces for which there are no clear precedents (or only speculative ones). One of the most thoroughgoing is Ockeghem's *Missa Au travail suis*, a four-voice work that revisits the two-tier scoring of the earlier fifteenth century.[2] Not only do the upper and lower pairs of voices occupy practically the same ranges (with tenor and contratenor bassus constantly crossing), but the top voice consistently behaves like the triplum in the earlier set-up, finishing a fifth above the final at cadences, while the voice beneath it invariably cadences with the tenor and has more consecutive fifths with the top voice than is typical for the mid-to-late fifteenth century (Example 11.3). This unambiguous 'triplum function' of the top voice strongly suggests that Ockeghem must have become acquainted with two-tier scoring (perhaps through direct contact with Du Fay, who had known it in his youth). Yet this is no stylistic throwback, because there is no distinction between the speeds of the upper and lower pair (a defining feature of the older style). Instead, the setting is characterized by a kaleidoscopic interplay between different pairings of voices, in which two-part-writing predominates. Equally *sui generis* is Obrecht's dazzling house of cards, *Missa Sub tuum presidium* (*c.*1503?), which begins in three voices with the c.f. as the top voice and adds a new voice with each movement, culminating in the seven-voice Agnus dei. Each movement adds at least one c.f. to those already present, ending with one of the best-known Marian chants, *Regina celi*, which is placed on the final Agnus dei like a cherry on a cake. The trick of keeping something in reserve for the last section had about fifty years' history when this Mass was written, but few examples are more delightful.

Although that Agnus dei is Obrecht's only surviving seven-voice music, it is with his generation that the attitude to scoring began to change. Coinciding with the gradual move towards four distinct vocal ranges, five- and six-voice writing became more common, alongside individual pieces for even greater numbers. Whereas the previous examples concern the internal arrangements of relatively few voices, after 1500 composers' attention to scoring and texture shifted towards the expansion of musical space. Here also Ockeghem may have led the way, although the thirty-six-voice canonic motet known to be his is lost (it cannot be the motet *Deo gratia* included in the Collected Edition of his work, whose distribution of the thirty-six voices into four choirs differs from contemporary accounts of Ockeghem's piece). These often incorporate canonic writing, which anyway features prominently with Mouton and La Rue, and in Josquin's five- and six-voice works (*Pater noster/Ave maria, Petite camusette*, and several concluding Agnus dei settings in Mass cycles; but his authorship of a twenty-four-voice motet *Quis habitat*, ascribed to him in its only printed source, is very unlikely). As noted in Chapter 3, the taste for sonic blockbusters in the later Renaissance was fuelled as much by princely love of display as genuine musical appreciation. The expansion of musical space parallels the growing state of knowledge of the known world and the cosmos during this period, which saw the first known circumnavigation of the globe (1519–23) and the dissemination of Copernicus' theories concerning the solar system. Be that as it may, approaches to scoring in the fifteenth and sixteenth centuries are audibly worlds apart. Interpreting this transformation requires that we consider the changing technical resources that helped bring it about.

Much of the polyphonic landscape between 1450 and 1550 is defined by the interplay of two paradigms, c.f. composition and imitation. Imitation was already a known quantity in 1450, and pieces were still being written around a c.f. a century later. But each plays a crucial role in structuring musical discourse: concretely, each fundamentally affects how voices relate to each other.

Texture types: polyphony with and without cantus firmus

At the very start of this book, I drew attention to the role of the c.f., not merely as a structural element but as the metaphorical 'lungs' of the music,

Example 11.4 Du Fay, *Ave regina celorum III* (beginning). Translation: Hail, Queen of heaven, mistress of the angels.

the alternation of sections where it is present (usually in fully scored passages) or absent (reduced scoring) corresponding to inhaling and exhaling. The initial entry of a c.f. and the lower contratenor introduces four-voice texture for the first time. The resumption of duo texture when the lower voices fall silent sets up their eventual return and provides a context for interpreting what follows in terms of this alternation. But this strategy can be inflected: in some cases, the opening duo (always between the discantus and upper contratenor) is sometimes followed by a bassus entry, which takes over from the discantus (Example 11.4). This new pairing delays the entry of the tenor, which is then paired with the discantus when the full texture is first presented. The set-up's textural potential deepened when composers began using the tenor as the c.f. carrier at some points and as a 'free' voice elsewhere. This paved the way for another opening gambit, whereby a discantus–altus duo is immediately replicated at the octave by the lower pair of voices; only later, after a period of silence, does the tenor enter again, this time bearing the c.f. This antiphonal configuration grew so common as to become a cliché (Lassus parodies it at the start of the chanson *Quand mon mari vient de dehors* to evoke the crabby old husband of the title; it begins each movement of Josquin's famous *Missa Pange lingua*, but Example 11.4 is an intermediary step: the contratenor is the lower voice against the discantus and the upper voice against the bassus.) The possible variations on this are worth exploring, but the crucial point to note is the interplay between two levels of formal articulation: on the large scale, the alternation between full and reduced texture, and more locally, the permutations of voices in reduced sections. This interplay is a constant of c.f. structures in general.

The two levels are interdependent; they can interfere with each other or even merge. Example 11.4 is from the motet *Ave regina celorum* that Du Fay intended for his memorial. With its two sections in O and ₵, it is a classic statement of the two-part c.f. motet in the grand, post-*Caput* style. What marks out Du Fay's late style from his English models is the greater fluidity with which vocal combinations succeed each other, whether or not the tenor has the c.f. But as was seen at the very first tenor entry of his *L'Homme armé* Mass (Example 8.1 on p. 113), the smoothing or blurring of boundaries between full and reduced sections does not undermine the principle of their alternation, nor does it affect the c.f.'s structural function. On the contrary, the certainty of the return to full scoring gives the free voices licence to interact in more and more varied ways. In Du Fay's motet, the predictability of the first tenor entry is offset by the signed e♭' in the discantus. This surprise is the first indication of Du Fay's affective play against modal expectations; it neatly prefigures the piece's central moment, which happens much later in the work's second part: the plea to 'have mercy on the beseeching Du Fay', previously noted in Chapter 3 (Example 3.2 above, p. 33). Sealing the correspondence, both these entries begin on the same pitch and set the same word ('miserere').

In Obrecht's five-voice motet *Salve crux**, written about twenty-five years after Du Fay's, this textural fluency is even more marked. Example 11.5 shows an extended passage from its second section (which is here compressed for reasons of space) during which the c.f.-bearing tenor is silent until the very end. Initially, two voices in different ranges exchange imitative dialogue ('Crux est nostrae libra') and are answered by a different point of imitation in the other pair ('Sceptrum regis'). This antiphonal exchange (lower vs higher pair) is repeated in the following bars (not shown), whereupon two very short points of imitation are presented in the four voices from the lowest to the highest ('Tu scala tu ratis/Tu crux desperatis'). Then they join in a chordal statement (at 'tabula suprema'), cadencing on the final. Another antiphonal pair of statements follows (not shown), very similar to the first, then a chordal statement whose text and cadence ('regum diadema') corresponds and 'rhymes' with the previous one. Following Example 11.5 is a more extended, consistently imitative duo in triple time, and, to finish, the tenor enters as all the voices invoke the motet's object directly and solemnly: 'O Crux lignum triumphale' ('O cross, wood triumphant').

This passage can be reduced to just three texture types: antiphony (the alternation of two or more groups of voices), homophony, and what I will call 'independent part-writing'; however, the combination of these texture types is exceptionally fluid.

From the point of view of texture, the sections of *Salve crux* where the c.f. is present are just as varied as in the passages shown in Example 11.5, where it is absent. In the first major section, they tend to be fully scored: the motet's very first tenor entry is marked by a series of long chords, ensuring maximum impact for the first flush of full scoring. In the second part, voices drop in and out, deferring full scoring until the concluding invocation. The short final section is entirely in triple time, and fully scored throughout. (Thus, the mensural scheme of *Salve crux* conforms to the standard two-part layout with O and ₵, with the third section as a concluding flourish in triple time.) But there is a crucial difference: when the c.f. is present, the alternation of texture types seen in Example 11.5 is almost entirely absent, because the long notes of a c.f. impede it.

Mouton's *In omni tribulatione* (Example 9.2, p. 126 above) makes the same point: in the absence of a c.f., the motet consists of a succession of homophonic and antiphonal passages, and a concluding passage of independent four-voice part-writing. *In omni tribulatione* is typical of a type of motet without c.f. with which composers of Mouton's generation began to experiment early in their careers (i.e. from the mid-1470s), first in motets and a little later in secular music. (Perhaps the most famous example is Josquin's four-voice *Ave Maria ... virgo serena*.) An advantage of this approach was that although it didn't preclude the use of plainchant, the absence of a c.f. gave composers free rein with respect to texture and

Example 11.5 Obrecht, *Salve crux* (second part, excerpts). Translation: (a) The Cross is the measure of our justice, the King's sceptre, the rod of power. Heavenly Cross... (b) O ladder, O raft, last plank of those in despair... (c) [from Christ's limbs you have taken the beauteous] crown of kings.

entailed no expectations at all regarding scale. A tenor c.f. might still be appropriate for specific occasions, but the Medici Codex shows composers finding new ways of smoothing over the sectional implications of c.f. structures (or ignoring them altogether). Breaking up the c.f. and treating it as a two-voice canon (as in Josquin's *Inviolata, integra et casta es*; *Pater noster/Ave Maria*; or *Virgo prudentissima*) allowed it to run throughout the piece uninterrupted while accommodating changes of texture. Thus, the textural strategies that helped articulate c.f. structures began to develop independently of them.

Varietas: texture types and the role of imitation

Another key factor in differentiating musical textures is the role of imitation. We have observed it many times in passing; it is time to focus on it more closely.

Imitation consists in two or more voices duplicating identical or near-identical melodic material at given intervals of both time and pitch. The time-interval between the voices varies from just one pitch, a minim or a semibreve of original notation (this is 'stretto fuga') to a whole bar or several. The imitation itself can be brief or extend over several bars, but it eventually breaks off, typically to allow the voices to cadence. Beyond this basic definition, the many types of imitation have been closely studied.[3] Since I am concerned with the textural implications of imitation rather than its technical workings, I will simply refer to them as they arise.

Unlike canon, which is maintained throughout a section and is rigorously exact, the statements of a point of imitation can change to suit the contrapuntal context. (This is familiar in common practice from the distinction between 'real' and 'tonal' answers in fugues.) The beginning of Cipriano's *Da le belle contrade* (discussed in Chapter 10), in which only the point of imitation's basic outline is retained, shows how flexible it can be. In other respects, imitation and canon are closely associated and follow similar rules (Renaissance musicians used the same term, 'fuga', for both). Another mark of imitation is that its points (or 'modules') are usually separated from what precedes them by a rest or a held note. This feature is integral to imitative procedures from the start, in the early fifteenth century.

The relationship between imitation and texture types is worth examining further. First, there is an inverse relationship between the presence of a c.f. and the use of imitation; in other words, whenever the c.f. is heard (and particularly in full scoring), imitation is the exception rather than the rule. Although the second half of *Salve crux*'s third section has an extended point of imitation between the discantus and tenor, there is very little in the other voices, and nothing extended. But where the tenor is absent, imitation and repeated modules are the principal means of articulating textures. In Mouton's freely composed *In omni tribulatione*, it is present everywhere (apart from homophonic passages, by definition), since all its antiphonal exchanges consist of repeated two-voice modules, which may themselves be imitative. The generation born around 1450 is the first for whom imitative procedures are of fundamental technical importance. It is they who begin to experiment intensively with close-knit imitative modules that permit imitation between three, four, and more voices. But imitation is only one of several techniques based on repetition and duplication of material, such as sequence, ostinato, and what Gaffurius called 'the very famous procedure', in which outer voices move in parallel tenths against a middle voice in longer values (a procedure beloved of wind ensembles from the turn of the sixteenth century). First cultivated extensively by Busnoys, these features are ubiquitous from the 1480s, trailing off after 1500 as imitation becomes even more generalized. Though already less frequent in the slightly younger Mouton, they feature especially strongly with Obrecht, Agricola, Isaac, La Rue, Gaspar, Marbrianus de Orto (*c.*1460–1529), and a number of others, including Josquin. For them, imitation appears as a means to an end – the varied interplay of vocal combinations – not an end in itself.

This concern is inherited from the composers writing in the wake of the *Missa Caput* (including Du Fay, who was in mid-career when it was introduced). Chansons were fertile ground because of the need to mark off the beginnings of text lines, which points of imitation do especially well. All the same, in the list of the most popular songs of the 1450s and 60s, imitation features prominently in some and hardly at all in others.[4] Even when it is strongly present, it functions very differently from later 'modular' imitation, in which the voices are separated only by a couple of pitches: a point of imitation may consist of an entire phrase, however long (e.g. the opening phrases of Busnoys' *Je ne puis vivre ainsi* and Ockeghem's *Fors seulement l'actente*). The same applies to two-voice imitative episodes in Masses and motets with reduced scoring (particularly those of Busnoys: *In hydraulis* is full of them). The fact that composers mid-century experimented with disguised or 'embedded' imitation confirms it as an occasional resource rather than the pervasive presence it later became. The strong preference was for a variety of scoring and texture.

Variety also features in the contemporary theoretical discourse of the time. It is rare for Renaissance teachers to evaluate polyphony from what we would recognize as an aesthetic standpoint, and it is almost unheard of for them to do so in technical terms. A striking exception comes from Tinctoris, whose eighth rule from the *Book of the Art of Counterpoint* (1477) states that

> variety must be diligently sought for in all counterpoint ... now by one quantity [duration], now by another; now by one perfection [cadence?], now by another; now by one proportion [interval or sonority?], now by another; now by one conjunction [melodic interval?], now by another; now with suspensions, now without suspensions; now with *fugae* [imitation], now without *fugae*; now with pauses, now without pauses; now ornamented, now in simple values [*nunc diminutive, nunc plane*][5]

Although the meaning of Tinctoris' terminology is open to interpretation, the caution against relying too much on any one procedure explicitly includes imitation; in any case, the general point reinforces his other rules, and chimes – broadly speaking – with the music of his direct and younger contemporaries, including the generation born after 1450 such as Josquin, Brumel, and Obrecht. But notwithstanding differences of emphasis between generations in handling imitation, their composed music bears out the observation of variety as an aesthetic ideal, expressed in the interplay of voices. The classic expression of this is Ockeghem's five-voice motet *Intemerata Dei mater** (c.1480). A tour de force by any standards, its three sections can be described entirely in terms of our three texture types. The first section is dominated by independent part-writing: changes in the number and combinations of voices are not marked off from one another, but are free and fluid. The second focuses on antiphonal exchanges between high and low voices (and a brief homophonic passage). The third alternates passages of independent part-writing and prominent homophonic episodes. This schematic description does scant justice to one of the Renaissance's most individual creations; but the essential point is that *Intemerata* has no c.f. and vanishingly few instances of imitation. Even in antiphonal exchanges (which so often involve a recurring phrase or a two-voice imitative module) repetition of material is consistently avoided; on the contrary, Ockeghem gives his antiphonal exchanges audibly different material (for example, contrary vs parallel motion). In short, *Intemerata Dei mater* demonstrates that the handling of texture is central to Tinctoris' ideal of 'varietas'. But there is more: it shows that textural variety can be achieved without recourse to the intensive imitative and repetitive procedures of the late fifteenth century.

To call imitation a means to an end in no way downplays its significance. But that significance is best understood in terms of the changing approaches to scoring and texture discussed in this chapter. I have already observed that changes of musical style usually involve several parameters at once. The contrast between the sound worlds of the freely composed motets of the Medici Codex and *Intemerata Dei mater* could hardly be greater: the contrapuntal writing is simpler and the scoring more transparent (not least because the voices are more clearly differentiated in terms of range). Although the texture types are the same as those of *Intemerata*, their relationship is more audible because imitation helps to focus the ear through its introduction of shared material. This is variety of a very different sort from what Tinctoris had had in mind (his sixth rule of counterpoint concerns the avoidance of repetition, specifically of melodic figures). By 1500, imitative procedures had diversified well beyond what he would have known in 1475. But, although it is expressed very differently, the handling of texture is as pertinent an observation point for the period after 1520 as before.

The role of imitation in foregrounding contrapuntal processes may explain why it took hold as it did. Another reason has to do with the technique itself.[6] As expressed by John Milsom, the rules for stretto fuga are very simple: 'provided the leading voice sings a melody made only from the intervals of rising seconds, falling thirds [and] rising fourths ... or repeats the pitch on which it stands, a second voice can replicate it at the lower fifth and a unit [of pitch] later, giving rise to flawless counterpoint'. Although the rules governing imitation more broadly may be simply expressed, the resulting possibilities seem infinite. Willaert's *Saluto te, sancta virgo* (Example 5.5, p. 76 above) shows one of the more common procedures: the point of imitation at the lower fifth between the discantus and tenor is replicated a few bars later by the tenor and bassus. Rather than drop out, which would create an antiphonal effect, the higher pair continues freely; but rather than cadence with the lower voices, it begins a new point of imitation that is eventually carried over to the lower pair, which has fallen silent. This dovetailing effect allows several points of imitation to follow one another without a break: as one process ends, the other begins. Reduced to essentials, Willaert's opening gambit is a two-voice module that has been expanded to include four voices. Example 11.6 shows the opening of *Absalon fili mi* (variously ascribed to Josquin and La Rue) in which two statements of a two-

Example 11.6 Josquin/La Rue (?), *Absalon fili mi* (beginning). Translation: Absalom, my son...

voice 'interlock' (as Milsom calls it) overlap; that is, the gap between the second entry of the first pair (altus) and the first entry of the second (tenor) is shorter than the gap between the two voices of the initial pair. Therefore, this module (or 'fuga subject', in Milsom's elegant term) is replicated against itself in two ways: after one pitch at the fourth below, or after three at the fifth below.[7] The ingenuity of such contrapuntal inventions is another factor in the spread of imitation beyond two-voice constructs to four, five, six, or as many as available. (The deliberately 'off-centre' quality of the beginning of Agricola's *Si dedero* (Example 9.1, p. 121 above) comments indirectly on the standardization of such imitative modules: the entry of the tenor is half a bar later than the previous entry leads one to expect, and its opening pitch results in a seventh sounding against the bassus.) It is no accident that the move towards generalized or 'pervasive' imitation coincides with an increase in the usual number of voices and of 'outsized' scorings of twelve, twenty-four, thirty-six voices or more.

English exceptionalism: the Eton Choirbook and beyond

While continental composers were still experimenting with five-voice writing, composers of the British Isles had been handling it fluently for some time. English and Scottish music after 1450 cannot be precisely charted because of the wholesale destruction of native sources during the Reformation and the Protectorate. English music had become less accessible to continental scribes with the end of the Hundred Years' War (1336–1453), which put an end to the constant to-and-fro of English princes and their courts on the mainland. As the music of Power, Dunstaple and their contemporaries survives only in continental sources, the record for subsequent generations is very patchy. A lone Burgundian source transmits a few Masses by Walter Frye, a key figure for this period. The next major source for sacred music is the Eton Choirbook, a partly dismembered but still sizeable volume of Marian antiphons copied just after 1500, whose repertory spans the previous half-century (including brand-new pieces). Of the composers whose music it transmits virtually nothing would be known otherwise. This includes several figures whose reputation would certainly be far greater had more of their music survived: Walter Lambe, Richard Davy, and John Browne. Eton gives only an incomplete account of their work: the absence of any Mass music is a major loss. (The music of the Scotsman Robert Carver, preserved independently, is similarly individual.) But what survives shows that English polyphony post-*Caput* developed on very different lines from the continent. What comes across most clearly from the Eton repertory is the exceptional proficiency of boy trebles, far surpassing the few clear continental examples.

Most Eton antiphons preserve a c.f. structure with two main sections in O and C, but the differences with continental music are almost entirely to do with the issues explored in this chapter. The alternation of vocal combinations and texture types on the continent is replaced by a kind of panel structure: reduced sections typically consist of chains of extended, self-contained episodes for specific scorings. Antiphony is very rare; homophony is confined to chordal statements at key words; independent part-writing is the norm. Describing this style in terms of what it lacks is not meant as a negative value judgement, for the diversity of scorings of these individual panels far exceeds anything found in continental practice: extended duos between the highest treble and the lowest bass, for example, or the so-called 'gimell' scoring with the treble voice split into two. Although changes of scoring are less frequent than in continental music, the greater wealth of textural possibilities is exploited to great effect in the best Eton music; and, because more voices are usually involved, the impact of the contrast between full and reduced scoring is that much greater. In short, it seems that English composers were sensitive rather earlier to the potential of texture on a broad canvas than their continental colleagues. It is especially acute in Browne's surviving works, no two of which have exactly the same scoring. Not only does Eton contain more music by him than by any other composer; an uncommonly high proportion of it is for more than five voices. The choirbook's index also records several four-voice antiphons with an overall range of nearly three octaves (including one by Browne), all of which have been lost. With the exception of Ockeghem's four-voice rondeau *Je n'ay dueil*, practically nothing comparable exists in continental music, and it is very short in comparison.

It is worth emphasizing that scale is the other distinguishing feature of this music: Davy's *O Domine celi terreque*, which lasts well over a quarter of an hour, is hardly unusual in context but dwarfs most continental motets and longer Mass movements of the time. The few multi-sectional works of comparable duration (such as Josquin's *Miserere*, and *Planxit autem David*) are unlike English music in nearly every other way. The parallel that is sometimes made with the Eton Choirbook repertory and contemporary perpendicular architecture gets at something essential: like the antiphons' two-part c.f. layout and the panel structure of reduced sections, the long, narrow chapel of King's College, Cambridge, has the simplest structure imaginable. Its plainness draws the viewer's eye upwards, towards the dazzling tracery of the fan vaulting above, which it is designed to support. (The plan of Eton College chapel is very similar though, if a fan vault was planned, it was not executed.) The same can be said of the texturally intricate music performed there, its exceptional sonic luxuriance accentuated by formal austerity.

Early Tudor polyphony post-Eton is better documented. Thanks to the survival of later sources we have Masses by Robert Fayrfax (c.1464–1521, one of the youngest Eton composers), Thomas Ashwell (c.1478–c.1513), and Nicholas Ludford (c. 1485–1557), whose music bridges the gap with John Taverner (c.1490–1545), and from Taverner onwards the record is even more detailed. Taverner deploys imitation more consistently than any Eton composer, and some of his late works suggest a gradual rapprochement of English music with continental practice – a trend that intensifies with the growing influence of continental figures established in England, such as the Fleming Philip van Wilder (c.1500–53). The large-scale antiphon continued until mid-century on a scale at times surpassing the longest examples in Eton (for example in the so-called Peterhouse partbooks, an incomplete set whose repertory has been largely recovered thanks to the systematic reconstruction of the lost material). Tallis' *Gaude gloriosa Dei mater* is usually regarded as one of the last and finest Marian English antiphons, in which imitation plays a more prominent role than ever.

Like that of many English composers, Tallis' output bears witness to the competing religious and political priorities of the later Tudors; the fact that he weathered these artistically more successfully than anyone is a testament to his exceptional range and invention. Along with the famous Lamentations, the motets in his joint publication with Byrd, *Cantiones sacrae* (1575), show how far the stylistic gap with the continent had been bridged. They also demonstrate sensitivity to scoring and texture on a par with Browne's, though expressed in a more understated way. The forty-voice *Spem in alium* is the one exception to that understatement, and we will turn to it presently; just as individual is the incomplete seven-voice *Missa Puer natus est*, probably composed in the mid-1550s. It is constructed on a c.f. tenor, but which has not the same function as before: its presence or absence has little perceptible influence on formal articulation and triggers no changes of texture. What is new in English terms is the consistent alternation of the three texture types. But the manner of their deployment is very different from what was observed earlier in this chapter; it is in fact much closer to the style of Tallis' continental colleagues. (The Mass may have been intended for the combined choirs of Queen Mary and her husband, Philip of Spain.) There is no extended writing for two or three voices; the presence of two trebles in the same range permits antiphonal effects and homophonic episodes even in fully scored passages; finally, reduced sections seldom last long, except where a fuga subject builds up the texture to achieve full scoring at the beginning of a major formal division (e.g. the 'Qui tollis' or the 'Pleni sunt caeli'). Whatever the presence of a c.f. was intended to convey to Tallis' audience, in musical terms, its use is largely symbolic. The sound world of the *Caput* Mass is a distant memory.

Pervasive imitation and its aftermath

I remarked in a previous chapter that a heightened emphasis on one parameter is often balanced by a corresponding stepping-down in the treatment of others. In early Tudor polyphony, long-standing formal conventions were fairly strictly adhered to (particularly regarding the role of the c.f. in the articulation of form), while contrasts in scoring and detailed vocal display were pushed very far. A similar situation obtains on the continent after 1520 with the so-called 'pervasive imitation' pioneered by the imperial master of the choirboys, Nicolas Gombert. Like the motet *Media vita* (Example 5.6, p. 77 above), most pieces by Gombert begin with an unfolding fuga subject, stated one voice at a time until all of them have entered. (In some cases, a countersubject is present, or a figure resembling the main subject but soon diverging from it.) It may be restated more than once in a given voice, but eventually a new subject is introduced (typically corresponding to a new text phrase), whereupon the process begins again. But rather than start the textural build-up from scratch, the new subject gradually displaces the old, so that the two processes are dovetailed. The process can be repeated indefinitely, resulting in a series of interlocking musical 'paragraphs'. Once the initial fuga subject is set up, full scoring persists until the end of the section. New entries are usually marked off with a rest, and occasional 'windows' of three- or four-voice writing introduce a touch of parallel motion by way of contrast; but these rarely last more than two or three bars. Antiphonal effects are also possible, but as in Tallis' seven-voice Mass, they are more often suggested by the call and response of voices in the same range than by actual division of the ensemble into groups.

Gombert's technique is sometimes said to derive from the style of Josquin, but that view seems to me problematic. While imitative and obsessively repetitive procedures characterize much of Josquin's output, they remain subordinate to the fluid approach to texture discussed in the previous section. This is true even of *Ave Maria ... virgo serena*, which is so often held up as the quintessence of his style: however prominent the role of imitation, the three texture types constantly alternate whereas with Gombert pervasive imitation is seemingly an end in itself. And his style was recognized as a radical departure in his own time: writing in the decades either side of his death, Hermann Finck (in his *Practica musica*, 1556) and Cosimo Bartoli (in his *Ragionamenti accademici*, 1567) remark on his avoidance of pauses and emphasis on fuga, Finck stating that Gombert's music was 'entirely different from what went before'.

A consequence of this thick scoring is the potential for false relations and passing dissonances on or off the beat, quite unlike anything found in Josquin (as in the last bar of Example 5.6, p. 77 above). Like salt (or perhaps yeast), these details leaven Gombert's ruminative textures, preventing them from becoming stodgy. His influence was considerable: pervasive imitation features strongly in the work of Thomas Crequillon (*c.*1505–*c.*1557) and Pierre Manchicourt (*c.*1511–64), who was praised by Lassus as 'very excellent and significant'. But perhaps the most enduring consequence of Gombert's music is its irrevocable turn away from the system of duos that characterized the first half of the Renaissance. In the later sixteenth century, chordal sonorities returned as an audible feature of even the most contrapuntal conceptions, but the dyadic framework that had underpinned centuries of polyphony became embedded into the polyphonic fabric itself.

Yet Gombert's radicalism was also a dead end. Privileging independent part-writing to the exclusion of other textural possibilities, using only imitation, was an extreme position that could not be sustained indefinitely. An instructive comparison is with the slightly older Willaert, whose style is more varied despite their shared taste for full and thick textures. Although strongly imitative, his early motets in the Medici Codex are nearer in style to Josquin and Mouton, and whereas Willaert adapted his style to the type of text being set, Gombert's chansons are often barely distinguishable from his motets. (*Je prens congié* is credibly contrafacted as *Lugebat David Absalon*, for instance.) The motets and madrigals of Willaert's *Musica nova* are as densely and contrapuntally conceived as Gombert's music, but they avoid pervasive imitation, in some cases avoiding imitation as nearly as possible. The sacred music of Cristóbal de Morales (c.1500–53) and Cipriano De Rore (near-exact contemporaries of Clemens, Crequillon, and Manchicourt) shows signs of stepping back from the more extreme consequences of Gombert's style in favour of greater textural variety. The reputation of Cipriano, and Morales' successful career both in Rome and in his native Spain, ensured a wide influence. Their reappraisal of Gombert's legacy sets the scene for the generation of the equally successful Palestrina and Lassus, whose modern-day reputation has led to other very fine composers of that generation being overlooked – notably the hyper-prolific master of the Imperial Chapel Philippe de Monte and his short-lived but extremely impressive predecessor, Jacobus Vaet (c.1529–67). In common with most of the composers born after 1520, fuga remains a primary resource but is expressed in a greater variety of ways; antiphonal effects and homophony are fully present, but the distinction between texture types is softened, so that they appear more seamlessly integrated. Example 11.7 illustrates this tendency at the most local level: a single voice is rhythmically displaced in a passage of otherwise chordal writing. Though something of a cliché, this simple little trick shows how homophony can be achieved without sacrificing the sense of forward motion.

A more detailed example of this smoothing over of texture types is Palestrina's six-voice motet *Dum complerentur* (Example 11.8), a fine example of his style. The opening text phrase is set antiphonally between a three-voice group (concluding on the final) and a four-voice response that reworks the initial statement but voices it differently. Though not a straightforward case of high vs low voices (as happens elsewhere), the two groups are registrally distinct nonetheless. The next phrase, a fully

Example 11.7 Tallis, *Lamentatione Jeremiae I*, 'Plorans ploravit' (excerpt). Translation: Jerusalem, Jerusalem, return [to the Lord thy God].

scored passage that is chordal in conception and effect, is tempered by occasional note-exchanges between voices (b. 6 of the example) and linear skips within the prevailing sonority (Quintus, b. 8). Then comes the first of several statements of the 'Alleluia' refrain, characterized by an extensively worked point of imitation. All six voices are involved and the texture is very animated, with voices dropping in and out and more than a hint of antiphony (at bb. 9–12) before full scoring resumes to conclude the passage. In all, the motet has four Alleluias, each with its point of imitation (and occasionally an associated countersubject, as with Gombert); the final section of both parts is identical, involving both a text phrase ('tamquam spiritus vehementis') and the concluding Alleluia, after the manner of responsories. This last text phrase is initially set as a homophonic four-voice figure and later recast as imitation and parallel motion. This integrated and flexible approach to texture is typical of an international late Renaissance style, extending to the generation of Byrd and Victoria, which also includes the Frenchman Eustache du Caurroy (1549–1609) or the Slovene Jacobus Gallus (also known as Handl, 1550–91), to name just two other important but now largely overlooked protagonists.

Example 11.8 Palestrina, *Dum complerentur* (beginning). Translation: When came the day of Pentecost, they were gathered together, saying, Alleluia

Gombert's focus on a single texture type to the exclusion of others has echoes in the later sixteenth century. The syllabic, rhythmically quantified system of the French *vers mesurés* is another style in which melismas and contrapuntal flourishes are almost entirely absent, all the voices moving together in stylized imitation of speech-rhythm (see Example 13.11 below, p. 207). Curiously, a similar evocation of the classical world led to very similar results in far-away Prague: Gallus' posthumous collections of *Moralia* (1596), setting didactic texts drawn from classical authors such as Ovid and Horace, have the same speech-like declamation throughout, combined with antiphony in the volume for eight voices in double choir. Where Le Jeune compensates for this single-mindedness by his gift for melody, Gallus relies on nervous, sinewy rhythmic patterns and subtle chromatic shifts. This also happens with the popularizing style of madrigal ennobled (in the mildest sense) by Willaert in the 1540s, which harks back in spirit to similar types of polyphony earlier in the century, achieving a completely different effect from Le Jeune or Gallus' consciously elitist and classicizing efforts, but with virtually the same means.

Antiphony and homophony are also the principal motors of the Italian experiments in polychoral writing, which reintroduce this chapter's third parameter, scale.

'O che nuovo miracolo': scale as exploration

It may simply be a coincidence that the Eton Choirbook, the earliest record of large-scale English antiphons, was copied just as continental composers began pushing against temporal boundaries in their music; in any case, the two currents' respective explorations of scale and space took very different forms. Josquin's *Miserere* has already been mentioned in this context, but an interest in breadth of design and a longer timescale is common to several continental composers at the turn of the sixteenth century. His generation was the last one to cultivate both the polyphonic *formes fixes* and the c.f. Mass cycle; the potential for these forms to grow to exceptional lengths seems to have been part of that last stage of their history. Certain rondeaus by Compère, Agricola, and Josquin last nearly ten minutes in performance and are unusually elaborate (for example Josquin's *Plus nulz regretz*, c.1507). Among Mass cycles, Obrecht's *Missa Maria zart* must be one of the longest before Beethoven's *Missa solemnis*; lasting nearly an hour and conceived on a grand scale, it is the composer's most ambitious surviving work and very likely one of his last. Though not quite as long (due to the loss of its Kyrie), Agricola's *Missa In minen sinn* has a similar density of ideas and comparable formal ambition, as though the bounds of what was usual were being deliberately tested. Already exceptional on account of its scoring, the sense of scale of Brumel's twelve-voice *Missa Et ecce terre motus* is amplified by the wealth of contrapuntal details: extended antiphonal exchanges, repeated phrases, moments of stasis, and ostinatos so extended that they anticipate twentieth-century minimalism. (The circumstances of its composition are conjectural, though a strong hint is connected with its c.f., which recounts the earthquake following Christ's death: the nickname given by his soldiers to Brumel's patron, the warlike Duke Alfonso I d'Este of Ferrara, was 'il Terremoto' – 'the earthquake'.) The expanded timescale of these pieces indicates a stepping-up of creative ambition, but their exceptional compositional resources are themselves a consequence of working on a broader canvas. These are early manifestations of what would later be called the sublime, the sense of awe and wonder on encountering something outside usual experience, in this case forms that have grown beyond what had previously been known. (In Romanticism that sense is typically associated with the contemplation of natural phenomena; the textural upheavals of Brumel's 'earthquake' Mass seem especially far-sighted.) A sense of wonder is crucial to subsequent explorations of scale, even though they developed along very different lines. So far as is known, nothing the size of *Missa Maria zart* was attempted again, and in England the end of Catholicism spelt the end of the large-scale antiphon. The later sixteenth-century concern with expansions of scale is not so much expressed temporally as spatially.

Judging by the examples cited earlier, composing for very large forces appears initially not to have been an end in itself but an extension of composers' interest in canonic writing. Soon, the emphasis was on numbers and how to mobilize them effectively. The loss of Ockeghem's thirty-six-voice work deprives us of essential information about this early history of polychoral writing, since his solutions to technical problems are never formulaic: the use of canon would have had implications for his handling of texture. Be that as it may, antiphonal writing between groups or choirs is not a feature of this early Franco-Flemish stage. It arose in northern Italy during the early sixteenth century in connection with psalm settings – a consequence of the chanting of psalm verses in antiphony, hence the term 'cori spezzati' (split choirs) associated with it. Willaert's adoption of the technique in his psalm publication (Venice, 1550) was not in itself innovative, but built on a firmly established practice. This continued in Venice under the Gabrielis (of whom the elder, Andrea, had sung in Munich under

Lassus, another early exponent), where it reached an exceptional degree of refinement, including the use of instruments, the presence of a basso continuo, and sophisticated use of spatialization whose cumulative splendour was unrivalled (except perhaps in Florence).[8] In the more conservative atmosphere of Rome, the technique did not catch on until the 1570s, although the influence of Palestrina ensured its survival beyond the point when it had fallen out of fashion in seventeenth-century Venice.

Venetian polychoral music could encompass any number of independent lines, but its principal resource was antiphony. As one might expect, composers of the calibre of Palestrina and Lassus were more inclined to integrate it within independent part-writing, but with few exceptions eight voices was their limit. This was a matter of choice rather than opportunity, in Lassus's case at least: annotations survive in his hand of an earlier sixteenth-century copy of Brumel's 'Earthquake' Mass, naming the singers on each line; and in 1568 he was involved in performances of several outsized works, a twenty-four-voice Mass by Annibale Padovano (1527–75) and the forty-voice motet *Ecce beatam lucem* and its companion Mass *Missa Ecco sì beato giorno* by Alessandro Striggio the Elder (mentioned in Chapter 3).[9] Striggio's pieces are particularly successful because his choirs are of different sizes and he makes full use of the textural contrasts this creates. To set off the now customary antiphonal effects, he is not afraid to prolong a single sonority for several bars at a time, with all the forces at his disposal; and contrapuntal details are limited to pithy motifs that can be distributed on a large scale. The emphasis on diversity, contrast, and splendour in these pieces was undoubtedly enhanced by the forces involved, which included over two dozen instrumentalists. Both the Mass and the motet were likely commissioned for the wedding celebrations of the heir to the duchy of Bavaria: Striggio had already written similar pieces for the ruling Medici family in Florence, where such extravagant showpieces were particularly appreciated. Most popular of all were the *intermedii*, staged musical interludes sandwiched between the acts of plays. These theatrical set-pieces soon grew more elaborate than the plays themselves, their hugely elaborate stage machinery bringing forth all manner of *meraviglie* (marvels): fire-breathing pythons, airborne mythological figures, sailors in their ship, a dolphin, and so on. The music was similarly designed to astonish: at the most famous of these extravaganzas, the *intermedii* for *La Pellegrina* in 1589, the cast included several dozen musicians including over three dozen instrumentalists, divided at one point into two groups of fifteen voices and, at another, seven choirs. The sixth and final *intermedio* culminates in a song in praise of the newly wedded grand-ducal couple, to a tune that became famous throughout Europe as the *'ballo del Granduca'*, 'O che nuovo miracolo' ('Behold the new miracle'). Although Striggio had by that time retired, he had been a key figure in the development of the *intermedio*, and his Mass and motet are best understood in this light. Although the Bavarian commission was undoubtedly intended for liturgical performance, the wedding was a public event and a state occasion, a projection of the power of the ruling family; not only the centrepiece of the festivities, but their principal motivation. The splendour of the music was required to be on a par with the secular entertainments. All this was taking place at the height of the Counter-Reformation, whose artistic productions share in the same aesthetic intention, to stir the onlooker to wonder.

As an aesthetic strategy, the projection of contrasts to maximum effect is typically associated with the Baroque, and it is no accident that these experiments should have taken place in Florence, a crucible of artistic experimentation throughout this period. Nor is it surprising that Striggio prioritized the technical resources (antiphony and a homophonic 'wall of sound') that made those effects possible, in preference to learned contrapuntal displays: some of the fiercest criticisms of polyphony originated in the talking shop of the *Accademia Fiorentina*. All the same, Striggio would have been surprised by one unintended consequence of his work. According to a contemporary report, the performance of his forty-voice works in London led one of Tallis' patrons to challenge him to respond to the Italian's work. The result, famously, was *Spem in alium*.[10]

Tallis incorporated more than a few nods in Striggio's direction – not least the periodic 'walls of sound', which sound almost like direct quotations. But *Spem in alium* is a very different kind of piece, for, in accepting the challenge, Tallis seems to have challenged himself to integrate the imitative writing that Striggio conspicuously avoids; in doing so, he achieved a spatial effect that is likewise absent from his Italian model. His formal plan is at once clear and sophisticated, with two interlocking, complementary processes. The forty voices consist of eight five-voice choirs, most likely disposed in a circle; thus, the fuga subject that begins the work slowly 'pans' round the ensemble, eventually coming literally full circle. This is soon followed by a first 'wall of sound' episode (at 'praeter in te'), which lasts just a few bars. A second fuga subject then makes its way round; it is shorter than the first and involves fewer voices at any one time. A second wall of sound follows (at 'et omnia peccata omnium' – 'the sins *of all*'), which is correspondingly longer than the first. More or less at the midpoint of the piece comes an extended antiphonal episode (at 'Domine

Deus, creator caeli et terrae'), with contrasting blocks of voices separated by 180 degrees. After a brief homophonic jolt (at 'respice') a final fuga subject is launched (at 'iniquitates nostra'), shorter again than the second and also 'shallower', in that still fewer voices sound together; the final *tutti* is correspondingly longer than the others and moves through several chords, bringing the piece to a close. The simple expedient of making the waves of imitation progressively shorter and shallower and the walls of sound correspondingly longer introduces an audible element of process, which makes the piece's form very tangible. The panning effect of these imitative passages introduces new spatial possibilities: counteracting the sharp contrasts of full and antiphonal texture, it moves slowly and gradually, and then speeds up with each new occurrence. Not only are all three texture types present, each is endowed with its own spatial character, which evolves over the course of the work. In short, *Spem in alium* is not all 'shock and awe'; Tallis more or less exhausts the ensemble's spatial potential in one compact statement, leaving Striggio's more modern-sounding piece far behind, conceptually speaking. There is a certain irony in this, for it was nearly 400 years before musical space was explored again so explicitly or systematically. (To anyone acquainted with the modern score edition of Tallis' work, the opening systems of György Ligeti's orchestral work, *Lontano* (1967), will look very familiar.) The case for the modern pertinence of Renaissance music can begin – or end – with *Spem in alium*.

Chapter 12 | Understanding musical borrowing

The story is told by a contemporary biographer of Holy Roman Emperor Charles V that towards the end of his life he was presented with a book of polyphony by the composer Francisco Guerrero (1528–99) and had his musicians sing from it. Afterwards he called his chaplain and said, '*Oh hi de puta* ('son of a bitch'), he's a crafty thief, that Guerrero; he's stolen this bit from so-and-so, and this other one from so-and-so.'[1] This colourful anecdote is very revealing. First, it shows that the emperor's easy familiarity with his entourage evidently extended to music, since he could recall specific passages by ear and from memory. Second, it underscores the degree of musical literacy that composers could expect of their patrons and audiences. Third, the role of the listener in this anecdote is crucial. Owen Rees has speculated that Guerrero's supposed 'lifts' may have been deliberately designed to flatter Charles by quoting from pieces previously composed in his honour. Judging by the emperor's reaction, the ploy worked; in his comment one senses an admiring, perhaps even affectionate recognition of his skill, for, as a connoisseur like Charles would have known, citing previously composed polyphony was perfectly commonplace. But if Guerrero did indeed expect his 'theft' to be uncovered, was he really 'stealing'? After all, incorporating pre-existing music (the subject of this chapter) was literally the foundation of polyphony itself.

Previously, I described polyphony as 'adornment' of the liturgy. This is not just a figure of speech. The origin of Western polyphony lay in adorning plainchant with added voices, initially through extemporization and later in notation. A useful analogy is with the precious materials, creative ingenuity, and workmanship that went into countless sacred objects, from the buildings and their materials, clothed in marble, to silver and golden chalices, bejewelled and enamelled reliquaries, illuminated bibles, chant books, and books of polyphony. The comparison with an illuminated bible or book of hours is particularly apt: as the vessel of the divine Word, the time and expense lavished on it signalled the preciousness of what it holds. The same can be said of the highly trained performers who sang and adorned the plainchant, using the only musical instrument in divine creation, the human voice. Before going further, it is worth pointing out that the widely used term 'musical borrowing' does not apply equally well to all polyphonic situations. It puts the emphasis on the end product (polyphony) rather than the starting point (chant), whereas in the earliest stages of polyphonic practice, plainchant was not 'incorporated' into polyphony; polyphony was added to the plainchant. Only when polyphony is written down and circulated (effectively becoming an end in itself) is the reference to 'borrowed' chant truly appropriate. The Latin phrase *cantus prius factus* (literally a 'song previously made', or 'music previously composed') accounts for all the techniques discussed in this chapter.

Chant paraphrase and cantus firmus

By the start of our period, there were two principal ways of setting plainchant.[2] The first was the so-called 'paraphrase' method, whereby the chant appears typically in the discantus, with the lower voices in support. As the term denotes, the chant is not quoted strictly but is ornamented to a greater or lesser extent, in note-values typically as fast as those of the lower voices. Example 12.1 shows the beginning of the antiphon *Alma redemptoris mater* as set by Du Fay and Ockeghem, respectively. (The notes of the plainchant are marked with a cross.) Du Fay's setting begins unusually, with the chant entirely on its own for the whole first phrase. Rhythms are smooth and placid, forming roughly equal phrases, which continue when the lower voices enter. The number of added notes (that is, notes extraneous to the chant) is small. By contrast, Ockeghem's setting has more added notes and a more unpredictable course rhythmically. The chant's outline is clearly recognizable, but there is more incident and the clear phrase-structure of Du Fay's setting is avoided; what is more, the chant is not in the highest voice but in the one just below, and, when the top voice enters, its soaring phrases threaten to upstage it. The two settings point to clear differences between the two composers, but more fundamentally, they are located at opposite points on a continuum between strict and free approaches to musical borrowing. The distinction is crucial not least because composers' treatment of borrowed material (strict or loose, sequential or random) is often a good indicator of their approach to other matters of style and form. Another element of paraphrase technique is for the chant to 'migrate' from one voice to another. This initially happened when it moved outside the range of the voice in which it started. Finally, Du Fay's setting, though relatively

Example 12.1 (a) Du Fay, *Alma redemptoris mater* (beginning); (b) Ockeghem, *Alma redemptoris mater* (beginning). Translation: Loving mother of the Redeemer…

straightforward, is not the simplest way of paraphrasing chant; hymns, for example, were usually set in a syllabic, note-against-note style that could easily have been improvised.

The second way to set plainchant is by now very familiar, as a cantus firmus in the tenor. Initially (as in the English *Caput* Mass or the slightly earlier *Missa Alma redemptoris mater* by Leonel Power), this entailed a typically stricter approach than chant paraphrase, with fewer or no added pitches and slower note-values than the surrounding voices. This made it more difficult to identify the chant by ear, especially with the introduction of the lower contratenor, which placed the chant in the middle of the texture. This was compounded by the English composers' habit of using just a few pitches of the chant, often beginning or ending mid-phrase in a seemingly arbitrary manner (a survival of the earlier practice of tenor or isorhythmic motets). Finally, the durations assigned to the chant pitches were typically the same across all the movements of a Mass. But there is a more fundamental difference between c.f. and paraphrase technique: whereas with the latter, the plainchant is typically identical to the liturgical text being set, in most music with a c.f. the two are not the same. This was also characteristic of earlier motets, whose texts were written for specific occasions and therefore unconnected with the liturgy. To sum up, paraphrase and c.f. technique emerge out of quite distinct traditions. This is most obvious when the two are heard in close proximity, for example a c.f. Mass cycle and a set of Propers performed alongside each other: unless they are freely composed, Propers settings invariably paraphrase the chants associated with their texts.

The differences between paraphrase and c.f. techniques in the early Renaissance could hardly be greater, but by the second half of the fifteenth century, the two had begun to merge. In many plainchant c.f. Masses by continental composers post-*Caput*, the presentation of the plainchant is not fixed but changes from movement to movement, and the other voices sometimes 'shadow' the c.f. material in the tenor, usually in tandem with it. Although the c.f. remains 'fixed' in the tenor, its treatment has the flexibility of paraphrase. All these features are found in Du Fay's later plainchant Masses, *Ecce ancilla/Beata es, Maria* and *Ave regina celorum*.[3] They are already found in the motet on which the *Missa Ave regina celorum* is based, in which c.f. and paraphrase techniques also cross over (but in reverse, since it is a c.f. motet whose principal text is that of the plainchant). The merging of the two techniques undoubtedly reflects continental composers' more flexible approach to plainchant usage; but that shift itself reflects a new departure in the selection of *cantus prius facti*.

Masses: from cantus firmus to model

As mentioned in Chapter 8, deriving new music from pre-existing polyphony was not an entirely new phenomenon, but Du Fay is usually credited with the first Mass cycle to take the tenor of a polyphonic song as a c.f. in his *Missa Se la face ay pale*. It is a typically bold synthesis of elements from the English c.f. Mass and the isorhythmic motet: in the long movements of the Gloria and Credo, the tenor of Du Fay's chanson is stated three times in the tenor voice of the Mass. A verbal instruction specifies that the first statement augments the written note-values of the song tenor by a factor of three, the second by a factor of two, and the final one as notated (that is, as fast as the other voices). This recalls another feature of isorhythmic motets, in which the notated material in the tenor is subject to accelerating repetitions. But the use of a song tenor as a c.f. introduces two fundamental changes of approach compared with plainchant. The rhythmic layout of a plainchant c.f. is a matter for the composer, but a polyphonic song tenor comes with its durations pre-determined. Of course, the composer of the new work may choose either to treat the song tenor strictly or to paraphrase it, in which case its rhythmic profile can be altered as well as its pitches. But in *Se la face ay pale*, Du Fay opts for a strict approach, preserving the rhythms of the song tenor exactly as they are. This may have been a nod to the strict approach to chant c.f. of English composers, but it also expresses a new and radical idea: the essence of the *cantus prius factus* is located as much in its notation as in its sound. This idea will have profound consequences. The second major consequence of deriving a c.f. from pre-existing polyphony is the potential to use more than one voice of the model. One of the most memorable passages of Du Fay's song is its final melisma, in which all three voices exchange a triadic motif. This moment is alluded to nearly every time that the Mass tenor reaches this point of the song (as in Example 12.2).

That the earliest known instance of a Mass cycle based on a polyphonic model so fully expresses the phenomenon's potential qualifies *Missa Se la face ay pale* as one of music history's miracles – unless earlier experiments in this direction have been lost. In any case, the composers growing up under Du Fay quickly seized on those possibilities. In the Kyrie of Ockeghem's *Ma maistresse* cycle, the song's tenor is transposed down an octave in the lower contratenor; and, in the Gloria, its discantus appears transposed by the same interval in the tenor. In the Sanctus of Obrecht's *Missa Fortuna desperata*, the song tenor appears transposed at the upper

Example 12.2 (a) Du Fay, *Se la face ay pale* (excerpt). Translation: [since she to whom I belong/ can plainly see/ that] I cannot live without her; (b) Du Fay, *Missa Se la face ay pale* 'Confiteor' (excerpt).

fifth in the discantus of the opening section, then at the lower octave in the bassus of the 'Osanna'. In theory, any voice of the model could be used as a c.f. in any voice of the Mass, though usually the model's tenor and discantus were preferred; but, in his own *Missa Fortuna desperata*, Josquin also uses the contratenor, closing the circle of correspondences set up in Obrecht's Mass. In tandem with the treatment of single voices as cantus firmi, a great many Masses incorporate elements of their models' complete polyphonic fabric, following Du Fay's example in *Missa Se la face ay pale*. The 'Kyrie II' of Obrecht's *Fortuna desperata* cycle has a complete statement of the song's tenor and quotes all three voices together at the beginning, middle, and end. At these moments, the model itself comes briefly into focus and becomes recognizable in its own right. Each of these developments has far-reaching implications.

The popularity of polyphonic *cantus prius facti* did not spell the end for plainchant-based cycles. Pierre de La Rue's extensive Mass output includes a significantly higher proportion of chant-based Masses than is the case with other prominent Mass composers, a fact that may have contributed to his later reputation for seriousness.[4] His choice of chants appears to have been highly specialized, not to say idiosyncratic: the splendid *Missa de septem doloribus* incorporates several, some of which have yet to be identified. Writing during a period that saw the standardization of plainchant throughout the Catholic Church, Palestrina's usage is more conventional, but his enormous Mass production testifies to a continued interest in it. Meanwhile, the rise of polyphonic models poses a fundamental problem: how did the phenomenon come about in the first place? And why did composers choose for this purpose secular songs, whose typical subject matter is not divine worship but love, longing, and desire?

The aesthetics of borrowing: the model as analogy

To make sense of this, we need to step back to the polytextual tenor motets of earlier centuries. In his treatise *On the manner of composing tenors in motets*, the mid-fourteenth-century theorist Egidius de Murino advises that one should take the tenor from a passage of chant whose text is relevant to the new work's subject matter or destination.[5] Though clear enough, the instruction leaves open the precise nature of the relationship, which can be straightforward or indirect. Thus, the c.f. of Du Fay's *Nuper rosarum flores*, 'terribilis est locus iste' ('this place is awe-inspiring', the opening words of the Introit for the consecration of a church), was unquestionably appropriate to the consecration of Florence's great cathedral. Many cases of chant borrowing are similarly straightforward. In some cases, the occasion of a Mass's composition has been conjectured on the basis of its c.f. Frye's chant-based *Missa Flos regalis* may have been performed (if not actually written) in connection with the marriage in 1466 of Duke Charles of Burgundy and the 'royal flower' ('flos regalis') Elizabeth of York, sister of King Edward IV of England – the association of flowers with virginity making the analogy all the more fitting for a nuptial Mass. Analogy was an essential component of medieval imagination and imagery: nearly every kind of flower, animal, colour or number (and other things besides) held some kind of symbolical significance, representing a human attribute, behaviour, or situation. Medieval heraldry, the 'science' of coats-of-arms, was founded on a complex network of analogical relationships.

This attitude provides the key to reading secular song texts in a sacred light. We have already observed it in Richafort's Requiem, where the jocular reference in Josquin's *Faulte d'argent* to the 'pain unequalled' of being short of cash becomes a comment on the 'torments of the damned' mentioned in the plainchant c.f. But the most widespread analogy of all links the Virgin Mary with the idealized lady of chivalry, so often represented as simultaneously desirable and unattainable.[6] Recall Compère's singers' motet, *Omnium bonorum plena*, addressed to the Virgin and placing the singers under her protection. Its c.f. is one of the greatest hits of the 1460s, *De tous biens plaine*. The motet's opening words are a literal translation of those of Hayne's song: '[my lady is] replete with every virtue'. Its continuation could equally apply to the Virgin as to her earthly equivalent: 'everyone owes her tribute of honour, for she is as full of valour as ever was any goddess'. The famous song's appropriateness to its new context would have been self-evident to the singers involved: they all would have recognized it.[7] Another common topic of love poetry is the disconsolate, abandoned lover. If the lover is female, the topic is ideally suited to motets dealing with Mary's contemplation of Christ's Passion: its classic expression, Binchois' *Comme femme desconfortée*, is the c.f. for Josquin's *Stabat mater*, and Johannes Urrede's *Nunca fue peña mayor* ('Never was there greater sorrow') furnishes the tenor of *Memorare, mater Christi* by Matthaeus Pipelare (*c*.1450–*c*.1515). Pipelare's scoring of his motet for seven voices adds another symbolic dimension, since that number was commonly associated with Mary. Both motets are fitting sonic equivalents of the *pietà* of sculpture and painting. If the proposed equivalence between human and divine love seems surprising, it should be remembered that in the other arts it could be drawn still more forcefully: at the French royal court in Ockeghem's time, the painter Jean Fouquet represented the Virgin Mary suckling the baby Jesus with one breast exposed, choosing as his model the official mistress of King Charles VII, Agnès Sorel (and he seems not to have been the only Renaissance painter to memorialize a patron's mistress in this way).

However, more often, the lover is male, which sets up a different analogy. One of the most compelling instances concerns the *Missa Se la face ay pale*, so often cited as the earliest surviving Mass based on a secular c.f., which has convincingly been linked with Masses celebrating the acquisition of the so-called 'Shroud of Turin' by the ducal family of Savoy, Du Fay's patrons in the early 1450s.[8] Long thought to have been the cloth used to wrap Christ's body after the crucifixion, the Shroud bears the faint imprint of a man's bloodied hands, feet, face, and side. In Anne Walters

Robertson's ingenious reading, the opening words of the chanson are transferred from the courtly narrator lamenting his estrangement from his beloved to the pallid figure of Christ addressing the faithful, for love of whom he lays down his life: 'If my face is *pale*, the cause is love…'. The appropriateness of the song in its new context speaks for itself. Christ shifts from subject to object in Josquin's motet *Tu solus qui facis mirabilia*, whose Latin text incorporates the opening (French) words and music of one of Ockeghem's most famous chansons: 'D'un aultre amer / nobis esset falacia/ D'un aultre amer / magna esset stultitia' ('to love another / would be for us an error / to love another / would be a great folly'). Here, the faithful are equated to the female narrator protesting her love for a man, that object being equated to Christ. Finally, Christ has been proposed as the 'armed man' underlying the most famous Renaissance c.f. of all. Andrew Kirkman and others have pointed out a wealth of references to Christ as a warrior (in the fight against the devil), including Masses in which the celebrant wore chain mail and a sword at his belt, like the classic *homme armé*, the knight.[9] (A similar analogy obtains in Regis' setting, which uses plainchants from the Office for another divine warrior, the archangel Michael, alongside the *L'Homme armé* tune.) Like most analogical situations, this one can be read several ways: later in the Renaissance, the *L'Homme armé* tune may have become associated with Charles V. If the original analogy of *L'Homme armé* Masses were indeed with Christ, it would have been all the more complimentary to the warlike emperor. We will consider the history of this famous tune presently; for present purposes, its exceptional longevity as a c. f. (over three dozen Mass settings before 1600) was undoubtedly facilitated by these multiple readings.

All these examples lead to the surprising conclusion that the choice of a song tenor was not primarily dictated by its popularity, significance, or attractiveness to the composer but by the pertinence of its text to the occasion, exactly as Egidius de Murino had advocated a century earlier; or perhaps that is not so surprising, given the enduring popularity of polytextual situations of all sorts. Even when composers began using the whole polyphonic fabric of a pre-existing work, subject matter was often a determining factor: among the first known instances of these 'imitation' Masses was a group composed by French court composers on Richafort's motet *Quem dicunt homines*, which recounts Christ's designation of Peter as prince of the apostles (in other words, the first pope). A credible conjecture is that these Masses were written for performance in the presence of the music-loving Leo X at his meeting with Francis I of France in Bologna in 1515. Yet there is little doubt that the choice of model could also be motivated by musical considerations, that composers had different attitudes towards the question, and that these attitudes changed over time. The five cycles chosen for Lassus' first extant book of Masses in 1570 are all based on chansons whose subject matter is difficult to square with any religious interpretation (despite the ingenious efforts of some scholars to do so). They include a monk's sexual escapades (*Frère Thibaut*), a drinking song (*La la, Maistre Pierre*), and the disgusting dietary habits of Renaissance pigs (*Je ne menge point de porc*). It is significant that this collection was published in Venice, for Lassus could hardly have got away with such a selection of models in Counter-Reformation Rome. More than once when introducing volumes of his sacred music, Palestrina felt obliged to apologize for even having written madrigals in earlier years, let alone using them as the basis for Mass cycles. Victoria's sole declared concession to secular materials was his martial *Missa pro Victoria*, which recalls Janequin's *La Guerre* and must have been intended for a specific occasion. Undoubtedly, Lassus used smutty songs because he liked them, but that isn't the whole story.[10] Like the choice of borrowed materials, the techniques to which composers subjected them reveal other motivations.

Homage, exchange, and competition: the *L'Homme armé* story

Renaissance composers constantly rubbed shoulders. They sang in the same institutions, and as their careers took them from place to place they might well have come into contact with colleagues whom they had known years previously.[11] (A familiar analogy is with the superstar footballers of today, the so-called '*galacticos*'.) For their princely patrons, government involved almost constant travel, and the court travelled with them, hence the regular opportunities to meet fellow singers and catch up with their work. Music also circulated far and wide along the trade routes, by post, or in the diplomatic bags of ambassadors. (A document recently discovered by Bonnie J. Blackburn has an envoy of Ercole d'Este writing home from the court of Hungary in the mid-1480s to say that he is pressing 'Sandrachino' – almost certainly Alexander Agricola – to finish a new Mass so that he can send it to the duke.[12]) These constant opportunities for interchange explain the extent of connections between pieces. They range from gestures of homage to an esteemed elder colleague (witness the countless references to Ockeghem and Busnoys by composers of the following generation), commemoration (e.g. Richafort's quotations from Josquin in his Requiem), musical 'letter-exchange' (de Monte's *Super flumina Babylonis*, addressed to Byrd, which elicited the response, *Quomodo cantabimus*), and emulation between contemporaries. None of these motivations is incompatible with the analogical or symbolic motivations mentioned earlier; were that not the case, the great number of Masses based on composers' own music would be puzzling indeed. Cases of emulation between composers are too many to list, but the long and splendid procession of Masses based on *L'Homme armé* (refer again to Example 4.1, p. 51) offers a concise yet detailed case study.[13]

The presumably monophonic origin of the tune itself is unclear; its earliest polyphonic setting may have been a lost chanson. Much debate surrounds the question of which composer initiated the 'cult' of *L'Homme armé* (the most recent proposals put Ockeghem, Du Fay, and Regis in the frame), but just as intriguing a question is, who composed the second? From the start, these Masses seem to have been written in a spirit of (presumably friendly) competition. A good place to begin is to compare their last Agnus dei sections: Ockeghem transposes the tune down an octave (a procedure of which he was fond), but Du Fay gives the tune first in retrograde and in augmentation, then in the 'right' direction in shorter note-values. Whichever came first, Busnoys' solution can be read as a response to either or both: he has the tune in inversion but starting on the same pitch (g), so that its sounding range is the same as Ockeghem's transposed version, but the technique he uses recalls Du Fay's solution.

There will be more to say about the notation through which these features are expressed in the next chapter; meanwhile, the *L'Homme armé* story continues thanks to a detail we observed in Chapter 4. Early on, the tune was known in both Dorian and Mixolydian versions. Du Fay, Regis, and Busnoys used the former exclusively, Ockeghem mostly the latter (except in the Agnus dei). Two composers of the following generation, Compère and Obrecht, seem independently to have hit on the idea of using the Phrygian mode, whose association with mourning effectively defuses its martial overtones. In every other respect, Obrecht modelled his Mass on Busnoys', to the point of transplanting Busnoys' c.f. wholesale, down to the number of rests between its segments. Josquin wrote two *L'Homme armé* Masses. I subscribe to the view that the one subtitled *Sexti toni* was a response to Compère and Obrecht and was composed first, as it completes the 'full house' of the four principal modal types by offering a Lydian version. His second Mass can be read as a summation of the entire *L'Homme armé* tradition up until that point. Its subtitle, 'super *voces musicales*' (roughly translated, 'on the degrees [of the hexachord]'), indicates that the tune is sung successively on *ut* (or C, in the Kyrie), then *re* (D, in the Gloria), *mi* (E, in the Credo), and so on up to *la* (A) in the Agnus dei. But there is a further twist, for the mode of the Mass as a whole is consistently Dorian. Josquin's ingenious ground plan comments on *L'Homme armé*'s previous history: all the available modes having been exhausted in previous cycles, it only remains for the tune itself to migrate, step by step. That one Mass alone was insufficient to explore the implications of that history suggests what status it had attained in the eyes of Josquin's contemporaries.

The suggestion that Josquin's *L'Homme armé* Masses were conceived as a pair is confirmed by their complementary approaches.[14] Whereas *Sexti toni* treats the tune isomelically (following the Masses of Du Fay, Regis, Compère, and Brumel), *Super voces musicales* follows the principle of the 'notational archetype' set out in the Masses of Ockeghem, Busnoys, and Obrecht, strictly following the tune's pitches and rhythms absolutely throughout. Together, they explore both main facets of the tradition, modal and mensural. But *Sexti toni* is retrospective in other ways. Its 'Agnus dei III' (that movement again) refers to an extraordinary moment in the same section of Busnoys' Mass (Example 12.3a), when the c.f. reaches its highest point: because the tune is presented in inversion, this becomes the lowest pitch. Busnoys underscores this exceptional registral moment by 'freezing' the counterpoint: the bassus is shadowed by just one voice in rhythmic unison before the others resume. (A crucial point, regrettably obscured in transcription, is that the combination of mensuration signs used by Busnoys seems to imply a slower semibreve beat than usual, whereby the c.f.'s exposed pitches are exceptionally long.) In Josquin's setting (Example 12.3b), the tune's

Example 12.3 (a) Busnoys, *Missa L'Homme armé*, 'Agnus dei III' (excerpt); (b) Josquin, *Missa L'Homme armé sexti toni*, 'Agnus dei III' (excerpt)

Example 12.3 (Cont.)

two phrases (A and B) are stated simultaneously – A backwards and B forwards – and then in retrograde (shades of Du Fay). Upon this framework, two unison canons unfold at a minim's distance – and suddenly stop, leaving the *L'Homme armé* voices exposed for the space of two bars before resuming their course. Just as Busnoys' beautifully stage-managed revelation of the tune referenced both Du Fay and Ockeghem, Josquin here audibly pays tribute to Busnoys himself and covertly acknowledges Du Fay, while outdoing them both – since the two sounding voices are pitch-retrogrades of each other. Technical as the description of it must be, in performance this 'freeze frame' – a sudden window of stasis amidst the scurrying unison canons' perpetual motion – is very powerful.

In all this there is more than a hint of one-upmanship; these self-conscious displays of ingenuity are yet another factor in *L'Homme armé*'s popularity. One passage came to obsess later sixteenth-century teachers: the 'Agnus dei II' of Josquin's *Super voces musicales* consists of a canon, whose single notated part is read by three voices simultaneously at different speeds (and three different pitch-levels). This elicited a response by Pierre de La Rue whose entire *L'Homme armé* Mass consists of a series of canons, usually involving two of the four voices. But in the 'Agnus dei II' he trumps Josquin's bid by deriving *four* sounding voices from the single notated one. (The mechanics of these canons will be considered in Chapter 13.) In addition, his canon begins by audibly citing the repeated notes and the rising fourth with which the famous tune begins. The *L'Homme armé* Masses of Josquin and La Rue embody the competitive spirit of Renaissance composers at its peak. Most of the cycles that followed stepped back from such overt ostentation, while retaining memory traces of it. The setting by Guerrero is modelled on the five-voice version of his teacher Morales, which appears to have rekindled the *L'Homme armé* tradition in the mid-sixteenth century; Palestrina's two settings are later still (pub. 1570 and 1582), and, especially when viewed as a pair, they make repeated reference to the tune's earlier history. The tradition's most enduring residual trace is the occasional use of abstruse canons within Mass settings, which is especially notable among Iberian composers after Guerrero. (This resonates with the feats of improvised contrapuntal skill that were so popular in Spain during this period.)

The Mass cycle and 'peak borrowing' circa 1500

The presence of a *cantus prius factus* of one sort or other shaped the Mass cycle from the very start and endured long after the technique waned in the early sixteenth century. But in the years before 1500 the notion of cycle becomes an end in itself, with the borrowed material its primary means of articulation. There is a palpable sense of composers building on conventions accrued over generations: the expository function of the Kyrie, the pairing of the Gloria and Credo (sometimes transposing the c.f. to a lower pitch-level in the latter), and the Agnus dei as a contrapuntal set piece. In addition, composers began exploring teleological (that is, goal-oriented) readings of the cycle's five movements, sometimes with the 'Hosanna' as a provisional end point and sometimes with the Agnus dei as a summary. Reading the Mass cycle *across* the five movements was a novelty. It is not even implied in early English cycles like *Caput*, in which the same basic formal plan is repeated across all five movements but with no sense of progression. Examples are found in the Masses of Regis and Ockeghem (notably the latter's *Missa Prolationum*, discussed in the next chapter), but the trend reaches a climax in the next generation with the most prominent composers of Masses, Obrecht, La Rue, Isaac, Josquin, and Agricola.

The importance these composers attached to the Mass cycle is demonstrable in the use of 'signature' techniques peculiar to each of them. Josquin's so-called 'ostinato' Masses involve fashioning a very short motif from a verbal source: thus, the vowels of the name and title of Josquin's patron, 'Hercules dux Ferrarie' become the hexachord syllables '*re ut re ut re fa mi re*' (a technique later described by Zarlino as a 'subject carved from the words'). The motif is repeated dozens of times in the course of the work, albeit transposed onto three different hexachords (the tenor consists of nothing else, but in the 'Agnus dei I' it has the tune in retrograde). A similar technique accounts for the five-note 'subject' of Josquin's *Missa La sol fa re mi*, while the very concise *Missa Faisant regretz* quotes the first four pitches of the second half of Frye's chanson *Tout a par moy*. Josquin's penchant for ostinatos is well known, but in these Masses the ostinato is an end in itself: even the material of the free voices is overrun with them. But the three Masses explore the idea very differently. The contrast between the *Hercules* Mass's severe, foursquare architecture and the rhythmically free treatment of *Faisant regretz* is clear (an excerpt from the *Missa Faisant regretz* is discussed in Chapter 13). Josquin's ostinato procedures were widely copied. La Rue's *Missa Cum jocundidate* integrates the technique seamlessly within his own style, and Glarean claims that Obrecht, who briefly succeeded Josquin at Ferrara, composed a *Missa Hercules dux Ferrarie* of his own (tantalizingly, none survives). A later example is the similarly conceived *Missa Philippus rex Hispaniae* by Bartolomé de Escobedo (*c.*1505–63), born when Josquin's Mass was likely composed. The *La sol fa re mi* theme was also cited by later composers: Frescobaldi's version, one of his keyboard capriccios of 1624, was published over a century after Josquin's death.

An even stronger sense of goal-orientation informs Obrecht's so-called 'segmentation Masses'. A voice of a polyphonic song (usually the tenor) is cut up into segments, which are presented in sequential order over the course of the Mass.[15] Each segment is presented several times but progressively faster, recalling the technique used in isorhythmic motets. When this process has run its course, the tune is stated in its entirety as a concluding gesture in the Agnus dei. Even more so than in Josquin's ostinato Masses, the process unfolds over the course of the whole Mass, the sequential presentation of the chanson segments coinciding with the direction of time's arrow in the Mass itself.

Equally, the fundamental 'unifying' principle of the c.f. Mass is subverted: the Mass movements are unified only insofar as the segments come from the same song. It is all the more logical and necessary that their common origin is revealed at the very end. The final Agnus dei can also 'sample' several sounding voices of the polyphonic model together, which underlines the correspondence. As with Josquin's penchant for ostinato, Obrecht's liking for such large-scale designs is known from other Masses (recall the progression from three to seven voices in his *Sub tuum presidium*), but these are some of the most impressive – particularly *Maria zart*, which presents the monophonic tune in many guises, whether or not the tenor is present.

The inspiration for Obrecht's segmentation technique may well have come from an extrardinary 'cycle of cycles' from about 1470, comprising six anonymous Masses on *L'Homme armé* (known informally as the 'Naples' Masses, from the current location of their only source), in which the tune is segmented and then presented in a similar way. The resulting process is carried over across the first five cycles, and the final Mass uses the entire tune, anticipating Obrecht's practice in his Agnus dei settings. Another 'signature' approach to the Mass cycle comes from Agricola, several of whose Masses on polyphonic models (e.g. *Le Serviteur*, *Malheur me bat* and *In minen sinn*) combine the principal techniques associated with musical borrowing within a single work: paraphrase, strict c.f., and occasional 'sampling' of polyphonic quotations follow one another in seemingly random, kaleidoscopic fashion, in a manner quite unlike either Josquin or Obrecht. The impression is of the model moving in and out of focus: 'now you see it, now you don't'.[16] Again, the details of their treatment of borrowed materials summarize these composers' aesthetic priorities – continuity vs discontinuity, process vs ad hoc procedures, economy vs superabundance, and so on.

It is no accident that these self-consciously sophisticated approaches to the c.f. Mass should coincide with the expansion of scale discussed in the previous chapter. Both features are frequently associated with genres in the latter stages of their development (e.g. the isorhythmic motet at the turn of the fifteenth century and the symphony at the turn of the twentieth). Incidentally, the parallel that is frequently drawn with the symphony is attractive to a modern audience, but that is all the more reason to treat it cautiously.[17] Just as the choice of model was motivated as much by the event being celebrated as any musical consideration, so are the formal experiments just described rooted in the liturgy: the goal to which these structures tend is not some abstract or aestheticized 'finale' but the concrete moment of the elevation, which comes towards (but not at) the end of the

Mass. That is not to say that composers could not or did not think in terms of abstract designs; rather, the teleological features I have described are differently motivated from those of the symphony. A clearer parallel is with the *formes fixes*, which also grew to exceptional dimensions during this period before falling away: having furnished composers with their very first polyphonic models, they themselves began to incorporate borrowed materials from well-known songs of past generations. An intriguing example is the anonymous virelai *Si vous voullez que je vous ame*, from the recently discovered Leuven chansonnier. As shown in Example 12.4 (upper box), its

Example 12.4 (a) Ockeghem, *Ma maistresse* (beginning). Translation: My mistress and [my greatest friend]… (b) anon., *Si vous voullez* (beginning) Translation: If you wish [that I should love you]…

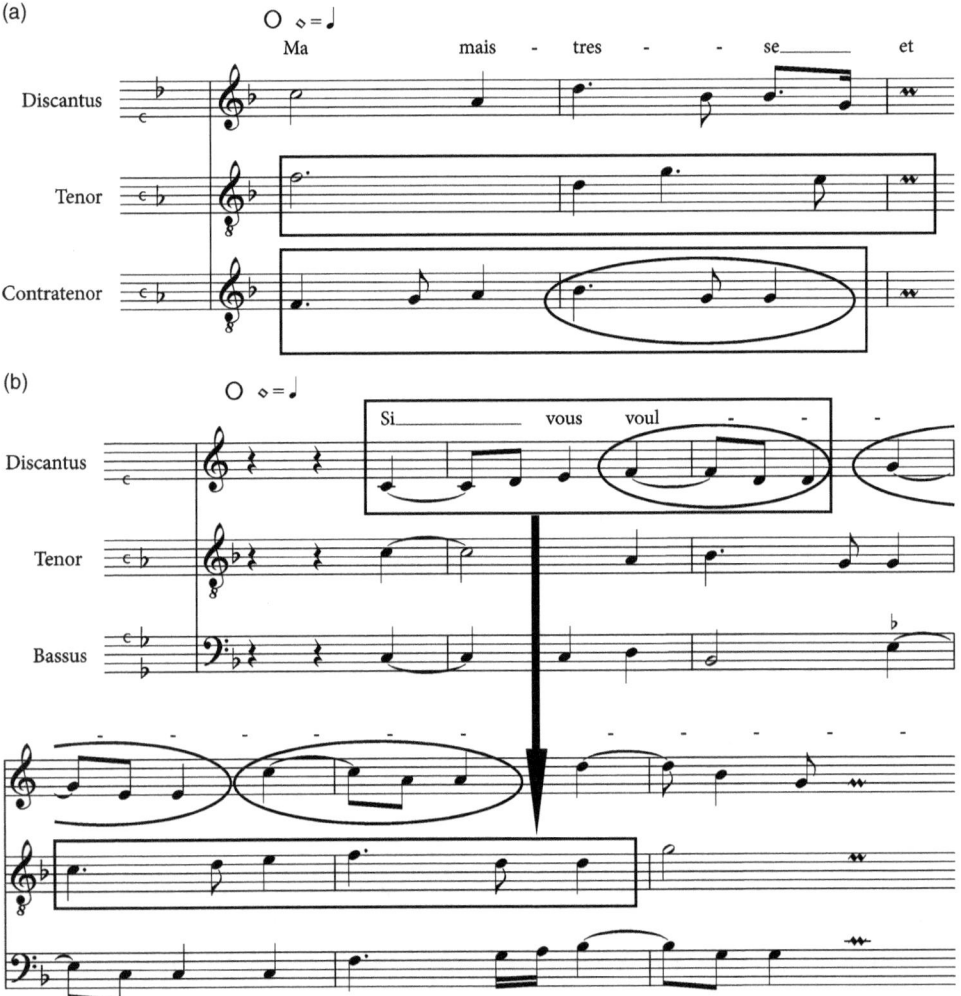

discantus' opening motif is taken from the contratenor of Ockeghem's virelai *Ma maistresse*, sequencing its second bar (circled); but in addition, the way it is deployed echoes the unusual imitation at the start of its famous model. Ockeghem has the tenor imitate the discantus by extending its opening pitch by just one semibreve; the tenor of the anonymous song does something similar, and its rhythmic shape replicates that of Ockeghem's tenor (lower box). It then returns to the beginning of the discantus, but this time at the distance of *seven* beats: where the discantus began on an offbeat (after two beats' rest), the tenor's imitation begins on the 'correct' part of the perfection (i.e. the downbeat). On the small scale appropriate to Tinctoris' *cantus parvus*, this is as sophisticated an instance of quotation as anything in the *L'Homme armé* tradition. Contemporary with these late *formes fixes* is the fashion for untexted polyphonic re-workings of famous rondeaus (e.g. *Le Serviteur, Comme femme, Fors seulement, De tous biens plaine, Fortuna desperata*) that began in the 1480s, and to which the same generation of composers contributed widely. It is unlikely that these 'arrangements' were intended to set the chansons' texts. The musical evidence (particularly the absence of any virelai settings, which would entail a repeat of the first section after the second) suggests that they were to be performed straight through. But their existence is proof that by 1500, the use of a *cantus prius factus* encompassed all the principal forms of polyphony.

The imitation Mass and the listener

The origin of the 'imitation' Mass was mentioned in passing in Chapter 8, perhaps a rare instance where we can pinpoint the birth of a major genre. In essence, composers at the French court – first among them Mouton, but also his pupil Willaert, Richafort, and others – began working not with just one voice of a model but with all the voices as they sound together. Although the basic premise was familiar to previous generations of composers, the imitation Mass represents a fundamental departure in several ways: where previously the polyphonic 'sampling' of models occurred either randomly or in tandem with tenor statements, and was therefore subordinate to c.f. technique, it was now the primary means of treating polyphonic models, and most often independent of a c.f. Two theorists writing twenty-five years apart (Pietro Pontio in the *Ragionamento di musica* (1588) and Pietro Cerone in *Il melopeo y maestro* (1613)) give very similar descriptions of it, which have been widely discussed: in a nutshell, each movement should begin and end with the corresponding material of the model, and the major internal sub-sections should begin with internal material (for instance, the beginning of a motet's second part). Because these writers' treatises are primarily instruction manuals, they set out rules of thumb rather than the practice of the most accomplished composers, which is considerably more varied. (Monteverdi's *Missa In illo tempore*, included in his famous 1610 print of Vespers music, was intended as a demonstration of his skill in what was by then considered as the old style of church music, the 'stile antico'.)

Although the transition from c.f. to imitation Mass was a function of the changed attitude towards borrowed material, it was also symptomatic of the new approach to texture noted in Chapter 11, notably the enhanced role of imitation in articulating texture types. This stylistic shift may be seen in the models chosen in the earliest imitation Masses, which favour motets over chansons. Like the ground rules of the imitation Mass itself, this seems to have been a collective decision on the part of the French court musicians; most of those motets were taken from within their own circle (with the exception of Josquin, already regarded as a canonic figure in the historiographical sense). That this seeming in-house experiment spread so widely and swiftly says much for the French court chapel's international reach.

Another significant distinction between c.f and imitation Masses is the relationship between the model and the derived work. In c.f. Masses, a single voice has been transplanted from its original context into a potentially 'alien' environment, where its identity and provenance may be entirely obscured; by contrast, imitation Masses typically insert *themselves* into the sound world of the model. Whereas the presence of a model in c.f. Mass cycles could be largely symbolic, the imitation Mass places its model's musical fabric front and centre. Example 12.5 shows the opening passages of the movements of the *Missa Ego sum qui sum* by Philippe Rogier (*c.*1561–96), chapel-master at the court of Philip II, alongside the start of the motet by Gombert on which it is based. Typical strategies include registral displacement or transposition (Gloria), inversion of the voices in a fuga subject and/or the addition of a voice (Credo), and the presentation of the fuga subject in a different contrapuntal context (Sanctus). For the beginning of the Agnus dei, Rogier draws on the model's 'Alleluia' refrains. This gradually looser treatment of the opening material is typical of imitation Masses. Thereafter, the model's ideas are rarely treated sequentially (an exception is Morales' *Missa Mille regretz*, which repeatedly quotes the

Example 12.5 (a) Gombert, *Ego sum qui sum* (beginning). Translation: I am who I am... (b) Rogier, *Missa Ego sum qui sum*, Kyrie (beginning); (c) Rogier, *Missa Ego sum qui sum*, 'Et in terra' (beginning); (d) Rogier, *Missa Ego sum qui sum*, 'Patrem' (beginning); (e) Rogier, *Missa Ego sum qui sum*, Sanctus (beginning); (f) Rogier, *Missa Ego sum qui sum*, Agnus dei (beginning)

Example 12.5 (Cont.)

famous song's discantus from end to end). Often, the composer's skill consists in weaving together ideas that do not follow one another in the model, either by direct juxtaposition or by ingenious connective material (cf. Lassus' *Missa Osculetur me*, based on his own motet; this strategy is difficult

Example 12.5 (Cont.)

to illustrate with musical examples). The Mass's closeness to or distance from its model is subject to constant re-evaluation. More or less extended passages are reworked with only surface changes, usually to fit the text of the Mass; or a familiar idea is taken in a completely new direction. This is especially true of fuga subjects (as Example 12.5 shows), their potential for re-working further enhanced by adding to (or more rarely subtracting from) the original scoring. Monteverdi took the unusual step of printing the fuga subjects of Gombert's motet (expressed as single voices) in a preface to his Mass. This is significant because the *Missa In illo tempore* takes far less account than usual of the totality of Gombert's sounding voices; instead, the fuga subjects are treated as starting points. In some cases, the nature of the relationship is still more abstract: the Mass Victoria based on his motet *O magnum mysterium* contains few direct quotations or even allusions, as though the distinctive atmosphere of the Phrygian mode were sufficient reference.

Arguably, however, the most radical consequence of the audible relationship between Mass and model is the space opened up for the listener. In Chapter 3, I suggested that the intended recipients of our fifteenth-century singer-composers' music were as much their fellow singers as their listeners (more evidence for this will be presented in Chapter 13). By its very nature, the imitation Mass presupposes the existence of an audience or listener in the modern sense of the term. Even without prior knowledge of the model, listeners could compare the composer's re-interpretation of the same material across the Mass's five movements; but if the model were known, the scope for observation significantly increased. It is as though the composer's working methods were laid open for evaluation; conversely, from the composer's perspective, the listener becomes an accomplice to be teased or impressed, an active subject whose expectations are confirmed or denied. (This implicit relationship is made explicit in Monteverdi's decision to 'show his work' by printing the subjects from which he drew.) In effect, the composer and listener engage in a kind of game, the game that Charles V (and possibly Guerrero) played at the beginning of this chapter. Other contemporary reports show listeners engaging with imitation Masses in just the same way. The use of risqué songs as Mass subjects noted earlier takes on a different colouring when viewed in this light. The Catholic Church was not alone in condemning the practice on the grounds that recognizing such songs during Mass was bound to distract the faithful. This mischievous perspective on the imitation Mass sets us up nicely for the next chapter, which involves game playing of many kinds.

Another subtle shift, to which the imitation Mass contributes significantly, is away from emulation as competition towards citation and the invocation of authority. This is suggested by the use of Josquin's works as models, which endured until the late Renaissance. A particularly sophisticated example is Cipriano's *Missa Preter rerum seriem*, based on one of Josquin's late motets. Cipriano adopts both its distinctive scoring (three pairs of voices, each in its own range) and the plainchant on which the motet is based, which alternates between the tenor and one of the top voices. But he adds a seventh voice, symbolically reinforcing the original's Marian connections and intensifying Josquin's dense, dazzling textures. But there is something else: Cipriano's added voice, also based on plainchant, has the text 'Hercules dux Ferrarie Quartus vivit et vivat' ('Ercole, fourth duke of Ferrara, lives: long may he live'). Though ostensibly a tribute to his current patron, this is Cipriano's reminder that Ercole's grandfather and namesake was the patron of Josquin, whose Mass *Hercules dux Ferrarie* was likewise named after him. In honouring Josquin, Cipriano declares his own artistic lineage, casting himself in the role of Josquin's heir and associating his patron in the gesture. Not since Du Fay incorporated the personal prayer of his motet into the *Missa Ave regina celorum* were humility and self-affirmation so effectively combined and projected. Years later, Lassus began writing 'imitation Magnificat' settings (another case of a personal 'signature').[18] One is based on *Preter rerum seriem*. Recalling both Josquin and Cipriano, the layering of allusions is unparalleled: a Magnificat based on a Mass imitating a motet founded on plainchant …

The limits of borrowing

The Mass cycle has attracted so much attention that it is easy to take the principle for granted and marginalize the many cycles whose movements are connected only loosely or not at all. Where Mass ordinaries are based on the chants of a feast (such as Easter or feasts for the Virgin), the mode varies from movement to movement, just as it did in Machaut's Mass a hundred years earlier. This is the case with the superb cycles on Marian chants ('De beata virgine') by Josquin and Brumel, whose texts are substantially troped. The same applies to ferial Masses, short, functional settings for everyday use, in which cyclical impulses are firmly subordinate to liturgical priorities, and Masses with multiple cantus firmi, which typically are linked liturgically (by the celebration of a given saint, for example) but not necessarily musically. Sometimes, Mass sections are linked by the most perfunctory devices – a head-motif, a common mode, or the briefest of local internal recurrences (as in Tallis' four-voice Mass). In some cases one can deduce an unnamed model, but the regrettable tendency is for such 'Sine nomine' Masses to slip beneath the radar of scholars and performers.

The popularity of *cantus prius facti* in general (and polyphonic ones in particular) accounts for the shared scribal habit of designating the model wherever possible, usually by entering its name at the start of the tenor line, which typically carries the borrowed voice. Famously, some Masses have an enigmatic title: apparently the first is Ockeghem's *Missa My-my* (one of its sources gives it the generic name 'quarti toni', or Hypophrygian). Several writers have pointed out striking similarities between its head-motif and the composer's virelai *Presque transi*. Although the connections between the two works go beyond this, the Mass has no c.f. and features no extensive quotations from the song, leading others to dispute the relationship. And yet, there are indications in other Masses (notably *Au travail suis*, which is explicitly so named) that Ockeghem was deliberately problematizing the notion of borrowing, by questioning how far removed a Mass can be from its model.[19] (This would be entirely consistent with his penchant for hiding his tracks.) Some subsequent Masses may conceal a polyphonic model beneath an enigmatic name: similar claims have been made for La Rue's *Missa Almana* (and his chanson *Pour quoy non*) and for Brumel's *Missa de Dringhs* (and his chanson *Tous les regretz*). Like the titles and the relationships, the motivation remains a mystery, but it anticipates the play with recognizability that the imitation Mass brings into the open. The movements of Palestrina's *Missa Papae Marcelli* also have ideas in common, but the connections are so generic that they need not even have been conscious.

In any case, the boundaries between quotation, allusion, memory trace, and coincidental similarity are notoriously hard to pin down. Many apparent points in common are the result of a shared mode or technical constraints (e.g. to do with imitation). The suggestion that thematic elements of Byrd's four-voice Mass derive from Taverner's *Mean Mass* may be an instance of 'intertextuality', a term as useful as it is misused. Some more demonstrable relationships lie outside the 'textbook' strategies of borrowing. Perhaps most common of all are local, isolated quotations of short phrases in song repertories, where a textual correspondence with a well-known chanson prompts the composer to cite the musical phrase that sets it. In some cases the correspondence has been 'reverse-engineered'; that is, the text has been written to accommodate the musical citation. Compère's rondeau *Au travail suis sans espoir de confort* is a pot-pourri or quodlibet of the opening words of famous songs, whose musical phrases are faithfully quoted in the setting. Sometimes a single phrase of a well-known work is cited for symbolic reasons: the second Hosanna of La Rue's *Missa de Septem doloribus* transposes the closing phrase of Josquin's *Ave Maria* ...

virgo serena down a twelfth from the discantus (where it is clearly audible) to the tenor, rendering it unrecognizable. That the words of the original, 'O mater dei, memento mei' ('Mother of God, remember me'), are underlaid in the tenor at this place seals the correspondence, but it appears to be the only such allusion in the entire Mass.

The fame of Josquin's early motet elicited multiple re-workings, ranging from La Rue's short quotation to entire Masses. One of the most remarkable is the motet by Senfl, which sets the same text (albeit contrafacted in one source). The label 'imitation motet' gets close to a description, without doing it full justice. Senfl takes not merely each section but each individual phrase, which may expand to fill an entire section. So extensively does he do this that Josquin's material grows to well over twice its original length, lasting over ten minutes in performance. This expansion is textural as well as temporal, Senfl adding two voices to the original four. Equally unusually (and contrary to the usual practice of imitation Masses), his approach is uncommonly rigorous: Josquin's ideas are treated broadly in the order in which they occur, and there is scarcely a bar that is not directly derived from it. This somewhat obsessive concentration enables Senfl to explore all the model's potential ramifications, indicating not just what the master did, but what he might have done. The term 'fantasia' is nearer the mark (a recent recording presents it very convincingly as an instrumental work). Given how well-known his model was, Senfl's overflowing invention can scarcely have failed to stir his listeners to admiration.

Not only does so-called musical borrowing lie at the heart of polyphony itself: re-working another composer's music was a fundamental part of compositional practice, a rite of passage, a way of framing one's identity and shaping others' view of it, a means of creative exchange between colleagues and listeners – aspects that enhance our appreciation. So it seems appropriate to conclude this chapter with a few examples of demonstrable borrowing that are not directly audible (or at least not immediately). Obrecht's wholesale transplantation of the c.f. of Busnoys' *L'Homme armé* Mass into his own cycle has already been mentioned. A century later, Victoria modelled his five-voice motet *Dum complerentur* on Palestrina's six-voice setting, mentioned in the last chapter. The strategy might be described as 'textural borrowing'. Victoria follows Palestrina's textural treatment of the text phrases (that is, homophonic, antiphonal, or imitative). This is difficult to illustrate with a single example, though the resemblance is striking when the two are placed side by side. It is especially clear where the text is set syllabically, for Victoria's adopts not only the original's accentual and rhythmic patterns but also any associated

Example 12.6 Victoria, *Dum complerentur* (excerpt). Translation: they were gathered together, saying, Alleluia, and suddenly…

antiphonal deployment (compare Example 12.6 with Example 11.7 on p. 162). The only passage that deviates from the model (perhaps to throw the observer off the scent?) is the opening phrase, which is set imitatively rather than homophonically. Despite differences of detail (e.g. the precise number of times a text phrase is repeated), the correspondences running through them are too numerous to be coincidental.

I finish with a more speculative but intriguing case, the relation of Monteverdi's *Missa In illo tempore* cycle to Rogier's *Missa Ego sum qui*

Example 12.7 (a) Rogier, *Missa Ego sum qui sum*, 'Kyrie II' (conclusion); (b) Monteverdi, *Missa In illo tempore*, 'Kyrie II' (conclusion)

sum, both of which are based on a motet by Gombert. One of the most striking passages of Rogier's Mass is the stepwise descending sequence that closes several of its movements and internal sections (Example 12.7a). This appears to be Rogier's invention, for it is absent in Gombert's motet;

Example 12.7 (Cont.)

besides, it doesn't occur either in Gombert's motet *In illo tempore* but happens again and again in Monteverdi's Mass (Example 12.7b).[20] It is not so much the descending motif itself (which is a commonplace of polyphony) as the fact that both composers state it more than once (for reasons of space, Example 12.7 shows only the point of greatest correspondence). Though not on a par with Gombert's, Rogier's contemporary reputation was greater than it is today (much of his known output having since been lost). Both Masses are based on identically scored and uncannily similar motets by the same composer, and both use exactly the same fuga subject at the start of the 'Christe' (which also occurs in their respective models). One suspects that Monteverdi's 'painstaking study and effort' in writing his work (as reported by his deputy chapel-master at St Mark's) included a close look at the music of Rogier, who was just a few years older.[21] Might this be a clever piece of misdirection on Monteverdi's part? We will never be sure, but there may be some truth in the well-rehearsed quip that 'good artists borrow; great ones steal'.

Chapter 13 | Canons, puzzles, games

In the previous chapter, the imitation Mass was proposed as a game in which the listener recognizes the model and observes its transformation at the hands of the composer. In this chapter, the idea of game playing shifts from the listener's perspective to include the composer and the performer. It assumes many guises, ranging from the audible – focusing on an intrinsically musical idea – to forms of notation that require decoding or compositional puzzles that lie behind the musical surface. Many of these games are not overtly humorous; certain forms of compositional problem solving are a test of ingenuity in which the abstruseness of the challenge and the elegance of the solution are equally important. But just as many games involve more than one person, most of these situations imply a recipient – someone who observes or participates either as listener or performer. The games brought together in this chapter deepen the act of listening to Renaissance polyphony and connect us to ways of thinking about music beyond the notes. They also bring together most of the themes of this book.

Playing with syntax: cadence

I begin with that most essential of contrapuntal structures, the cadence, which can be inflected in several ways. The most common is when the contratenor bassus fails to resolve onto the final, as in Example 13.1. In dyadic terms, both these cadences are technically complete, but their

Example 13.1 Evaded cadences (four-voice)

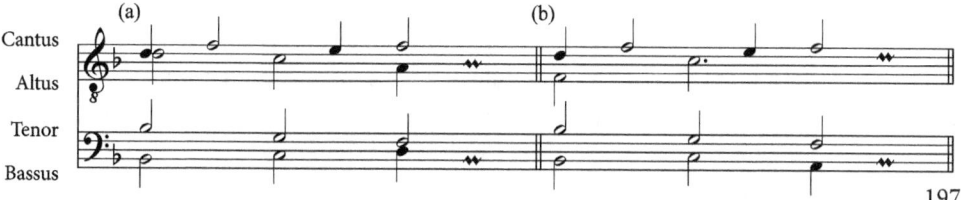

Example 13.2 Evaded cadences (two-voice)

Example 13.3 Agricola, *Allés regretz* (excerpt)

function is defused by the behaviour of the other voices. Cadences can also be evaded by the cadential voices themselves, as shown in Example 13.2: either voice (or both) may leap in another direction or onto another pitch in the same direction, or they can delay the final by means of a rest, or combine these alternatives in different ways.

While these examples of cadential evasion are commonplace, there are, other, subtler forms. Example 13.3 is from a textless setting by Agricola of a chanson tenor, with a discantus and a contratenor in the same range. In the first half of b. 2 of the example, the contratenor has the *cantizans* formula (complete with suspension) but with no corresponding *tenorizans* motion in either of the other voices. The converse happens at bb. 2–3: the tenor has the downward motion onto f, but there is no corresponding *cantizans*

Example 13.4 Agricola, *Comme femme desconfortée I* (beginning)

formula: the upper voices have already cadenced a beat earlier on B♭ (b. 2). At b. 3, they have another cadence on B♭, except that both the preparation and the resolution are off the beat. In Example 13.4, from another textless chanson tenor setting, a phrase is introduced against the cantus firmus in each of the free voices in turn: this phrase ends with a *cantizans* formula, complete with suspension, but only with the last statement (in the bassus) does it correspond to the motion in the tenor: it is as though the cadential materials were placed in spite of the tenor, whose role as the foundation of polyphony is pointedly negated. In the original notation, where there are no bar-lines and the voices are laid out separately, the deliberate misplacement of cadential material would have been especially obvious to the performers. The humour of these skilfully engineered situations arises from a sense of surprise and an appreciation of the composer's ingenuity.

A similar game is played on a broad scale in the Kyrie of Mouton's *Messe sans cadence*, which consistently (though not entirely) evades cadences, even at the ends of sections. Here, 'play' is not synonymous with jest, but with a demonstration of skill in response to a challenge. In other contexts, where ostentatious display would seem inappropriate (for example towards the conclusion of Tallis' penitential motet *Suscipe quaeso, Domine*), repeating a cadential gesture serves a rhetorical purpose; all the same, after a few repetitions the singers and the audience might have wondered how many the composer could get away with. As the most enduring cliché of polyphony, the cadence's potential to be subverted was exploited throughout the Renaissance. The last word on the subject goes to Lassus, whose sense of

Example 13.5 Lassus, *Psalmi David poenitentiales: Beati quorum*, 'Nolite fieri' (conclusion). Translation: [Be not as the horse and the mule], that hath no understanding.

humour is well attested in his surviving letters. One of the verses from his Penitential Psalms (again an unlikely place for a joke) illustrates the psalmist's injunction 'Be not as the horse and the mule, that hath no understanding' with a cadence that is indeed asinine in contrapuntal terms (Example 13.5).

Playing with material: hexachord games and ostinato

Another pervasive cliché of Renaissance polyphony is the hexachord.[1] In the last quarter of the fifteenth century, composers begin making explicit musical reference to it in significant number. The use of hexachord syllables in Senfl's *Lust hab ich g'habt* has already been mentioned, and also related examples in Josquin. (Although the 'subjects' of the *Missa Hercules dux Ferrarie* and *Missa La sol fa re mi* are hexachordally derived, they do not foreground the hexachord itself; the ascent of the *L'Homme armé* tune up the degrees of the hexachord in the *Super voces musicales* cycle comes closer to doing so.) Possibly the earliest recorded instance is the 'Agnus dei II' of Ockeghem's *Missa Quinti toni* (plausibly composed after 1470), in which the bassus's material consists entirely of a short up-and-down phrase (*ut re ut*), to which the syllable *mi* is added; each repetition adds a new pitch until *la* is reached (Example 13.6). The process is emphasized because the same basic profile is retained each time. Because such process-driven devices are atypical of his music, Ockeghem may have been responding to the composers of the next generation: Agricola's two extended fantasias, *Cecus non iudicat de coloribus* and *Pater meus Agricola est*, have similar

Example 13.6 Ockeghem, *Missa Quinti toni*, 'Agnus dei II' (contratenor bassus, excerpt)

incremental episodes, each time in a single voice (in *Pater meus* it takes the ascending/descending form seen in *Quinti toni*).

Alongside these 'cameo appearances' (including practically countless shorter ones) are pieces in which a process derived from the exposition of the hexachord unfolds over the entire work. Both halves of Isaac's motet *O decus ecclesie* restate a similar incremental process, first adding and ascending and then descending and subtracting, but in long notes and with no embellishment. Senfl takes a freer approach in a setting of *Fortuna desperata*, against whose tenor the top voice states the hexachord incrementally in both directions, but freely as regards pitches and rhythms. Long-note exposition is a feature of Brumel's Mass *Ut re mi fa sol la*, but instead of proceeding by increments, Brumel states the seven possible hexachords of the gamut (the three hard hexachords and the two natural and soft) in both directions, from the lowest to the highest.[2] Brumel's cycle is the first of more than two dozen hexachord Masses composed over the next two centuries. Palestrina's six-voice Mass is relatively rigorous: the second cantus consists almost entirely of unembellished ascending and descending statements, always on the same pitch-level (the highest hexachord of the gamut). Morales' approach is more radical: dispensing with constructivist processes, he treats the hexachord as a flexible fantasia subject, but in one sense his method is more rigorous than Palestrina's, for the subject permeates the voices as far as possible, sometimes all four simultaneously. Like Palestrina after him, he adds a canonic voice in the 'Agnus dei III', which though rhythmically free is suffused with hexachordal elements. Morales' Mass neatly marks the distance between the composers of the mid-sixteenth century and those active at the start of it. In this light, Palestrina's more formal approach (with the second cantus effectively functioning as a c.f.) may be viewed as retrospective.

Perhaps the most captivating hexachordal piece of all is Josquin's motet *Ut Phebi radiis*, which holds the most rigorous constructivism

Example 13.7 Josquin, *Ut Phebi radiis*, tenor and bassus: canonic pitch materials

and playful wit in perfect synthesis.³ At its heart is the incremental procedure described earlier, but this time also in canon: the bassus sings the pitches of the natural hexachord and the tenor those of the soft hexachord one pitch later, resulting in a string of thirds (Example 13.7). The statements have eight breve rests between them, and the canonic voices go up the hexachord in the first half and descend in the second. Above this severe scaffolding, the two upper voices sing a text whose twelve lines are divided into two seven-line stanzas, one for each half. The beginning of the text lines coincides with the ends of segments in the lower voices. The twist is in the text, whose classical and biblical allusions are obscured by apparent corruptions. Towards the end of the stanzas especially, it degenerates into nonsense, but one feature has survived the transmission process unscathed: the first syllable of the first line is *Ut*, the first two syllables of the second are *Ut re*, the first three syllables of the third are *Ut re mi*, and so on; the lines of the second stanza do the same in reverse, beginning with *La*. (The seventh and last line of each stanza is a textual extension of the sixth, a 'coda' of sorts, in which the game is suspended.) The upper voices, accordingly, both begin each text line by matching the pitch to the syllable, culminating in all six pitches in the penultimate line. In a marvellous touch, Josquin has all the three hexachordal types (soft, natural, and hard) run concurrently (Example 13.8). Plainly the text was written not just with music in mind but to accommodate exactly this process, like the text of Compère's quodlibet-rondeau *Au travail suis* mentioned in Chapter 12. Over many years, scholars have tried to correct the apparent mistakes in Petrucci's *Motetti libro quarto* (1505), but could it be that the nonsense syllables he transmits are garbled intentionally? To put the question differently, would a 'correct' text tell us any more about the relation between text and music in *Ut Phebi radiis* than we know already? It is oddly fitting that the text's meaning dissolves just at the point when it becomes superfluous from a musical

Example 13.8 Josquin, *Ut Phebi radiis*, first part (excerpt). Translation: As the running of the oar of Peter from the abandoned ship is a Divine law, So do you rule over all, [O Virgin Mary].

Note: Given the uncertain nature of the text and its transmission in its only source, the translation given here is conjectural.

point of view. For *Ut Phebi radiis* is a supremely elegant game of consequences, in which the words are the servants of the music rather than the other way around. At the risk of being misunderstood (given the number of technical *tours-de-force* his output contains, some of them far more impressive), I might name *Ut Phebi radiis* as my favourite piece by Josquin.

The foregrounding of specifically musical features is common to Josquin's direct contemporaries. In its successive form (*ut re mi fa sol la*), the hexachord is treated as a theme or motif; but in the years around 1500, musical techniques achieve 'thematic' status. Especially popular is ostinato, the repetition of a motif, usually consisting of just a few notes. Like the hexachord, ostinatos can be a short-term device for constructing a section, passage, or phrase; but they can also fuel an entire movement or work, Josquin's *soggetto cavato* Masses being the most highly developed examples. An especially popular procedure involves overlaying an ostinato against a c.f. (especially a voice from a chanson). Obrecht and Josquin were equally fond if it, as were Isaac, Agricola, and later Senfl; moreover, they competed with each other in its use. A virtuoso instance is the final Agnus dei from Josquin's *Missa Faisant regretz*. This is very likely a

Example 13.9 Josquin, *Missa Faisant regretz*, 'Agnus dei III' (beginning)

response to an untexted setting by Agricola of Frye's rondeau *Tout a par moy*, which sets the first four notes of the chanson tenor as an ostinato against the first half of the whole tenor, and does the same with the first four notes of the tenor's second half in the second part. Josquin's Agnus dei has the discantus of Frye's song (not the tenor!) in the top voice, while Agricola's four-note ostinatos are set against each other separately in the contratenor and tenor (Example 13.9). At over 500 years' distance, the boundary between emulation and rivalry can be hard to draw, but their contrasting approaches to borrowed material are emblematic of the two composers' styles. Whereas Agricola's setting is a plethora of contrapuntal detail and intricacy, three out of Josquin's four voices are entirely determined by a process. The stately pace of the ostinatos in this Agnus dei also sets it apart from the ostinatos of other composers, which are typically incisive and rhythmically driven. Their 'thematic' use of musical materials fell away with the passing of that generation, as imitation gained the upper hand. By 1520 it had largely disappeared from currency.

Playing with pitch

The subject of Renaissance chromaticism and expanded pitch treatment has been developed extensively. In 1946, Edward E. Lowinsky's *Secret Chromatic Art in the Netherlands Motet* placed it front and centre of a scholarly study. As others have since pointed out, how far any experiment with pitch was actually 'secret' is a moot point, given the quantity of music in which it features explicitly; but undoubtedly, seemingly straightforward notational situations may conceal more complex-sounding results. The examples on which I draw have a place in this chapter because pitch treatment is not merely a feature but arguably the actual 'subject' of the piece or passage. For this reason, Cipriano's famous *Calami sonum ferentes*, whose opening point of imitation ascends in semitones from B to e, does not fit this category, because its use of chromaticism is primarily illustrative and localized, just as in *Da le belle contrade*. In this, Cipriano is typical of most madrigal composers, for whom chromaticism is usually motivated by textual considerations. The case of Gesualdo is more ambiguous, since his texts so consistently lend themselves to the heightened chromaticism he favours (another example of the text being subservient to the musical idea). The following examples are also 'games of consequences', in that a straightforward premise leads logically to a paradoxical conclusion.

The long-standing tradition of transposed hexachords may have inspired *Passibus ambiguis/Fortuna desperata* (pub. 1553) by Matthias Greiter (c.1494–1550), which takes the first six notes of the famous song (*Ut ut re mi re ut*, in the soft hexachord) and transposes them eight times up a fourth to finish on an F♭ sonority – that is, on the pitch-level where it started, but sounding a semitone lower. This sets up a cascade of flats in the surrounding voices, most (but not all) of which are indicated by a cumulative system of key signatures. Towards the end of the piece a ♭♭ is indicated in the lower voices (B having been notated as flat from the start). The details of Greiter's life are suggestive of a lively character, and other surviving works confirm his penchant for musical jokes. *Passibus ambiguis* was published after his death, so when it was composed is unclear; it would be useful to know whether Greiter was familiar with Willaert's early motet *Quid non ebrietas*, whose underlying principal is similar.[4] Starting with a single signature flat, the tenor cycles through a series of signed flats (that is, placed against individual notes) on e', a, d', g, and c', which remain flattened for the rest of the piece. Midway through comes a downward leap of a fifth (onto f), shortly followed by an upward leap of a fourth (onto b). As notated, these two intervals are respectively diminished and augmented, and thus both forbidden; flattening the two pitches to make the intervals perfect prolongs the chain of flats. By the end of the piece, the tenor finishes on a notated e but sounds on d, an octave below the notated d' in the cantus. In terms of notation, *Quid non ebrietas* is even more economical than *Passibus ambiguis*, since its key signature never changes. Beyond those few signed flats, the piece bears no outward sign of its unconventionality, since the other voices are perfectly straightforward. (That said, a recording by the vocal ensemble Cinquecento has the tenor subtly adjusting his intonation at the crucial moment to remain within the framework of the other voices; Renaissance teachers focused on the implications of this passage for intonation rather than its notational usage.[5])

It is worth emphasizing that *Quid non ebrietas* is in a sense not a 'trick' piece, since correcting diminished fifths is perfectly standard behaviour. What can seem alien to modern observers is the conceptual distance it opens up between notation and sounding result, but, as will become clear in the following sections, to Renaissance musicians it was second nature. Besides, Willaert's predecessors may well have played similar games without recourse to accidentals. A case that has generated much discussion is the concluding sequence of the Kyrie of Obrecht's *Missa Libenter gloriabor*, in which the same principle – 'correcting' perfect consonances that are notated as imperfect – results in a final cadence on F♭ (Example 13.10). As Margaret Bent has observed, the fact that the Gloria is heard immediately afterwards is no objection, since the singers would simply have taken its opening pitch from the end of the Kyrie.[6]

The flat regions explored in these examples call to mind the possibility of expanded hexachord readings, but other ways of conceptualizing pitch had currency in the sixteenth century. Debates concerning intonation and tuning systems centred on the three ancient Greek genera, each of which divides the tetrachord differently (the diatonic into semitone, tone, and tone, reading upwards; the chromatic into two semitones and a minor third; and the enharmonic into two quarter-tones and a major third): a stated aim of Vicentino in constructing his *archicembalo* was to facilitate performances in all three. The three voices of *Qu'est devenu ce bel œuil* by Claude Le Jeune (c.1528–1600) extensively exploit the chromatic genus (Example 13.11). Though probably not intended as a demonstration piece, its melodic peculiarities come across with perfect naturalness when

Example 13.10 Obrecht, *Missa Libenter gloriabor*, 'Kyrie II' (conclusion)

Example 13.11 Le Jeune, *Qu'est devenu ce bel œuil* (beginning). Translation: What has become of that comely eye/that once lit up my soul with its rays/And in whom Love recovered its arrows, its torches, and its darts?

interpreted against the theoretical context. It is no coincidence that Le Jeune's chanson also conforms to another classicizing aspiration, the *vers mesurés à l'antique*.

Fugal canon

The distinction between encoded notation and sounding result in *Quid non ebrietas* reaches a peak of sophistication in that quintessentially Renaissance musical artefact: canon. This takes two principal forms, the first of which overlaps with the term's modern definition: two or more voices state the same material exactly, usually at a temporal distance and at a specified pitch-interval (which may be the unison). As mentioned in Chapter 11, this form of canon is closely related to imitation, with the difference that imitation may be looser than canon and is eventually discontinued, whereas a canon lasts for the duration of a piece or section. Because the rules governing imitation and this type of canon are also closely related, Renaissance musicians used the same term, 'fuga', for both; this has led Virginia Newes to propose the useful designation 'fugal canon' for these situations.[7] Another crucial difference is that in a canon only one voice is written down; all the sounding voices are read from the single notated part. The voice that starts first is sometimes called '*dux*', Latin for leader, and the one that follows '*comes*' ('follower', plural '*comites*'); this type of canon, with voices entering one after another, is sometimes called 'interval canon'. Typically, the place(s) where the comites begin singing is indicated by a 'sign of congruence', like the one seen a note or two into each voice of La Rue's *Ave sanctissima Maria* (shown in Chapter 2 as Illustration 2.1). Sometimes, the pitch-interval between the voices is given verbally (e.g. 'canon at the fourth above'), but not always: Illustration 2.1 gives no such indication, and the singers would have had to work it out for themselves. This is not as hard as it sounds, since the pitch-interval of most canons is a perfect interval, and the alternatives are easily exhausted; but even in this relatively straightforward type of canon (in the case of La Rue's motet and in *Ut Phebi radiis* at the fourth above), an essential piece of information is left to the singers to figure out.

A more sophisticated type of fugal canon is called 'mensuration' (or 'mensural') canon, alluded to in the previous chapter, in which the voices (whatever their number) start at the same time and gradually grow apart, reading the same notation simultaneously but under different mensural signs. If both voices are under the same prolational sign but one has a stroke and the other does not (say C and ¢), exactly the same music will sound, but one voice will move at twice the speed of the other. (By extension, if the signs are C and ¢2, the latter voice sounds at four times the speed of the former, since the stroke and the number 2 both denote diminution by half.) If the voices are under different prolational signs, the duration of notes longer than a semiminim may differ, depending on the application of the rules of perfection and alteration. (The difference between two readings of the same passage under O or C was shown in Example 6.1 above, p. 86): the presence of perfect breves and altered semibreves in the reading under O means that it lasts longer.) In the four-out-of-one canon from La Rue's *Missa L'Homme armé* (Example 13.12 and Illustration 13.1), the use of the signs O and ¢3 entails alteration and imperfection on the level of the semibreve and minim, respectively, whereas the other two signs (C and ¢) do not. (This is yet another respect in which La Rue appears to outdo Josquin, whose three-voice Agnus dei canon involves straightforward augmentation, with neither perfection nor alteration.) The starting pitch for each voice is shown by the placement of its mensuration sign: the higher on the stave the sign is placed, the lower the voice sounds. Here the singers are given all the necessary information, but in a way that presupposes their familiarity with the code. A successful performance from original notation involves a high degree of co-ordination, concentration, and possibly rehearsal; but to those not in the know, arriving at the correct result from the notation alone would present a considerable challenge. A barrier to the uninitiated, canonic notation visually expresses the singers' collective identity.

Just as continental composers lost no time in exploring potential uses of the *cantus prius factus* in the Mass cycle, it did not take them long to take the possibilities of fugal canon to mind-bending limits (an early, straightforward example is Du Fay's *Bien veignés vous* (Example 4.5b above, p. 62)). There are detailed surveys of canon technique in the literature; here I am less concerned with its technical workings than with what it tells us about how Renaissance musicians conceptualized polyphony. Perhaps the farthest-reaching example is Ockeghem's *Missa prolationum*, the likely forerunner of the three- and four-out-of-one canons of Josquin and La Rue. Written for four voices in double canon (that is, just two notated voices), its name reflects the fact that each of the four prolations appears in a different voice simultaneously. (Thus, a notated breve is worth anything between four and nine minims, depending on the sign involved.) Each section increases the canonic pitch-interval, which expands from the unison to

Example 13.12 La Rue, *Missa L'Homme armé*, 'Agnus dei II' (beginning)

the octave over the course of the Mass (a pattern that Palestrina remembered in his *Missa ad fugam*, and J. S. Bach in his *Goldberg Variations*); the sections utilize different combinations of mensuration and interval canons; finally, the time-interval between canonic voices ranges from just one breve to twelve. This unparalleled range of canonic possibilities showcases the mensural system's flexibility and the skill of those performing it. It is tempting to see in this remarkable work a possible audition piece for prospective singers at the French royal chapel. Even though its surviving sources transmit the Mass imperfectly, it is the supreme embodiment of the fundamental idea that notation and sounding result are two sides of the same coin, each perfectly expressing the other. Equally moving is how little these self-imposed restrictions seem to impinge on Ockeghem's distinctive melodic style.

Illustration 13.1 La Rue, *Missa L'Homme armé*, 'Agnus dei II'
Brussels, Koninklijke Bibliotheek/Bibliothèque Royale, Ms. 9126, f. 42 (reproduced with permission)

A few now famous canons notwithstanding (such as the thirteenth-century *Sumer is icumen in*), the technique appears only sporadically until after 1450, reaching a climax in the early years of the sixteenth century.[8] Its popularity among a wide, musically literate audience – attested by the printed anthologies consisting entirely of such pieces – testifies to the Renaissance taste for riddles of all kinds. The attraction of canons is two-fold: the intellectual satisfaction in solving a puzzle is reinforced by the shared sensory pleasure in the sounding of the same music in different voices simultaneously. Anyone who has sung canons from the original notation will have experienced the magical quality of a musical process audibly unfolding in real time.

Non-fugal and enigmatic canons

The second form of canon is less well known than its fugal counterpart but takes the principle of encoded notation further still. It is implicit in the origin of the word 'canon', which is Latin for 'rule'. Thus, in the phrase 'canon at the fourth below', the term denotes an instruction to the singers to read the notation in a certain way. In fugal canons, this generates an added voice or voices, but canons can prescribe all sorts of other ways of reading the notation. In the *L'Homme armé* Masses of Busnoys, Ockeghem, and Obrecht (and in Josquin's cycle *Super voces musicales*), the tune's different transformations are not written out: it is always presented in its original form (i.e. under major prolation, which entails augmentation in relation to the voices under minor prolation), while a verbal canon alerts the singer that it should be read back-to-front, inverted, read against itself, transposed, or however the composer wishes. Typically also, that instruction is itself expressed in a coded or cryptic fashion. The canon for Du Fay's 'Agnus dei III' says, 'Cancer eat plenus sed redeat medius' ('the crab goes [forwards] in full but returns by half'). Because crabs were mistakenly thought to walk backwards, the canon prescribes that the singers should first read the tune in retrograde and in full ('plenus') note-values, and then read from start to finish ('backwards', in crab terms) in halved values. This type of 'non-fugal' canon, so called because it does not usually generate additional voices, became a staple of c.f. Masses. It is typically associated with a *cantus prius factus* (typically a song tenor), which retains its original notated appearance but is transformed in performance according to the canon or verbal instruction. Non-verbal canons are thus doubly encoded: the music does not sound as notated, and the process by which one gets from notation to sound comes in the form of a riddle. In this respect, non-fugal canons are equivalent to the modern cryptic crossword.[9] (In his *Dictionary of Musical Definitions*, Tinctoris defines canon as 'the expression of the composer's intention under the cover of obscurity'.) Devotees of cryptic crosswords learn to recognize 'trigger' words signalling the operation to be performed (anagrams, for example). In the same way, for decades after Du Fay's example, the single word '*cancrizans*' – 'go like the crab' – became the clue for retrograde motion. Another feature of crosswords is that the solution is provided separately; from the very beginning of Petrucci's publishing venture, a 'resolved' version of the notation typically accompanied the encrypted one. Other printers followed suit, and soon music scribes began to do the same – partly out of convenience, but also because singers' familiarity with the rules of mensural notation were beginning to fade (even in prestigious institutions). In a few cases, such as the *Missa O quam glorifica* by Robert Fayrfax (1464–1521), the work's canons and original notation have had to be reconstructed on the basis of the surviving sources, which give only resolutions. (Fayrfax may have used several colours to signify different durations: blue is used alongside red and black in the Eton Choirbook, for example, to denote breves worth *five* minims.)

Counting the different durations arising from reading a *cantus prius factus* under different mensural signs, there are three levels on which non-fugal canons potentially encode the sounding result. The first is the verbal canon itself, which may give rise to all kinds of fanciful allusions, like the crab encountered earlier. Unsurprisingly, given the training of our singer-composers, biblical citations were especially popular: Christ's command 'Vade retro, Satanas' ('get thee behind me, Satan', found in several examples including La Rue's *Missa Alleluia*) is another way of prescribing retrograde; St Paul's saying that in the afterlife the faithful see God 'face to face' ('facie ad faciem', in Agricola's *Salve regina I*) denotes two voices singing the same material, one of them in inversion (i.e. 'facing' the other); and so on. Classical allusions and puns were also favoured: the legal tag 'de minimis non curat praetor' ('a judge is not concerned with trifles', from Josquin's *Missa Malheur me bat*) instructs the singer to omit all the minims in the original notation. There are hundreds of these canonic inscriptions, but I will mention a particular favourite: Manchicourt's *Regina celi* has the French instruction 'Sans souspirer, ne chantez poinct' ('Without sighing, don't sing at all'), which appears to makes no sense, except that 'souspir' was (and still is) the musical term for a minim rest, and 'poinct' ('at all') is a dot; therefore the singer must leave out all minim rests and dots of addition. In this case, because the *dux* sings the notation as written, the *comes*, paradoxically, finishes ahead of it. (A similar idea informs Moulu's chant paraphrase *Missa Alma redemptoris mater*, also called 'Mass with two faces' in some sources because it may be sung either as notated or in a shorter version, leaving out all rests longer than a minim.)

These examples and a few more give some idea how far composers might go in transforming the original notation.[10] In the anonymous *Missa L'Ardant désir* (c.1470), the tenor is instructed to read the notated song tenor while mentally removing all the stems; in another movement, by omitting any note that is followed by a higher pitch; and in a third, by inverting the note-values so that maximas become minims and longs become semibreves (and vice-versa), with only the middle value (the breve) remaining constant.[11] Perhaps the most prolific and sophisticated deviser of enigmatic canons was Obrecht. Two especially remarkable examples are from the previously mentioned *Missa Fortuna desperata*. The canon '*In medio consistit virtus*' ('Virtue lies in the middle way') instructs that the tenor begins both sections of the Gloria by singing the central note of the tenor of the song and then working outwards in both directions, first backwards from the midpoint to the start and then forwards from the midpoint to the end; the two sections of the Credo do the converse, working inwards, from the end backwards to the central note and then from the beginning to the centre. (These segments are separated by symmetrically disposed groups of rests.) Although the procedure sounds very arcane, in each movement the tune is initially unrecognizable but is then revealed halfway through as the retrograde yields to the 'prime'. The process culminates in the Credo statements, when the beginning of the famous tune is heard for the first time since the Kyrie. These moments, in which the unfamiliar is suddenly revealed as familiar, are part of the music's rhetorical effect (I will return to this point presently). In the Credo of his *Missa Grecorum*, the canon '*Digniora sunt priora*' ('The more worthy have precedence') prescribes an even more extreme procedure: all the longs of the song tenor are sung in the order in which they occur, then all the breves in order, and finally all the semibreves; then the same thing is done again, but in retrograde. (The Credo of the *Missa De tous biens plaine* has the same technique, but with a different canonic inscription.) Compared to all this, the retrogradations, inversions, and transpositions of earlier composers (and indeed later ones) appear straightforward indeed. Obrecht's canon has more in common with modern post-serial techniques than with fugal canon (the cut-up technique of the novelist William S. Burroughs (1914–97) comes to mind). It is not merely that the distance between notation and sounding result has become a chasm; paradoxically, in 'solving' Obrecht's riddle, the singers create an insoluble one for the listener, who has no chance of identifying the original material – even a very famous song like *De tous biens plaine*. Finally, Obrecht's 'cut-up' technique gives rise to otherwise nonsensical melodic intervals, such as sevenths and ninths; yet this seemingly random musical result is arrived at through rational procedures (or at least ones that can be described in a few words). Bearing in mind these aesthetic ramifications, the attraction of these techniques to our singer-composers is easy to understand.

Such paradoxes are typical of non-fugal canons and have led to the perception of an overly cerebral, calculated approach to composing. Undoubtedly in some cases the complexity of the canons is the most remarkable thing about them. Although the *Missa L'Ardant désir* is a very distinctive piece, the sounding results of its canonic manipulations are rarely striking in themselves. The same is true of the anonymous motet *Ut heremita solus* in Petrucci's *Canti C* (1502), whose verbal canons have only recently been deciphered.[12] Its attribution to Ockeghem is doubtful for stylistic reasons (at least in the version transmitted by Petruccci), but its extreme complexity anticipates later canonic devices in works by Spanish composers such as Alonso Lobo (1555–1617), Sebastian de Vivanco (1551–1622) and others stretching into the seventeenth century. The prejudice against canon (especially the enigmatic variety) as 'paper-music' was widespread among writers of the Enlightenment and persisted into the twentieth century, when the same kinds of objections were levelled at serialism. But this view passes over the conceptual elegance of so many of these examples, in which the *cantus prius factus* retains its (visual) notated form throughout the Mass but is transformed sonically in a variety of ways, satisfying the aesthetic criterion of diversity out of unity; it ignores the dramatic potential of those moments of revelation, when the borrowed material is heard in its pristine form (recalling the moment of revelation at the elevation); and crucially, it discounts entirely the element of game playing: some of these musical situations, such as being instructed to sing 'nonsense' intervals, are after all inherently humorous.

Puzzles and *Augenmusik*

The potential disconnection between eye and ear is inscribed within the mensural system. It was sufficiently familiar for singers to distinguish between situations where the two are held in balance and those when that potential is taken to extremes. An outstanding example of *Augenmusik* ('eye-music') is the canon for the Sanctus of the *L'Homme armé* Mass of Marbrianus de Orto. The first five notes of the tune are stated in different mensurations, which appear ahead of the notes themselves (Example 13.13). As with La Rue's four-out-of-one canon, the placement of mensural signs on the stave indicates the pitches on which the statements are sung; but here, the ordering of the signs duplicates the sequence of the

Example 13.13 De Orto, *Missa L'Homme armé*, Sanctus, tenor in original notation (beginning)

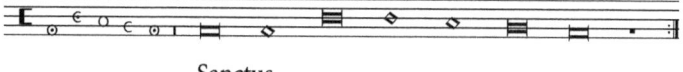

Sanctus

tune's first five pitches. Beyond observing that the statements of the tune cycle through all the available species of fourth (on *ut*, *re*, and *mi*), this subtlety would escape most listeners, but de Orto's singers would have recognized it as a particularly economical instance of *Augenmusik*. Gustave Reese noticed many years ago that in the 'Et incarnatus' of Obrecht's *Missa Maria zart* (a section in which the c.f. is silent), the semibreves of the bassus part pick out the first half of the borrowed tune's pitches; a few years later, it was shown that its second half appears in the semibreves of the discantus. These pitches are interspersed among other durations, such that both voices have the outward appearance of being 'freely composed'; the tune is present despite being neither audible nor visible. This detail is reminiscent of the gargoyles and other motifs that medieval stonemasons placed in the uppermost recesses of gothic cathedrals, hidden from all but God. A similar intention may have motivated Obrecht; equally, it may have amused him to conceal his borrowed material from his singing colleagues and challenge them to discover it. Needless to say, these motivations are not mutually exclusive.

That these examples belong to the world of games in the broad sense is borne out by the wealth of evidence of musical puzzles incorporating visual references in the later Renaissance. In view of Katelijne Schiltz's extensive study, it would be superfluous to consider them here in detail. Particularly popular topics were the cross, as the primary symbol of the Christian faith; the circle, whose history in polyphonic notation stretches back to the turn of the fifteenth century; and the use of colours to distinguish between different levels of code. While not all these musical riddles make great music, the fact is itself significant, for it shows that music's visual dimension was acknowledged as an attribute in itself. In other words, music notation was not simply a vehicle for conveying a desired sounding result, but belonged to the world of ideas and representation, along with words, images, and other signs. The use of black notation as a signifier of death and mourning (independent of its mensural implications) is a straightforward illustration of this idea; a later, more complex expression of it is the literally extraordinary *Atalanta fugiens* (1617) by Michael Maier (1569–1622), former physician and alchemist at the court of Emperor Rudolf II (Illustration 13.2). It consists of fifty 'fugues' or short canons – note the reference to the technique in the work's title (*fugiens*, 'fleeing') – each based on a well-known plainchant Kyrie. These pieces illustrate a complex allegory, which unfolds in the texts they set. The two canonic voices represent a male and a female character, Atalanta and Hippomenes, and the c.f. symbolizes an apple that comes between them. None of them is mentioned in the texts, which describe various alchemical processes with which Maier was intimately familiar. Each piece is framed (metaphorically) by a woodcut illustration and an epigram; the woodcut represents the text directly, while the epigram comments on it obliquely. Maier's association with the mystical society of Rosicrucians (Erik Satie was a much later, occasional adherent) adds another layer of symbolism. The combination of poetic text, epigram, and illustration places *Atalanta fugiens* within the enormously popular Renaissance puzzle genre known as *emblema*, in which the different components reflect (typically indirectly) on a moral or philosophical question. But Maier's integration of music in *Atalanta fugiens* is unique; the fact that as a composer he was barely competent is beside the point. Its late date notwithstanding, *Atalanta fugiens* is entirely consistent with Renaissance practice and the projection of music's place within it.

Playing with numbers

The mention of alchemy, magic, and mysticism leads back to the contentious subject of music and number.[13] Their close theoretical relationship is most clearly seen in isorhythmic motets, in which succeeding statements of the tenor material are sung at different speeds according to numerical proportions, creating sections of different lengths. These proportions express the most perfect harmonic relationships (e.g. 3:2:1 or 6:4:3:2) and are sometimes indicated by different mensural signs (this being the inspiration for subsequent adaptations of the technique in the early Renaissance). Pieces whose structure is articulated by repeated statements of the same material under different mensural signs will typically exhibit numerical patterns as a result. This is true of the earliest c.f. Mass cycles by English composers (the plan of Leonel Power's *Missa Alma redemptoris mater* is exemplary in its clarity, as are Dunstaple's many isorhythmic motets); an equally clear and elegant later example is John Browne's *Stabat mater*, whose first part has 450 semibreves under O and whose second has 360 semibreves under C, a proportion of 5:4 (corresponding to the acoustic interval of the minor third). Works written in an academic context often reflect music's status as a science of number through proportional number patterns. This was almost certainly the motivation for Fayrfax's *Missa O quam glorifica*, composed as part of the required exercises for the award of the Doctorate at the University of Cambridge in 1504. Proportional schemes based on c.f. structures will often alternate periods of presence and absence of the c.f. (the latter consisting either of silence or of material unrelated to the c.f.). More broadly, any formal scheme

Illustration 13.2 Michael Maier, *Atalanta fugiens*, fuga/emblema XLV (Oppenheim: Johann Theodor de Bry, 1617), pp. 188–9
Bayerische Staatsbibliothek München, Musikabteilung, Res/4 Alch. 54 (reproduced with permission)

based on large-scale repetition will generate numerical patterns of some kind (such as the consistent alternation in Josquin's *Missa Hercules dux Ferrarie* of eight-breve statements of the subject and eight-breve periods of silence between them). Busnoys' *In hydraulis* is built on repetitions of a very simple

Illustration 13.2 (Cont.)

ostinato under very simple proportions, mirroring its Latin text, which opens with a description of the myth of Pythagoras' discovery of those very ratios. The ostentatious use of Greek terminology was a compliment to the erudition of Busnoys' dedicatee, Ockeghem. *In hydraulis* is steeped in the world view of music as science.

As a rule, the simpler the proportions in play, the likelier they are to have been intentional; conversely, the more complex they are, the more likely speculative. Although a fair quantity of surviving music fits the sorts of straightforward proportional patterning just described, most of it does not. This is the first problem that confronts anyone interested in the matter. The second concerns different sorts of number symbolism, several examples of which have been mentioned in this book, usually connected with scoring. While many seven-voice pieces have a Marian connection, some do not, and conversely, seven-voice pieces make up a tiny proportion of Marian polyphony. The use of thirteen voices in Robert Wylkynson's canonic *Jesus autem transiens* plainly refers to the text, which relates to Christ and the twelve apostles (12+1, of which one is the 'leader'); but how to explain the nineteen voices of Robert Carver's *O bone Jesu*? The number is surely connected with the circumstances of its composition, but because these are unknown, any attempt to explain it (or deduce the occasion) can easily lead down blind alleys. A third difficulty has to do with the sources. Any speculation based on counting notes, for example, is fraught with risk because one cannot be sure to what extent the surviving sources accurately reflect the composer's intentions; that said, all three sources of Du Fay's early motet *Vasilissa ergo gaude* (c.1420) give the tenor a hundred pitches and a total of 700 for the three upper voices, as Jaap van Benthem has shown.[14] The same goes for the practice known as gematria (which assigns numerical values to letters, where A=1, B=2, etc.), which has led some to identify coded 'signatures' or dedications on the basis of composers' names and the number of notes or syllables of the text. But spelling in the pre-modern period was far from stable, and the received modern spelling of names is sometimes contradicted by contemporary sources (as with Obrecht, whose name is consistently spelt 'Hobrecht' in the archival documents pertaining to his family). These potential pitfalls bring to mind the great Bach scholar Alfred Dürr's caution that numerological investigations are all too often 'foredoomed to success'.

It could also be objected that even demonstrable proportional relationships are not directly audible. But the embodied perception of time is not fixed but culturally determined, at least to some extent; it is not impossible that medieval and Renaissance musicians were capable of temporal distinctions that we can no longer perceive. Although the issue of music and number needs careful handling, it is true that composers could and did extrapolate from the grand cosmological model to more speculative forms of number manipulation (as the example of *Vasilissa ergo gaude* suggests). The durations of the c.f. pitches of the *Missa Puer natus est* seemed entirely arbitrary until Joseph Kerman's discovery that Tallis assigned the numbers 1 to 5 to each vowel in order (1 for A, 2 for E, and so on to 5 for U).[15] We shall probably never know Tallis' reasons for the procedure, let alone what canonic instruction (if any) could have described it, but this example returns us to the realm of game playing of the speculative, puzzle variety. The random distribution of the *Maria zart* tune in Obrecht's Mass implies the existence of other similar hidden gems, which we can hardly hope to recover except by happy accident. I believe this all the more having had the good fortune to uncover a particularly neat example. Obrecht's short motet *Hec Deum celi* paraphrases its plainchant material in breves in no fewer than three of its five voices (Example 13.14). The technique is suggestive of canon, but it is inexact: slight discrepancies between the voices prevent their being derived from a single notation. The reason for these adjustments is explained by counting the number of breves of c.f.: the pitches have been adjusted to create alternating segments of c.f. and silence. In the discantus II, the nineteen segments are symmetrically disposed so that there is the same number of segments (9) and the same number of breves (33) either side of the central segment of three sounding breves (in bold type, Figure 13.1). The number of total sounding breves and breves of silence is in a ratio of 46:23, or 2:1. But adding the central segment to the first group (Figure 13.2) gives two unequal 'halves' (36 and 33 breves) in

Example 13.14 Obrecht, *Hec Deum celi*, 'canonic' voices. Translation: [A virgin conceived] the God of heaven and Lord of earth...

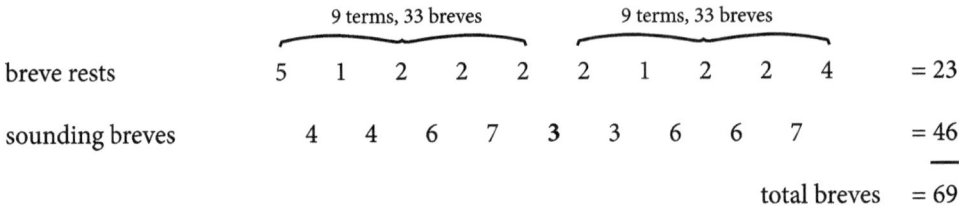

Figure 13.1 Obrecht, *Hec Deum celi*, discantus II: numerical structure

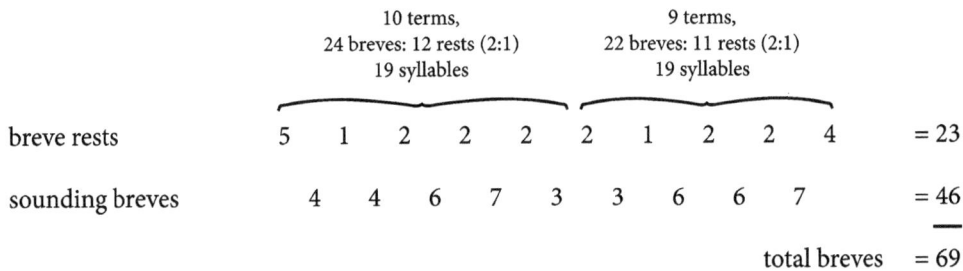

Figure 13.2 Obrecht, *Hec Deum celi*, discantus II: alternative numerical structure

which the ratio of sounding breves to silence is the same as in the motet as a whole (24:12 and 22:11, or 2:1).[16] It seems a fitting conclusion to this chapter that a deliberately inexact canonic construction conceals a hidden number game. At the very start of this book, I posed the question why polyphony was ever formally written down, given the proficiency of our singer-clerics in extemporizing it. Perhaps the idea for *Hec Deum celi* occurred to Obrecht as he coached his choirboys through the day's chant, but it is nearly unthinkable for such a musical *fantasia* to have been extemporized. Once fixed in Obrecht's mind, its details would almost certainly have required working out in writing.

Chapter 14 | Performance practice: a brief introduction

One of the most perplexing issues concerning Renaissance music can be summed up in a simple question: how can two performances of the same piece sound so entirely different? The question will occur to anyone approaching the music for the first time, and also to more experienced listeners. The beginning of modern research into performance practice coincides roughly with that of sound recording, yet one only has to listen to recorded performances of standard repertory made fifty or seventy-five years ago to realize how far tastes have evolved during that period. Thus, an answer to the initial question introduces two separate but related factors: the recovery of the evidence that survives, and the tastes and assumptions that influence how it is interpreted. In this chapter I aim at a succinct account of both, with a focus on concrete examples and the more typical situations. This brings specific observations from previous chapters directly into play.

What the sources don't tell us: aspects of pitch

The Renaissance saw a gradual acceleration in the shift from a predominantly oral culture to a written one. In oral cultures, the scope for variation in the transmission of texts is far greater: manuscript readings of a given piece may vary considerably, a tendency that persisted well into the age of printed music. Modern editorial principles and choices result in different versions, most obviously depending on which source has been chosen as the basis for a given edition. Not infrequently, the variants go beyond surface details. Relatively common instances include the addition of a fourth voice to a three-voice original; the transmission of a different contratenor (often in just one source) or even two, altus and bassus; or the addition or omission of one of the Agnus dei sub-sections in a Mass. (The phenomenon of contrafacta has already been discussed.) Compared to the relative stability of musical texts in later repertories (which, it may be claimed, is more apparent than real), such variants are striking reminders of musical practice in an age before the *Urtext*.

Editorial choice also accounts for differences in the applications of the rules of *musica ficta*, whose implications can be very far-reaching: the decision to inflect one pitch can set off a chain reaction affecting the surrounding voices for bars on end, as in the Kyrie from Obrecht's *Missa Libenter gloriabor* discussed in the previous chapter (Example 13.10). On certain principles there is general agreement, such as the raising of the 'leading note' at cadences; but even then, the contrapuntal context can give rise to considerable ambiguity. In many other cases, the existence of a 'correct' solution is highly debatable, and the possibility of deliberate ambiguity cannot be discounted. Where the 'tonal colouring' of a given passage varies because of editorial intervention, the effect can be very noticeable, particularly when that moment illustrates an affect in the text or when the piece itself is well known. In any case, of all textual variants the decisions concerning 'editorial ficta' are the most likely subjects to change in performance, since experienced musicians (and even not so experienced ones) will make their own decisions; those who perform from original sources make such choices as a matter of course. Clear evidence that the situation was just as fluid during the Renaissance comes in the shape of lute intabulations of polyphonic pieces, which are by their nature prescriptive as to pitch. Where several intabulations exist of the same piece, they often differ significantly – not to say radically – in their moment-to-moment interpretation of accidentals; such variant readings suggest that the notion of a single 'correct' solution misinterprets contemporary practice.

The question of editorial ficta is one of many where the modern expectation of unequivocal solutions is not borne out by evidence. It raises yet again the distinction between emic and etic: even in cases susceptible of multiple solutions, Renaissance singers would instinctively have known what to do and would likely have been far more accepting of potential ambiguities. The problem lies not in what the musical sources fail to tell us but in our ability to interpret them. What we have lost is not so much factual knowledge (which can be recovered to an extent) but practical experience of the system from within, the emic assumptions that underlay the notation and did not require notating. The same goes for most aspects of performance practice that perplex scholars and performers of today.

As explained in Chapter 5, the introduction of high clefs (*chiavette*) made explicit what had been implicit previously, namely, that notated pitch-levels corresponded to no absolute pitch-standard.[1] Downward transposition of *chiavette* would have been taken as read, the precise interval being dependent on the modal context. This is worth insisting on, because even today professional ensembles interpret the notated pitch-levels of *chiavette* literally – that is, as indicating absolute pitch – resulting in noticeable shifts of range from one piece to the next and changes of personnel. This can be heard in most recordings of Lassus' *Lagrime di San Pietro* and Palestrina's sacred madrigal cycle of Song of Songs (*Canticum canticorum*) settings. Given that this is one of the few aspects of performance practice on which there is near-unanimous agreement, it is regrettable that the misapprehension is so widespread. Choices of pitch-level in the period before *chiavette* should likewise be treated pragmatically, dependent on the voices available: since the vocal compass of Renaissance music rarely exceeds two-and-a-half octaves, there is nearly always scope for flexibility. Not only does a tone or semitone in either direction affect 'singability'; it can radically alter an ensemble's timbre. Two categories constitute special cases. Where a piece's overall compass pushes or exceeds three octaves (as in the more lavishly scored pieces of pre-Reformation England from the Eton Choirbook up to and including Tallis), the amount of 'wriggle-room' either side of notated pitch is correspondingly narrow, but worth experimenting with nonetheless. Then there is the substantial body of pieces transmitted in very low clefs (from Du Fay to Lassus). In all these cases, notation at a higher pitch would have been possible; it is therefore reasonable to suppose that these low clefs were a signal to performers to sing as low in their ranges as they could comfortably manage. (Ockeghem's five-voice motet *Intemerata Dei mater* is a useful test case because of its many recordings: the difference of pitch-standard between the lowest and highest is at least a fourth.)

The question of pitch leads naturally to the issue of tuning (also called temperament).[2] Of all performance-practice-related issues it is the subtlest and the least discussed, although there are signs this is changing, not least due to the growing interest in tuning within other repertories (e.g. New Music). The near-stranglehold of equal temperament on modern-day performance practice has long since been broken in Baroque performance, which sports a wide variety of tuning systems. Around 1500 the centuries-old Pythagorean tuning system (which privileges acoustically pure fifths) was gradually superseded by mean-tone tuning, which compromises the purity of fifths in favour of more consistently tuned major thirds. Few vocal ensembles explicitly address the issue, preferring a pragmatic approach. For instrumentalists the issue poses itself more pressingly: the frets of viols and lutes can be adjusted, and each individual fret can be split onto two different positions, which allows for any number of enharmonic tunings. Most soloists and instrumental ensembles adapt their tuning systems to the repertory or even the individual piece, depending on chromatic peculiarities.

Related to intonation (but to some extent separate from it) are the investigations of octave division, mentioned in Chapter 4. Both come together in the manufacture of keyboard instruments, which accommodated split black keys, alternative B#/C and E#/F, and equal divisions of the octave beyond the semitone.

Perhaps the best way to become attuned to the potential of tuning is to listen to performances of solo lute and organ repertories, which most clearly focus the ear on fine intervallic distinctions. The oldest functioning organ, one of a pair in the Basilica of San Petronio in Bologna, was constructed *c.*1475 and includes most of its original stops (and like its younger sister, built in 1596, it is tuned to mean-tone temperament). Although solo instrumental performance is beyond the scope of this chapter, one of the most evocative aspects of historically informed interpretation is the opportunity to hear period instruments capable of playing polyphony – organs, stringed keyboard, and lutes – in this repertory.

Tempo and modern performance practice

The question of tempo was considered from a notational standpoint in Chapter 6, but a few remarks are in order on their practical implications. First and foremost, mensuration signs, like most of the symbols pertaining to pitch, indicate relative values only, not absolute ones. This explains the significant variation in tempo choices in performance. It has been claimed that the tempos adopted for the majority of modern performances of medieval and Renaissance music are much too fast,[3] but in truth there is still less certainty than usual on this point. Concerning relative tempos there are firmer footholds, perhaps the firmest of which is the intended relationship of O to ¢: for all the differing views as to its interpretation and practical application, then as now, the evidence that the semibreve under ¢ should be 'somewhat faster' than (but *not* twice as fast as) the semibreve under O is overwhelming. But the practice of modern ensembles is not always consistent with the available evidence. Even more questionable is the widespread habit of adopting a markedly slower beat in the Gloria of the Mass at the phrase 'qui tollis peccata mundi' (which is usually preceded by a sectional close) and reverting to a faster tempo at the words 'quoniam tu solus sanctus'. This is especially prevalent in performances of Mass cycles after 1520, even when the mensuration (¢) remains unchanged. The practice is of long standing: it can be traced through recordings at least to the early twentieth century and is in all likelihood earlier still, but it cannot be taken for granted that changes of mood in the text were overtly 'illustrated' in this way at the time. The same modern performances often take a much slower tempo for the Agnus dei even though (again) the same mensuration is commonly used at the start of all five sections. This is not to claim that local inflections of a basic tempo never happened, and still less to advocate that they are 'inauthentic', but to point out that the notation simply does not support such stark contrasts in tempo. These examples differ from other categories of performance practice discussed so far, in that concrete information contained in the notation is widely disregarded in modern performance for reasons of unspoken aesthetic choice – a situation more prevalent than performers (and even some scholars) may care to admit. In making this observation, I don't presume to sit in judgement; I have been at pains to show how personal preference (mine included) influences our choices and how we interpret the available evidence. To conclude on the subject of tempo, I offer two contrasting quotations from composers of different periods: 'I myself have never believed that my blood and a mechanical instrument go well together' (Johannes Brahms, on the subject of metronome markings);[4] and yet, 'there can be no doubt, that the perfection of playing consists principally in understanding the tempi' (Girolamo Frescobaldi in the preface to his *First Book of Toccatas* (1615)). There is much to be gained by holding these two potentially contradictory ideas in mind simultaneously.

Scoring and texting, voices and instruments: a historical view

But perhaps the most audible cause of variation in performances of Renaissance music is that the overwhelming majority of sources do not specify the forces involved: as explained in Chapter 5, voice-names denote function rather than voice-type (exceptions to this rule, such as those specifying boys' voices, are few and far between); by extension, they don't indicate whether instrumental or vocal performance is intended. Furthermore, and for some time after the advent of print, texting varies greatly between sources. In chanson manuscripts and printed collections, it is common for the full text to appear in just one voice (usually the discantus) and only fragmentarily or with just the first few words (called an 'incipit') in the others. But some sources of secular music (most famously the very first polyphonic print, Petrucci's *Odhecaton*) give no words at all beyond an incipit, which merely functions as a label. Texting is generally fuller in sources of sacred music, though a fragmentary approach in at least some of the voices is noticeable there also.

The issue of texting is relevant because, at first blush, the presence of texts might seem to indicate vocal performance, and its absence the use of instruments. For much of the twentieth century this assumption was carried over into performance practice. Instrumental participation in polyphony was widely regarded as self-evident – first in secular music, and then, albeit more gradually, in sacred music. The fact that the lower voices carried the least text suggested an analogy with the instrumental 'accompaniment' in later music of a text-carrying top voice. This view was supported by external evidence: the depictions of music making in medieval iconography, notably late medieval altarpieces showing varied groups of instruments being played together, and the growing field of research into medieval instruments. But it was also suggested by the many leaps and large intervals of contratenor lines, which were considered unidiomatic for singers and contrasted sharply with the syllabic and stepwise movement of the discantus and tenor. (Incidentally, instruments could be a stable point of reference at a time when pitching and tuning in vocal ensembles was unreliable.) Further support for instrumental participation came from the early fifteenth-century song repertory, a common feature of which was the absence of text for the first few bars, even in the top voice (as in Example 6.2, p. 89 above). The conclusion seemed obvious that these textless 'introductions' were inherently instrumental. All of which led scholars and performers to propose veritable 'orchestrations' of Renaissance polyphony, scored for voices and instruments drawn from all the available families, including percussion. Not coincidentally, Anton Webern's quasi-serial orchestral arrangements of the six-voice ricercar from Bach's *Musical Offering* are exactly contemporary with the onset of the 'voices and instruments' hypothesis. (Webern himself had transcribed a volume of the *Choralis Constantinus* for his PhD and was a close student of the 'Art of the Netherlanders'.)

The co-existence of voices and instruments is ubiquitous in most recordings of sacred and secular polyphony made between 1930 and 1975; towards the end of this period, however, the use of instruments became more flexible and discriminating, especially in secular music, where there tended to be fewer performers on individual lines. During the late 1970s, a considerable body of evidence was adduced in favour of a cappella performance of polyphony, both sacred and secular.[5] Because much of this research was led by scholars of the English-speaking world, a number of whom were themselves performers, all-vocal performance became especially popular among English groups of the following decades;

in continental Europe the trend was not quite so pronounced, but still perceptible to the extent that ensembles that had previously mixed voices and instruments began to experiment with all-vocal performance (especially for sacred polyphony), beginning with the Early Music Consort of London's *The Art of the Netherlands* (1976). This wave of research and performance coincided with the growing influence of the 'early music movement' and the fashion for its more problematic corollary, 'authentic performance', which soon extended to the late Baroque, Classical, and Romantic periods. Although many of the claims surrounding 'authenticity' are now discredited, the trends in performance practice and the interest in Renaissance polyphony it helped launch persist. Many of the ensembles that sprang up in those years are still active today.

Much of the documentary evidence supporting the 'a cappella heresy' (as it was known by some of its detractors) was not new; some of it had been published decades earlier but largely ignored because its conclusions were unfashionable;[6] other existing evidence was subject to fresh scrutiny. It was noticed, for example, that many iconographical representations of the earlier Renaissance showing singers and players (notably of organs) in the same picture implied a degree of separateness between them, which cast doubt on the assumption that they were necessarily used together; this re-reading was supported by evidence that in some church institutions the use of instruments, even the organ, was banned (as at Cambrai Cathedral in Du Fay's lifetime).[7] The same scholars pointed to the wealth of illustrations of singers in clerical garb gathered around a lectern in groups of no more than a dozen (and often less) with not an instrument in sight. More fundamentally, the aim of much of that iconography was not factually accurate representation but was driven by other considerations (not excluding, for example, demonstrating the skill of the artist). Thus, many Renaissance depictions of a variety of instruments playing together were intended to glorify the patron who had so many musicians on his payroll. Sometimes, the singers and the instrumentalists appearing in the same picture plane were depicted as quite distinct. I do not cite these examples to support the 'a cappella' side of the argument, since there is also firm evidence in the other direction (not least the use of the *bajón* or dulcian to support the bass in vocal ensembles), but rather to show how the same documents can be read in support of very different conclusions. But it doesn't follow from this observation that 'anything goes': as scholars insisted at the time and have ever since, interpreting artefacts from another culture (including our own historical past) requires that we take account of what can be known about the circumstances of their production. Otherwise we are liable to draw incorrect conclusions, especially given the tendency for interpretations to be coloured by aesthetic preferences and habits of thought.

It is good to keep this conclusion in mind when considering how different performance options reflect underlying assumptions and interpretations about the music. In the chanson repertory, for example, an approach combining voices and instruments might take the top line vocally and give the lower voices to instruments; this works particularly well where the lower voices are in the same range and together support the top line. Another option is a sung discantus–tenor pair with an instrumental contratenor (or contratenors): this draws attention to the relationship of the sung voices as the basis of the contrapuntal framework and points out the functional distinction between the stepwise tenor and the angular contratenor. As we have seen, this distinction explains why instruments were often used on contratenor lines before the 'a capella heresy' took hold. One of the new movement's innovations was to challenge the assumption that such lines are vocally unidiomatic (which, incidentally, might reasonably be claimed of Bach's vocal writing); they are readily performable by agile singers, either texted or vocalized on a neutral vowel (as are the 'instrumental introductions' of early fifteenth-century songs, mentioned earlier), as heard on recordings by the Gothic Voices and the Orlando Consort.[8] For those favouring an all-vocal approach, untexted vocalization resolves a further difficulty: whereas the word underlay of the discantus is usually straightforward, getting the text to fit the contratenor and sometimes even the tenor in three-voice songs can pose real difficulties. As a result of these changing perspectives, all-vocal performance of both texted and untexted parts became the new orthodoxy in the song repertory from 1980 onwards. It is no accident that assumptions about idiomatic vocal writing had undergone similar scrutiny from other quarters in the years leading up to the 'a cappella heresy', not least contemporary music and non-Western music: there is a direct parallel a generation earlier, with the coincidence of Webern's orchestration of Bach and the heyday of the 'voices-and-instruments' approach to polyphony. Quite simply, all-vocal performance was a notion whose time had come, and the reconsideration of the evidence was as much a reflection of changing aesthetic priorities as an end in itself.[9]

The impact of the 'a cappella hypothesis' on performances of sacred polyphony was, if anything, still more far-reaching and enduring than for secular music. Where previously doubling the cantus firmus by an organ or sackbut was not seen as controversial, to this day many ensembles are reluctant to combine voices and instruments in the same piece unless explicitly supported by documentary evidence. Variation between ensembles is more likely to hinge on the matter of personnel: whether female voices or male falsettists are used on the top lines (or, more rarely, child trebles), or how many voices are used on each part. At the height of the fixation on 'authenticity', the use of female sopranos was excused on the grounds that they were more reliable than child trebles; but, as the obsession with reproducing the performance conditions expected by the composer waned, the participation of female sopranos was viewed less apologetically. Considerable research has been undertaken on the membership of polyphonic ensembles, but most of it can give only a general indication. That a given chapel choir had an average of fifteen singers on the payroll, for example, does not necessarily mean that they would all have sung at the same time. (Echoing the point made earlier, the sole purpose of these payrolls was to record those present so that they were paid.) In the rare cases where concrete examples exist, modern ensembles can be reluctant to act on them: the ordinances of Charles the Bold (1469) concerning the membership of his chapel specified six falsettists against seven singers for all the other parts combined in four-voice polyphony.[10] Despite this clear evidence on behalf of one of the great connoisseurs of the time, this distribution has hardly ever been tried out by modern-day ensembles, and never in a recording (possibly for economic reasons, and the difficulty in assembling so many countertenors). In any case, the notion of a single 'correct' solution does not stand up to scrutiny, for one simple reason. Compositions circulated the length and breadth of Europe, and it is in a sense striking how consistent the copies of an individual piece can be across such a wide geographical span; on the other hand, performance conditions were known to be extremely diverse, even between neighbouring institutions. Composers would not have expected that those under which a given piece was first performed would be replicated hundreds of miles away. Bearing this in mind, the aims of modern performers can be rethought, privileging not so much the performance conditions a given composer envisaged (which are unknowable in most cases) as ones that he would have recognized.

Again, this is not to suggest that all performance options are equally valid from a historical perspective; some are more plausible than others. But the challenge posed by the 'a cappella hypothesis' stimulated ensembles that used voices and instruments (and instrumental ensembles more generally) to refine their approach. Where instruments had been deployed with a view to maximum effects and contrasts of colour, research into instrumental consorts resulted in a more selective approach to instrumental combinations, and a greater sensitivity to musical syntax: where once it was common to hear lines doubled at the octave or even placed in the wrong octave, this now happens more rarely. Extreme variety of instrumental combinations (known informally as the 'kitchen-sink' approach by *its* detractors) was replaced by groupings into families and the sort of matched pairings described in previous chapters. This more discriminating approach was supported by independent evidence (mentioned earlier) for the performance of motets by wind bands, even during Mass. As a result, the standard of performance on early instruments improved significantly throughout the 1980s and 1990s, and is now at least on a par with that of vocal ensembles. This is true of more intimate chamber ensembles as well as the polychoral repertoire of the later Renaissance, in which voices and instruments are integrated on a spectacular scale.

'The past is a foreign country': strategies of de-familiarization

A central problem in the reading of history (or, more accurately, the telling of it) is the tension between 'nearness' and 'distance': whether the description of history should make it seem nearer to our own lived experience or, on the contrary, unfamiliar and alien. It's a dilemma with which historians have long wrestled. Although there is not the space to summarize the question here, I mention it because it directly underpins the 'telling' (i.e. the performance) of any music of the historical past – not just in philosophical but in strictly practical terms. Before combining voices and instruments became an orthodoxy in the early twentieth century, a cappella performance appears to have been standard, albeit on a much larger scale, in line with the fashion for large choruses in Handel and Bach and the vogue of semi-professional choral societies in England and Germany. When it was first proposed, the 'voices and instruments' set-up was therefore a novelty, as was the 'a cappella hypothesis' when its turn came. With novelty came an impression of exoticism and unfamiliarity, echoing the modernist sense that the telling of history should emphasize its distance from us. (As the writer L. P. Hartley famously expressed it in his novel *The Go-Between*, 'the past is a foreign country; they do things differently there'.) Two seemingly unrelated approaches illustrate this common impulse: the practice of 'liturgical reconstruction', in which sacred music is presented as part of the liturgical action for which it was designed, including plainchant in Catholic ritual or the interventions of the congregation in Reformation worship; and alternative methods of vocal production, which are especially de-familiarizing because they focus on the most potently evocative instrument of all.

Vocal production and the 'oriental hypothesis'

The cultivation of alternative approaches to vocal production constitutes a narrow but influential trend within medieval and Renaissance performance. Frequently it appears alongside a set of associated practices, including microtonal inflections and portamento, improvisations in free or loosely structured time (often over a drone), and the use of percussion. This 'oriental hypothesis' (as it has sometimes been called) draws on medieval descriptions of ornamentation in the execution of plainchant and the undoubted influence of Arab and Byzantine cultures in Europe, which reached its highpoint during the period of the early Crusades. Although largely speculative, it is founded on well-documented monophonic traditions past and present, not least the Jewish and Near Eastern styles of cantillation that gave rise to the trend's occasional nickname. Collectively, these trends are more widely applied in music of the medieval period, when contacts between East and West were at their most dynamic, but their influence on fifteenth-century repertories is somewhat attenuated. The most striking of these features is undoubtedly the re-imagining of vocal timbre, for which direct parallels survive up to the present day, from the singing style of monks from the Mediterranean islands of Corsica and Sardinia to the rural traditions of central Europe, notably Bulgaria and Romania. (Given these European associations, the 'oriental' label is misleading at best and at worst lazy shorthand for exoticism in general.) Not coincidentally, extemporized polyphony is a shared feature of these European traditions. Such models are audible to a greater or lesser extent in the work of ensembles from the 1960s onwards, notably Musica Reservata, the Studio der Frühen Musik, and Ensemble Organum, all characterized by a full-throated delivery, augmented in the case of Organum by an overtly nasal quality. Though its singers were audibly trained in the modern English choral tradition, the early recordings of the all-vocal consort Gothic Voices feature a hyper-focused sound achieved through a combination of precise tuning and identically formed vowels. The intended effect is the diametrical opposite of Organum's (microtonal ornamentation is notably absent, for example) but the particular concern with vocal production is very similar; both are audibly different from the sound of classically trained singers. This is defamiliarization at its most radical. Undoubtedly also it is speculative, but while hard documentation from the period is lacking, there is some intriguing, albeit indirect, iconographical evidence. Medieval representations of singers, such as those in the margins of the early fifteenth-century Codex Chantilly or the grand books of hours of John, Duke of Berry (d.1416), sometimes give them strained expressions, even grimaces. In some cases the artist's intention may have been playful caricature, but this is clearly not the case with the angel-musicians in the van Eyck brothers' Ghent altarpiece (1432), several of whose faces are visibly strained.[11] Although we cannot know what contemporary ideals of vocal sound might have been (the descriptions of medieval and Renaissance writers are frustratingly imprecise), these representations hint at something far removed from modern-day preferences and techniques. Another audible strategy of defamiliarization is that of 'period pronunciation': until relatively recently, Latin was typically pronounced not in the 'Italianate' manner widely heard today but following the pronunciation of the local language (a tendency still discernible with modern German vocal ensembles.) In some cases the effect is startlingly disorienting, especially when the text is very familiar, like that of the Mass: recordings of fifteenth-century English polyphony by the Binchois Consort and the Orlando Consort are a case in point. Like the experiments in vocal production just described, they express the essential 'otherness' of Renaissance culture.

Given that vocal production and pronunciation so radically affect the sounding result, it is worth drawing attention to another consideration that has had little impact on recorded performance so far despite overwhelming pictorial evidence. A fundamental component of the modern sound of Renaissance polyphony is a reverberant acoustic, the result of concert and liturgical performances taking place mostly in the nave or the crossing of churches (at least partly for financial reasons). This results in an atmospheric wash, in which contrapuntal detail is easily downplayed in favour of a homogeneous ensemble and sonority. But contemporary representations of polyphonic performances (especially in the earlier Renaissance) often situate them in the far more intimate space of side-chapels or the private chapels of princely residences, sometimes hung with tapestries – conditions that would strongly mitigate the tendency to reverberation and radically affect the feeling of ensemble. This is not to claim that a broad acoustic is 'historically inaccurate' in all circumstances, but to point out that its strong association today with a 'churchy' sound is unlikely to have held such sway at the time. (Some of the spaces in use today cause recording engineers considerable problems because of the conflicting priorities of a balanced, naturalistic overall sound and the capture of contrapuntal details.) This simple example shows how far unspoken biases and habits colour our expectations, however much we might think or even wish it otherwise.

Liturgical reconstruction: programming and the future of Renaissance music

The historical search to recreate the 'original' performance conditions of music began with the details of the music but soon extended to the circumstances of the performance itself. During the Renaissance, sacred music formed part of a liturgical action, a ritual event within which it fulfilled what we today would call an aesthetic function. Of course, a ritual is itself a performance, so the music is doubly aestheticized, a performance framed within another. Most recordings made before 1980 (and since) present the sections of Mass Ordinary settings without a break. But in the actual liturgy, a considerable time elapses between the Gloria and the Credo, and the Sanctus is immediately preceded by the very lengthy plainchant preface. It is a very different dynamic from the unbroken five-movement cycle, whose components were further separated by the singing of the Propers in chant or polyphony, of motets or other paraliturgical music, and even chansons, all of which are documented in contemporary reports. Liturgical reconstruction presents polyphony in something more nearly reflecting its original context, including the interventions of the celebrants and the participation of the congregation in Protestant services. Inevitably it entails a degree of compromise (since actual Masses could last for hours), but its aesthetic effect clearly aligns it with other strategies of defamiliarization: the unfamiliar context in which the music is presented actively resists the 'symphonic' reading of the Mass cycle that consecutive performance encourages in modern listeners.

Although staged or semi-staged recreations of the Mass liturgy are very rare, the format is almost perfectly suited to recording, which can evoke the atmosphere of an occasion on which specific pieces are known to have been performed (or can plausibly be hypothesized), leaving visual details to the listener's imagination.[12] A similar approach can serve for secular occasions as well, though this happens more rarely. One notable exception is the repertory of Florentine *intermedii* composed as staged intervals between theatrical entertainments at the Medici court of Florence. A full replication of the elaborate costumes and stage machinery would be prohibitively expensive today, but the listener's imagination can be stimulated with the help of contemporary reports and the designers' very detailed surviving drawings.

The trend has left its mark on programming and recording: even without invoking liturgical reconstruction, ensembles sometimes present a pair of Ordinary and Propers cycles that can plausibly be performed alongside each other, for instance. The interleaving of Mass Ordinary sections with other music makes the wider point that recordings are no longer invariably treated as the sonic analogue of a printed publication. There is little evidence that motet or madrigals prints were ever intended to be sung or played through consecutively. (On the other hand, a similar cautionary note may be in order concerning the tendency to treat recordings as analogues of the concert programme – an assumption, whose implicit basis is currently undermined by the prevalence of streaming services, which calls into question the concept of the discrete recording project or album.) A growing awareness of the fluidity of local performance practices has fostered greater sensitivity to the possible ways of performing and recording sacred music. To take just one example, it is possible to hear Palestrina's music re-imagined not as he might have heard it but a few decades later, alongside organ toccatas by Frescobaldi or songs by Carissimi, as part of a Christmas Mass in Rome;[13] or again, differently ornamented renderings of Allegri's *Miserere*, which boasts a nearly unbroken history of performance at the Sistine Chapel from his own time to the present day.[14] (Such trans-historical approaches are now an occasional feature of recordings of the common-practice repertory.) If the term 'authenticity' is now better avoided, one can instead speak of 'authenticities'. The age of streaming and online self-publication brings with it re-imaginings and re-mixes of music of every period, including Renaissance polyphony. The re-purposing of previously composed music has thus come full circle, being more prevalent today than at any time since its high-water mark, the period covered in this book. Then as now, these re-imaginings combine and confront different tastes and trends, not all of them conforming to received notions of fifteenth- and sixteenth-century music; but, as each generation reinterprets the past in its own image, it is heartening that Renaissance polyphony remains in the mix.

Notes

1 Introducing Renaissance polyphony

1. Reese, *Music in the Renaissance*; Brown and Stein, *Music in the Renaissance*; Atlas, *Renaissance Music*; Perkins, *Music in the Age of the Renaissance*; Freedman, *Music in the Renaissance*; Strohm, *The Rise of European Music*; Vendrix, *La Musique à la Renaissance*; *European Music*, ed. Haar; and Lütteken, *Music of the Renaissance*.
2. Vendrix, 'L'Impossible Renaissance'.
3. e.g. Perkins, *Music in the Age of the Renaissance*, 34–6.
4. For a musically grounded counterargument, Lütteken, *Music of the Renaissance*, 6–9.
5. *Johannes Tinctoris, Complete Theoretical Works*, http://earlymusictheory.org/Tinctoris/#; (accessed May 2019).
6. e.g. Atlas, *Renaissance Music*, 3–4. Le Franc's and Tinctoris' statements are explicitly conflated in Brown and Stein, *Music in the Renaissance*, 7–8. For a critique of both (and of their modern reception), Wegman, 'New Music' and Wegman, 'Johannes Tinctoris'.
7. Wegman, 'Petrus de Domarto'.
8. Brothers, 'Vestiges of the Isorhythmic Tradition'.

2 Making polyphony: sources and practice

1. First proposed in Small, *Musicking*.
2. Smith, *The Performance*, 4–19.
3. Bent, Margaret, 'Polyphonic Sources, *c*.1400–1450' and Schmidt-Beste, Thomas, 'Polyphonic sources, *c*.1450–1500', both in *Cambridge History of Fifteenth-Century Music*, ed. Busse Berger and Rodin, 617–39 and 640–62; see also the entries under 'Sources' in *Revised New Grove* [Grove Music Online: www.oxfordmusiconline.com/grovemusic]; Schmidt-Beste and Leitmeir, *The Production and Reading of Music Sources*; van Orden, *Music, Authorship*; and Bernstein, *Print Culture*.
4. *Treasury*, ed. Kellman.
5. Williamson, *Eton Choirbook*, 22.
6. Alden, *Songs*.
7. Boorman, *Ottaviano Petrucci*.
8. Bernstein, 'Financial Arrangements' and Bernstein, 'Publish or Perish?'.
9. Wistreich, 'Singing and Sociability'; Wegman, 'From Maker to Composer', 409–13.

10. On what follows, Canguilhem, *L'Improvisation polyphonique*. See also Busse Berger, Anna Maria, 'Oral composition in fifteenth-century music' and Canguilhem, Philippe, 'Improvisation as Concept and Musical Practice in the Fifteenth Century', both in *Cambridge History of Fifteenth-Century Music*, 139–48 and 149–63.
11. On plainchant, see Hiley, *Gregorian Chant*.
12. Canguilhem, 'Singing upon the Book'.
13. Edwards, Warwick, 'Agricola's Songs Without Words – the Sources and the Performing Traditions', in *Alexander Agricola*, ed. Schwindt, 83–121 (at 99–105).
14. Schubert, Peter, 'Counterpoint Pedagogy in the Renaissance', in *Cambridge History of Western Music Theory*, ed. Christensen, 503–33.
15. A rare recorded instance is *Alessandro Striggio: Mass for 40 and 60 Voices*, Le Concert Spirituel dir. Hervé Niquet, Glossa, 921623, El Escorial, 2012, which includes motets by Corteccia (c.1502–71) echoing techniques of polyphonic extemporization. See also Canguilhem, 'Towards a Stylistic History', 64–8.

3 Makers of polyphony

1. Prins, Jacomien, 'Music and Science', in *Cambridge History of Sixteenth-Century Music*, ed. Fenlon and Wistreich, 441–73, and Herlinger, Jan, 'Medieval canonics', in *Cambridge History of Western Music Theory*, ed. Christensen, 168–92; and Vendrix, *La Musique à la Renaissance*, passim.
2. Bower, Calvin M., 'The Transmission of Ancient Music Theory into the Middle Ages', in *Cambridge History of Western Music Theory*, 136–67.
3. Haar, 'The Courtier'.
4. Tomlinson, *Music and Renaissance Magic*; also Voss, Angela, 'Music and magic', in *Cambridge History of Sixteenth-Century Music*, 474–503.
5. On hostile attitudes towards polyphony, Wegman, *The Crisis*.
6. This is the sixth of the 'effects' of music detailed in his *Compendium of Music's Effects*, c.1475.
7. On singers' formative years, *Music Education*, ed. Murray, Weiss, and Cyrus, and *Young Choristers*, ed. Boynton and Rice.
8. Starr, Pamela, 'The beneficial system and fifteenth-century polyphony', in *Cambridge History of Fifteenth-Century Music*, ed. Busse Berger and Rodin, 463–75.
9. Kirkman, Andrew, 'Johannes Sohier *dit* Fede and Saint-Omer: A Story of Pragmatic Sanctions', in *Essays on Renaissance Music*, ed. Fitch and Kiel, 68–79.
10. Magro, 'Premièrement'.
11. Higgins, 'Parisian Nobles'.
12. Sherr, Richard, 'The Papal Chapel in the Fifteenth Century', in *Cambridge History of Fifteenth-Century Music*, 446–62; Dean, 'Listening to Sacred Polyphony'.
13. Blackburn, 'The Virgin in the Sun'.

14. Planchart, *Guillaume Du Fay*, 302–14 and 415–19; Nosow, 'Song and the Art of Dying', 542–6.
15. Wegman, 'From Maker to Composer', 426–8.
16. Wegman, 'From Maker to Composer', 461–9.
17. Wegman, 'From Maker to Composer', 435.
18. Polk, Keith, 'Instrumental Music in the Fifteenth Century', in *Cambridge History of Fifteenth-Century Music*, 745–54; also Coelho and Polk, *Instrumentalists*, and the essays in *Instruments and their Music*, ed. McGee.
19. Bowles, 'Haut and Bas'.
20. Gentile Bellini, *Procession on the Piazza San Marco* (1496).
21. Coelho and Polk, *Instrumentalists*, 149–53.
22. Canguilhem, 'Improvisation as Concept', in *The Cambridge History of Fifteenth-Century Music* 150–51.
23. Blackburn, Bonnie J., 'Professional Women Singers in the Fifteenth Century: A Tale of Two Annas', in *Cambridge History of Fifteenth-Century Music*, 476–85.
24. Wegman, 'From Maker to Composer', 414–15.
25. On Aleotti, Bowers, Jane, 'The Emergence of Women Composers in Italy, 1566–1700', in *Women Making Music*, ed. Bowers and Tick, 116–67, and Stras, *Women and Music*, passim.; and on music in convents (but with emphasis on the seventeenth century), Monson, *Disembodied Voices* and Kendrick, *Celestial Sirens*.
26. Newcomb, Anthony, 'Courtesans, Muses, or Musicians? Professional Women Musicians in Sixteenth-Century Italy', in *Women Making Music*, ed. Bowers and Tick, 90–115; Newcomb, *The Madrigal at Ferrara*; and, most recently, Stras, *Women and Music*.

4 Pitch: an overview

1. The view articulated in the following sections draws on Part 1 of Mengozzi, *Renaissance Reform*. Other accounts (cited here and in the endnotes to Chapter 3) may differ in their emphasis on certain points.
2. Busse Berger, *Medieval Music and the Art of Memory*.
3. Hiley, *Gregorian Chant*, 43–4.
4. For a useful summary see Crook, *Lasso's Imitation Magnificats*, 85–146.
5. For a practical demonstration, Smith, *Performance*, 28–47.
6. Mengozzi, *Renaissance Reform*, 82.
7. Collins Judd, Cristle, 'Renaissance Modal Theory: Theoretical, Compositional, and Editorial Perspectives', in *Cambridge History of Western Music Theory*, ed. Christensen, 364–406.
8. Smith, *Performance*, 95–7.
9. On Du Fay's authorship of chant, Haggh, 'The Celebration' (also Planchart, *Guillaume Du Fay*, 542–9); and on his being consulted about chant, Planchart, *Guillaume Du Fay*, 251–4.
10. The classic study is Berger, *Musica ficta*.

11. Berger, *Musica ficta*, 2–55.
12. Mengozzi, *Renaissance Reform*, 95–6.
13. Rasch, Rudolf, 'Tuning and Temperament', in *Cambridge History of Western Music Theory*, 193–222.
14. On the project to reconstruct such an instrument (with 31 keys per octave!), www.projektstudio31.com/ (accessed May 2019).
15. Schubert, 'Hidden Forms'.

5 Voice-names, ranges, and functions

1. Powers, 'Tonal Types' and 'Is Mode Real?'.
2. Sparks, 'Problems of Authenticity'.

6 Mensural notation, duration, and metre

1. Busse Berger, *Mensuration and Proportion*, and (most recently) DeFord, *Tactus, Mensuration*.
2. Zazulia, Emily, 'The Transformative Impulse', in *Cambrige History of Fifteenth-Century Music*, ed. Busse Berger and Rodin, 587–601.

7 Genre, texts, form

1. Lütteken, Laurenz, 'The Work Concept', in *Cambridge History of Fifteenth-Century Music*, ed. Busse Berger and Rodin, 55–68, and the bibliography cited there; and, in addition, the subsequent English translation of Lütteken, *Music of the Renaissance*.
2. This view largely informs Goehr, *The Imaginary Museum*, and Bürger, *Theory of the Avant-Garde*; from the Avant-Garde perspective advocated by Bürger, it is only in a later period that '[t]he artist ... develops a consciousness of the uniqueness of his activity' (Bürger, 47).
3. Kirkman, *The Cultural Life*, 26–8.
4. Vander Straeten, *La Musique*, vi, 87.
5. Edwards, 'Agricola's Songs' (at 118–19).
6. On contrafacta, Oettinger, *Music as Propaganda*, 89–136, and Freedman, *The Chansons of Orlando di Lasso*.
7. Edwards, 'Understanding Fifteenth-Century Chansonniers' (at 191–205).
8. For a range of views, the essays in *The Motet around 1500*, ed. Schmidt-Beste.
9. In the 'Dichiaratione' appended to the *Scherzi musicali* (1607).
10. See the section devoted to Humanism in *Cambridge History of Fifteenth-Century Music*; also Palisca, *Humanism*.
11. Edwards, Warwick, 'Text Treatment in Motets around 1500', in *The Motet around 1500*, 113–38.
12. Bloxam, M. Jennifer, 'Obrecht as Exegete', in *Hearing the Motet*, ed. Pesce, 169–92.

8 'Cantus magnus': music for the Mass

1. Kirkman, Andrew, 'Structure and Meaning in the Mass: the *Ordinarium Missae* and beyond', in *Motetti Missales Between Devotion and Liturgy*, ed. Pavanello and Filippi, 19–36.
2. Kirkman, *The Cultural Life* and 'The Polyphonic Mass in the Fifteenth Century', in *Cambridge History of Fifteenth-Century Music*, ed. Busse Berger and Rodin, 665–99.
3. Fallows, *Dufay*, 199–207; Planchart, *Guillaume Du Fay*, 594–603.
4. Wright, *The Maze*, 175–7; also Fallows, 'The Last Agnus dei'.
5. Fallows, 'The Last Agnus dei'.
6. On the Propers in general, the essays in *Heinrich Isaac*, ed. Burn and Gasch.
7. Planchart, *Guillaume Du Fay*, 501–35.
8. Wagstaff, 'Music for the Dead'.
9. Rees, *The Requiem of Tomás Luis de Victoria*.
10. Milsom, 'Sense and Sound'.

9 'Cantus mediocris': the motet

1. Cumming, *The Motet*; *Hearing the Motet*, ed. Pesce; and the essays in *The Motet around 1500*, ed. Schmidt-Beste and in *Mapping the Motet*, ed. Rodríguez-García and Filippi.
2. Nosow, *Ritual Meanings*.
3. See the essays in *Motet Cycles between Devotion and Liturgy*, ed. Pavanello and Filippi.
4. Edwards, 'Alexander Agricola and Intuitive Syllable Deployment' (at 409).
5. *The Medici Codex*, ed. Lowinsky; Rifkin, 'The Creation of the Medici Codex'; Shephard, 'Constructing Identities'.

10 'Cantus parvus': secular music

1. Fallows, *A Catalogue*.
2. Page, *Discarding Images*, 163–9.
3. On this piece and its context, Gilbert, Adam Knight, 'Heinrich Isaac, Ludwig Senfl, and a Fugal Hexachord', in *Canons*, ed. Schiltz and Blackburn, 111–23.
4. On the composer, Cœurdevey, *Roland de Lassus*; also *Orlandus Lassus*, ed. Bossuyt, Schreurs, and Wouters; and the seminal work, Holmes, *The Polyphonic Motets*.
5. On the composer, *Clément Janequin*, ed. Halévy, His, and Vignes.
6. Gómez, 'The Ensalada', and Preciado, 'La Cancion'.
7. Bryan, 'Extended Play', esp. 139–41.
8. Planchart, 'Cipriano de Rore's *Da le belle contrade*' and McClary, *Modal subjectivities*, 104–13; on Cipriano, the essays in *Cipriano de Rore*, ed. Owens and

Schiltz, and in *Journal of the Alamire Foundation*, 9/2 (2017) and 10/1 (2018); and on different approaches to the madrigal, Einstein, *The Italian Madrigal*; Newcomb, *The Madrigal at Ferrara*; and McClary, *Modal Subjectivities*.

9. On sexual allusion and imagery in the madrigal, Macy, 'Speaking of Sex'.

11 Scoring, texture, scale

1. Kreitner, 'Very Low Voices'; Meconi, 'The Range of Mourning'; also Gallagher, *Johannes Regis*, 173–98.
2. Fitch, *Johannes Ockeghem*, 140–58.
3. See Milsom, John, 'Making a Motet: Josquin's *Ave Maria ... Virgo serena*', and Cumming, Julie and Schubert, Peter, 'The Origins of Pervasive Imitation', both in *Cambridge History of Fifteenth-Century Music*, ed. Busse Berger and Rodin, 183–99 and 200–28, and the bibliography cited there.
4. Fallows, David, 'The Most Popular Songs of the Fifteenth Century', in *Cambridge History of Fifteenth-Century Music*, 787–801 (at 792–8).
5. On this passage, see Luko, 'Tinctoris', whose translation I have adapted; see also Cumming, 'From Variety to Repetition', for a different analysis of *varietas* and imitation in this period.
6. Milsom, 'Making a Motet' (at 193).
7. Milsom, John, 'Surface, Structure and "Style" in *Absalon fili mi*', in *Essays on Renaissance Music*, ed. Fitch and Kiel, 261–71.
8. On musical space and architecture, see Howard, Deborah, 'Architecture and Music in Fifteenth-Century Italy', in *Cambridge History of the Fifteenth Century*, and Howard and Moretti, *Sound and Space*, 17–29, and the bibliographies cited there.
9. Moroney, 'Alessandro Striggio'.
10. Stevens, 'A Song'.

12 Understanding musical borrowing

1. Rees, 'Guerrero' (at 47).
2. This reading stems from Sparks, *Cantus Firmus*.
3. Fallows, *Dufay*, 207–14; Planchart, *Guillaume Du Fay*, 603–22.
4. Meconi, *Pierre de La Rue*, 52 and 131 (and 99–133, *passim*.).
5. Kirkman, *The Cultural Life*, 79.
6. Bloxam, M. Jennifer, 'A Cultural Context for the Chanson Mass', in *Early Musical Borrowing*, ed. Meconi, 7–35, and Rothenberg, David J., 'Marian Devotion in the Fifteenth Century', in *Cambridge History of Fifteenth-Century Music*, ed. Busse Berger and Rodin, 528–44, and the bibliography cited there.
7. Rothenberg, *Flower of Paradise*, 163–78.
8. Robertson, 'The Man with the Pale Face'.

9. Warmington, Flynn, 'The Ceremony of the Armed Man', in *Antoine Busnoys*, ed. Higgins, 88–130; Wright, *The Maze*, 159–205, 282–8, and 328 n. 16; Kirkman, *The Cultural Life*, 98–134.
10. Crook, 'The Sacred and Secular'; Owens, 'Lasso's Ritual Reading'.
11. Rodin, *Josquin's Rome, passim*.
12. I thank Prof. Blackburn for permission to cite this document in advance of the publication of its details.
13. Rodin, Jesse, 'The *L'Homme armé* tradition', in *The Cambridge History of Fifteenth-Century Music*, 69–83, and the bibliography cited there.
14. *The Josquin Companion*, ed. Sherr, 53–69, and Fallows, *Josquin*, 148–60.
15. Wegman, *Born for the Muses*, from 234–5 *passim*.
16. Fitch, 'Agricola and the Rhizome'.
17. For opposing views, Kirkman, *The Cultural Life*, 3–25, and Fallows, 'The Last Agnus dei'.
18. Crook, *Orlando di Lasso's Imitation Magnificats*.
19. Fitch, *Johannes Ockeghem*, 39–93, and Kirkman, 'The Polyphonic Mass', 691–4.
20. David Trendell, introductory note to *Rogier: Missa Ego sum qui sum & Motets*, King's College London Choir, dir. David Trendell, Hyperion CDA67807, London, 2010.
21. Kurtzman, *The Monteverdi Vespers*, 40–1 and *passim*.

13 Canons, puzzles, games

1. Gilbert, 'Heinrich Isaac'.
2. Fuhrmann, 'A Humble Beginning?'.
3. Fallows, *Josquin*, 218–22; van Benthem, 'A Waif'.
4. Bent, 'Diatonic *Ficta*', 16–20.
5. Cinquecento, *Willaert: Missa Mente tota & motets*, Hyperion CDA67749, London, 2010. The passage is at track 11, from 0:53 to 0:56.
6. Bent, 'Diatonic *Ficta*', 34–40.
7. Newes, Virginia, 'Mensural Virtuosity in Non-Fugal Canons *c*. 1350 to 1450', in *Canons*, 19–46.
8. See the essays in *Canons*.
9. Schiltz, *Music and Riddle Culture*, 1–93.
10. Schiltz, *Music and Riddle Culture*, 93–193.
11. See Wegman, 'Another Mass'; also *Music & Letters*, 71 (1990), 631–5.
12. Lindmayr, 'Ein Rätseltenor Ockeghems'.
13. Elders, *Josquin*, 83 ff.
14. Fallows, *Dufay* (rev. ed.), 310.
15. Kerman, 'The *Missa Puer natus est*' (at 127–32).
16. Fitch, 'For the Sake of His Honour'.

14 Performance practice: a brief introduction

1. See the essays in Bowers, *English Church Polyphony* and Fallows, *Songs*.
2. Duffin, *How Equal Temperament Ruined Harmony*.
3. Segerman, 'A Re-Examination'. Slower than usual tempos characterize recordings by Cappella Pratensis under Rebecca Stewart.
4. Sherman, Bernard D., 'Tempos and Proportions in Brahms: Period Evidence', *Early Music* 25 (1997), 463–78 (at 463).
5. Page, *Music and Instruments* and *Studies*, ed. Boorman.
6. e.g. Hibberd, 'On "Instrumental Style"'.
7. McKinnon, James W., 'Fifteenth-Century Northern Book Painting and the *a cappella* Question: An Essay in Iconographic Method', in *Studies*, 1–17.
8. As formulated decades earlier in Hibberd, '"Instrumental Style"'.
9. *Authenticity*, ed. Kenyon, and the essays in the first section ('In Theory') of Taruskin, *Text and Act*.
10. Fallows, David, 'Specific Information', in *Studies*, 109–57 (at 110–17); also Fiala, David, 'Music and Musicians at the Burgundian Court in the Fifteenth Century', in *Cambridge History of Fifteenth-Century Music*, ed. Busse Berger and Rodin, 427–45.
11. Seebass, Tilman, 'The Visualisation of Music through Pictorial Imagery in Late Medieval France', in *Studies*, 19–33 (at 30–1).
12. An example audiovisual liturgical reenactment of a performance of a Renaissance Mass (Obrecht's *Missa Saincte Donatiane*) by the ensemble Cappella Pratensis can be accessed at https://sites.williams.edu/obrechtmass/mass/(accessed January 2020).
13. *Palestrina Mass "Hodie Christus Natus Est"*, Gabrieli Consort and Players, dir. Paul McCreesh, Deutsche Gramophon, 437 833-2, Hamburg, 1993.
14. *Music of the Sistine Chapel*, Taverner Consort, dir. Andrew Parrott, EMI Reflexe, CDC 747699 2, Hayes (Middlesex), 1987.

Glossary

ANTIPHONY   Technique deriving from psalmody (chanting) involving the distribution of musical material or (in performance) musical space into two or more groups

ASCRIPTION   The naming of the composer of a work in manuscript and printed sources (see also ATTRIBUTION)

ATTRIBUTION   The proposal of a composer's authorship of a work outside manuscript and printed sources (typically by scholars; see also ASCRIPTION)

AUTHENTICITY   For the purposes of this book, a now contested term denoting the performance practice of musical repertories from the pre-recording era, aiming to reproduce the performance conditions that the composer would have heard or had in mind (see 'H.I.P.')

CANON ('FUGAL' or 'INTERVAL', also 'MENSURAL')   Procedure whereby more than one sounding voice is derived from a single written one

CANON ('NON-FUGAL' or 'ENIGMATIC')   Procedure whereby the intended sounding result (usually in a single voice) differs from the literal notated reading and must be deduced by the singer(s)

CANTUS FIRMUS   (*abb.* 'c.f.') Literally, 'fixed song'; a line of pre-existing material (originally plainchant) in relation to which the other voices are composed. In larger-scale motets or Masses, it is typically stated several times (see also CANTUS PRIUS FACTUS).

CANTUS PRIUS FACTUS   Literally, 'song previously made', broadly synonymous with CANTUS FIRMUS

CHANSON   (Fr., 'song') Term applied to all French-texted secular music of the Renaissance until the *air de cour* in the late sixteenth century

COMES   (Lat., 'follower', pl. 'comites') In fugal canon, designates the voice or voices following the DUX

CONTRAFACTUM/CONTRAFACTA   Text(s) adapted to a pre-existing polyphonic work

COUNCIL OF TRENT   Plenary sessions of the Catholic Church convened from 1545 to 1562 in response to the criticisms and challenges of Reformed movements; this included recommendations concerning the use of polyphony in the liturgy (see also COUNTER-REFORMATION)

COUNTER-REFORMATION   The Catholic Church's formal and informal responses to the criticisms and challenges of Reformed movements during the period *c*.1540–1620, leading to reforms in the church's doctrines, organization, liturgical practices, as well as responses within the arts

DUX (Lat., 'leader') In fugal (interval) canon, the voice that sounds first or (in mensural canon) that finishes first

ELEVATION Point of the LITURGY at which the bread and wine of communion are held in Catholic teaching to be transformed into the body and blood of Christ, signalled by the celebrant's raising of the host and chalice for the congregation to see

EMIC The observation and description of a culture according to the standpoint and modes of functioning inherent to that culture (see also ETIC)

EPIGRAM Brief text in prose or verse, sometimes with a moral or pedagogical purpose; for the purposes of this book, a verse with satirical or risqué subject matter, often with a 'punchline' at or near the end

ETIC The observation and description of a culture according to standpoints originating outside that culture (see also EMIC)

FORMES FIXES (Fr., 'fixed forms') Term applied to French poetic texts with refrains and other recurring features; after 1440 the principal forms set to music are the rondeau, virelai, and ballade (the latter very rarely after 1450)

FREELY COMPOSED With reference to music borrowing, denotes any material (either an individual voice or a polyphonic section or passage) not derived from a designated or identifiable model

GEMATRIA A category of number-mysticism in which numerical values are assigned to terms (typically names) on the basis of their letters (where A=1, B=2, C=3, etc.)

GLOSS Commentary on a sacred or authoritative (e.g. classical) text, often by a recognized authority or source

H.I.P. ('historically informed performance') Current within musical scholarship and performance in which the performance of past musical repertories (especially from the pre-recording era) is grounded on the critical study, evaluation, and interpretation of available historical documentation

HOMOPHONY The sounding of voices together in rhythmic unison, usually associated with the simultaneous sounding of the same text

HUGUENOT French adherent of Protestant (Reformed, typically Calvinist) faiths

HUMANISM Philosophical and aesthetic current traditionally seen as originating in the Renaissance period; for the purposes of this book, it denotes the Renaissance's pre-occupation with rediscovering and appropriating the learning and culture of the 'ancient' (Graeco-Roman) world, principally through the study of its literary texts.

IMITATION 1. Procedure involving the replication in more than one voice of melodic material at a given time- and pitch-interval; 2. The derivation of a work on a polyphonic MODEL by quoting its polyphonic modules (i.e. all voices sounding together) rather than isolated voices (see also PARODY)

INDULGENCE Papal dispensation remitting individuals from purgatory for a specified period, relating to sins for which absolution has not been sought or obtained. The sale of indulgences (a practice that arose during the Renaissance) was one of the Reformed movement's principal criticisms of the church.

INTERTEXTUALITY Term from literary theory denoting interrelationships between texts, whether intentional or unintentional. Its use in discussions of Renaissance polyphony usually pertains to cases of intentional borrowing or the modelling of one work on another.

ISOMELISM The recurrence of a melodic outline, with its local and rhythmic details changed, often used with reference to cantus firmus design

ISORHYTHM The recurrence of a short rhythmic pattern, known as 'talea' (sometimes associated with a recurring melodic pattern, known as 'color') as the structuring element of one or more voices of a work, typically a motet

JUST INTONATION The tuning of intervals according to mathematically exact ratios, typically of the numbers 2, 3, 5

LITURGY, LITURGICAL HOURS Set of prescriptions regarding the timing, order, form, actions and content of Catholic worship throughout the day (hours) and year (calendar)

MODEL Polyphonic work serving as a basis for a subsequent polyphonic work (see also MUSICAL BORROWING, IMITATION, CANTUS FIRMUS, CANTUS PRIUS FACTUS)

MUSICAL BORROWING The intentional derivation of newly composed musical material from a pre-existing source

ORDINARY (also 'Mass Ordinary') Parts of the liturgy whose texts are fixed throughout the liturgical year (though some are omitted at certain times, e.g. during Lent); typically designates the Kyrie, Gloria, Credo, Sanctus and Benedictus, and Agnus dei

PARALITURGICAL Parallel to or associated with, but not formally part of, the liturgy

PARAPHRASE The composed ornamentation or embellishment of a line of pre-existent material (typically a CANTUS FIRMUS), as opposed to its strict quotation (see also ISOMELISM)

PARODY Now contested term synonymous with IMITATION when used in the context of musical borrowing

PROPERS Parts of the liturgy with a prescribed form, whose texts change according to the feast being celebrated

PYTHAGOREAN TUNING A tuning system that derives all other intervals from the ratio of the perfect fifth (3:2)

REFORMATION First successful pan-European wave of challenges to the hegemony of the Roman Catholic Church, initiated in German-speaking lands by Martin Luther in 1517 and subsequently followed by others, especially in the period 1520–70

RHETORIC Classical term denoting effective (persuasive) speaking or writing, associated in particular with the use of figures of speech, some of which are transferable to music

TELEOLOGY, TELEOLOGICAL Interpretations of phenomena in terms of their purpose or goal; for the purposes of this book, the notion of goal-orientation (e.g. viewing the cadence as a final point of arrival, or the reading of history and historical events in terms of determined points of arrival)

TEMPERAMENT (also 'tuning') The practice of adjusting or modifying the tuning of 'pure' intervals to inflect the sounding of chords (and, by extension, the playing of scales or keys)

TROPE Passage of text interpolated within a standard liturgical text (and by extension, in music, its setting in plainchant)

Bibliography

Alden, Jane, *Songs, Scribes, and Society: The History and Reception of the Loire Valley Chansonniers*, New York and Oxford, 2010

Alexander Agricola: Muzik zwischen Vokalität und Instrumentalismus: Trossinger Jahrbuch für Renaissancemusik 6, ed. Nicole Schwindt, Kassel, 2007

Antoine Busnoys: Method, Meaning, and Context in Late Medieval Music, ed. Paula Higgins, Oxford, 1999

Arnold, Denis, *Giovanni Gabrieli and the Music of the Venetian High Renaissance*, Oxford, 1979

Atlas, Alan W., *Renaissance Music: Music in Western Europe, 1400–1600*, 2 vols., New York and London, 1998

Authenticity and Early Music: A Symposium, ed. Nicholas Kenyon, Oxford, 1989

Benham, Hugh, *Latin Church Music in England, 1460–1575*, London, 1977

Bent, Margaret, *Counterpoint, Composition, and Musica Ficta*, New York and London, 2002

  'Diatonic Ficta', *EMH* 4 (1984), 1–48

  Dunstaple, London, 1971

  'The Grammar of Early Music: Preconditions for Analysis', in *Tonal Structures*, ed. Cristle Collins Judd, 15–59

Berger, Karol, *Musica ficta: Theories of Accidental Inflections in Vocal Polyphony from Marchetto da Padova to Gioseffo Zarlino*, Cambridge, 1987

Bernstein, Jane A., 'Financial Arrangements and the Role of Printer and Composer in Sixteenth-Century Italian Music Printing', *AM* 63 (1991), 39–56

  Print Culture and Music in Sixteenth-Century Venice, New York, 2001

  'Publish or Perish? Palestrina and Print Culture in 16th-Century Italy', *EM* 35 (2007), 225–35

Beyond Contemporary Fame: Reassessing the Art of Clemens non Papa and Thomas Crecquillon. Colloquium Proceedings, Utrecht, April 24–26, 2003, ed. Eric Jas, Turnhout, 2005

Binchois Studies, ed. Andrew Kirkman and Denis Slavin, Oxford and New York, 2000

Blackburn, Bonnie J., 'For Whom Do the Singers Sing?', *EM* 25 (1997), 593–609

  'On Compositional Process in the Fifteenth Century', *JAMS* 40 (1987), 210–84

  'The Virgin in the Sun: Music and Image for a Prayer Attributed to Sixtus IV', *JRMA* 124 (1999), 157–95

Boorman, Stanley, *Ottaviano Petrucci: Catalogue Raisonné*, Oxford and New York, 2006

Bowers, Roger, *English Church Polyphony*, Aldershot, 1999

Bowles, Edmund A., '"Haut and Bas": The Grouping of Instruments in the Middle Ages', *MD* 8 (1954), 115–40

Brooks, Jeanice, *Courtly Song in Sixteenth-Century France*, Chicago, 2000

Brothers, Thomas, 'Vestiges of the Isorhythmic Tradition in Mass and Motet, ca. 1450–1475', *JAMS* 44 (1991), 1–56

Brown, Howard Mayer and Stein, Louise, *Music in the Renaissance*, 2nd ed., Upper Saddle River, NJ, 1999

Bryan, John, 'Extended Play: Reflections of Heinrich Isaac's Music in Early Tudor England', *JM* 28 (2011), 118–41

Bryant, David, 'The "cori spezzati" of St Mark's: Myth and Reality', *EMH* 1 (1982), 165–86

Burckhardt, Jacob, *The Civilization of the Renaissance in Italy*, London, 1995. Orig. pub. 1860 as *Die Kultur der Renaissance in Italien*

Bürger, Peter, *Theorie der Avantgarde*, Frankfurt, 1974, trans. *Theory of the Avant-Garde*, trans. Michael Shaw, Manchester, 1984

Burstyn, Shai, 'Pre-1600 Music Listening: A Methodological Approach', *MQ* 82 (1998), 455–65

Busse Berger, Anna Maria, *Medieval Music and the Art of Memory*, Berkeley and Los Angeles, 2005

Mensuration and Proportion Signs: Origins and Evolution, Oxford, 1993

Butt, John, *Playing with History: The Historical Approach to Musical Performance*, Cambridge, 2002

Caldwell, John, *Editing Early Music*, 2nd ed., Oxford, 1995

The Cambridge History of Fifteenth-Century Music, ed. Anna Maria Busse Berger and Jesse Rodin, Cambridge, 2015

The Cambridge History of Sixteenth-Century Music, ed. Iain Fenlon and Richard Wistreich, Cambridge, 2019

The Cambridge History of Western Music Theory, ed. Thomas Christensen, Cambridge, 2002

Canguilhem, Philippe, *L'Improvisation polyphonique à la Renaissance*, Paris, 2015

'Singing upon the Book according to Vicente Lusitano', *EMH* 30 (2011), 55–103

'Towards a Stylistic History of cantare super librum', in *Studies in Historical Improvisation: From Cantare super librum to Partimenti*, ed. Massimiliano Guido, Abingdon and New York, 2017

Canons and Canonic Technique, ed. Katelijne Schiltz and Bonnie J. Blackburn, Leuven, 2007

Cazaux, Christelle, *La Musique à la cour de François Ier*, Paris, 2002

Cipriano de Rore: New Perspectives on His Life and Music, ed. Jessie Ann Owens and Katelijne Schiltz, Turnhout, 2016

Clément Janequin: un musicien au milieu des poètes, ed. Olivier Halévy, Isabelle His, and Jean Vignes, Paris, 2013

Coelho, Victor and Polk, Keith, *Instrumentalists and Renaissance Culture, 1420–1600: Players of Function and Fantasy*, Cambridge, 2016

Cœurdevey, Annie, *Roland de Lassus*, Paris, 2003

Companion to Medieval and Renaissance Music, ed. Tess Knighton and David Fallows, Berkeley and London, 1992

Cristóbal de Morales: Sources, Influences, Reception, ed. Owen Rees and Bernadette Nelson, Woodbridge, 2007

Crook, David, *Orlando di Lasso's Imitation Magnificats for Counter-Reformation Munich*, Princeton, 1994

'The Sacred and Secular in Post-Tridentine Church Music: De Rore, Lasso, and the Magnificat *Da le belle contrade*,' *JAF* 10 (2018), 45–72

Cumming, Julie, 'From Variety to Repetition: The Birth of Imitative Polyphony,' *YAF* 6 (2008), 21–44

The Motet in the Age of Du Fay, Cambridge, 1999

Dean, Jeffrey, 'Listening to Sacred Polyphony c.1500', *EM* 25 (1997), 611–36

DeFord, Ruth I., *Tactus, Mensuration, and Rhythm in Renaissance Music*, Cambridge, 2015

Dobbins, Frank, *Music in Renaissance Lyons*, Oxford, 1992

Duffin, Ross W., *How Equal Temperament Ruined Harmony (and Why You Should Care)*, New York, 2007

Early Musical Borrowing, ed. Honey Meconi, New York, 2004

Edwards, Warwick, 'Alexander Agricola and Intuitive Syllable Deployment', *EM* 24 (2006), 409–25

'Understanding Fifteenth-Century Chansonniers', *JRMA* 138 (2013), 187–205

Einstein, Alfred, *The Italian Madrigal*, 3 vols., trans. Alexander H. Krappe, Roger Sessions, and W. Oliver Strunk, Princeton, NJ, 1949

Elders, Willem, *Josquin des Prez and his Musical Legacy: An Introductory Guide*, Leuven, 2011

Symbolic Scores: Studies in the Music of the Renaissance, Leiden, 1994

Eroticism in Early Modern Music, ed. Bonnie J. Blackburn and Laurie Stras, London, 2016

Essays on Renaissance Music in Honour of David Fallows: Bon jour, bon mois et bonne estrenne, ed. Fabrice Fitch and Jacobijn Kiel, Woodbridge, 2011

European Music, 1520–1640, ed. James Haar, Woodbridge, 2006

Fallows, David, *A Catalogue of Polyphonic Songs, 1415–1480*, Oxford and New York, 1999

Dufay, rev. ed, London, 1987

Josquin, Turnhout, 2009

'The Last Agnus dei', in *Polyphone Messe im 15. und 16. Jahrhundert: Funktion, Kontext, Symbol*, ed. Andrea Amendola, Daniel Glowotz, Jürgen Heidrich, Göttingen, 2012, 53–63

'The Performing Ensembles in Josquin's Sacred Music', *TVNM* 35 (1985), 32–64; repr. in Fallows, *Songs and Musicians*, No. XII

Songs and Musicians in the Fifteenth Century, Aldershot, 1996

Fenlon, Iain, *Music and Patronage in Sixteenth-Century Mantua*, 2 vols., Cambridge, 1980–2

Fisher, Alexander J., *Music, Piety and Propaganda: The Soundscapes of Counter-Reformation Bavaria*, New York, 2014

Fitch, Fabrice, 'Agricola and the Rhizome: An Aesthetic of the Late Cantus Firmus Mass', *BTM/RBM* 59 (2005), 65–92

'"For the Sake of His Honour": Obrecht Reconsidered', *TVNM* 48 (1998), 150–63

'Hearing John Browne's Motets: Registral Space in the Music of the Eton Choirbook', *EM* 36 (2008), 19–40

Johannes Ockeghem: Masses and Models, Paris, 1997

'The Renaissance', in *The Cambridge Companion to French Music*, ed. Simon Trezise, Cambridge, 2015, 49–68

Freedman, Richard, *The Chansons of Orlando di Lasso and Their Protestant Listeners: Music, Piety, and Print in Sixteenth-Century France*, Rochester, 2001

Music in the Renaissance, New York and London, 2013

Fuhrmann, Wolfgang, 'A Humble Beginning? Three Ways to Understand Brumel's Missa Ut re me fa sol la', *JAF* 7 (2015), 22–49

Gallagher, Sean, *Johannes Regis*, Turnhout, 2010

Goehr, Lydia, *The Imaginary Museum of Musical Works: An Essay in the Philosophy of Music*, Oxford, 1992

Gómez, Maricarmen, 'The Ensalada and the Origins of Lyric Theater in Spain', *CD* 28 (1994), 367–93

Haar, James, 'The Courtier as Musician: Castiglione's View of the Science and Art of Music', in *Castiglione: The Ideal and the Real in Renaissance Culture*, ed. Robert W. Hanning and David Rosand, New Haven, CT, and London, 1983, 165–89

Essays on Italian Poetry and Music in the Renaissance, 1350–1600, Berkeley, CA, 1986

The Science and Art of Renaissance Music, ed. Paul Corneilson, Princeton, 1998

Haggh, Barbara, 'The Celebration of the "Recollectio Festorum Beatae Mariae Virginis", 1457–1987', in *Trasmissione e recezione delle forme di cultura musicale. Atti del XIV congresso della Società Internazionale di Musicologia, Bologna 1987*, ed. Angelo Pompilio et al., Turin, 1990, 3, 559–71

Harley, John, *Thomas Tallis*, Abingdon and New York, 2016

William Byrd: Gentleman of the Chapel Royal, Abingdon and New York, 1999

Harper, John, *The Forms and Orders of Western Liturgy from the Tenth to the Eighteenth Century*, Oxford and New York, 1991

Harrison, Frank Ll., *Music in Medieval Britain*, London and New York, 1958

Hearing the Motet: Essays on the Motet of the Middle Ages and Renaissance, ed. Dolores Pesce, New York and Oxford, 1997

Heinrich Isaac and Polyphony for the Proper of the Mass in the Late Middle Ages and Renaissance, ed. David Burn and Stefan Gasch, Turnhout, 2011

Hibberd, Lloyd, 'On "Instrumental Style" in Early Melody', *MQ* 32 (1946), 107–130 (repr. in *Instruments and their Music*, ed. McGee, 455–78)

Higgins, Paula, 'Parisian Nobles, a Scottish Princess, and the Woman's Voice in Late Medieval Song', *EMH* 10 (1991), 145–200

Hiley, David, *Gregorian Chant*, Cambridge, 2009

His, Isabelle, *Claude Le Jeune, v. 1530–1600: un compositeur entre Renaissance et baroque*, Arles, 2000

Holman, Peter, *Four and Twenty Fiddlers: The Violin at the English Court 1540–1690*, Oxford, 1993

Holmes, Sherlock, *Some Remarks on the Polyphonic Motets of Lassus*, London, 1896

Howard, Deborah, and Laura Moretti, *Sound and Space in Renaissance Venice: Architecture, Music, Acoustics*, New Haven, 2009

Instruments and their Music in the Middle Ages, ed. Timothy J. McGee, London and New York, 2016

Janin, Barnabé, *Chanter sur le livre: Manuel pratique d'improvisation polyphonique de la Renaissance, 15ème et 16ème siècles*, Langres, 2012

Jeppesen, Knud, *The Style of Palestrina and the Dissonance*, 2nd rev. ed., Copenhagen, 1946

Johannes Ockeghem: Actes du XLe colloque international d'études humanistes, Tours, 3–8 février 1997, ed. Philippe Vendrix, Paris, 1999

The Josquin Companion, ed. Richard Sherr, Oxford and New York, 2000

Judd, Cristle Collins, *Reading Renaissance Music Theory: Hearing with the Eyes*, Cambridge, 2000

Kendrick, Robert, *Celestial Sirens: Nuns and Their Music in Early Modern Milan*, Oxford, 1996

Kerman, Joseph, 'The *Missa Puer natus est* by Thomas Tallis', in *Write All These Down: Essays on Music*, Berkeley, 1994, 125–38

Kirkman, Andrew, *The Cultural Life of the Early Polyphonic Mass: Medieval Context to Modern Revival*, Cambridge, 2010

Kreitner, Kenneth, *The Church Music of Fifteenth-Century Spain*, Woodbridge, 2004

'Very Low Voices in the Sacred Music of Ockeghem and Tinctoris', *EM* 14 (1986), 467–79

Kurtzman, Jeffrey, *The Monteverdi Vespers of 1610: Music, Context, Performance*, Oxford, 1999

Leech-Wilkinson, Daniel, *The Modern Invention of Medieval Music: Scholarship, Ideology, Performance*, Cambridge, 2002

Le Huray, Peter, *Music and the Reformation in England 1549–1660*, London, 1967

Lindmayr, Andrea, 'Ein Rätseltenor Ockeghems: des Rätsels Lösung', *AM* 60 (1988), 31–42

'Listening Practice', colloquium in *EM* 25 (1997), 591–714

Lockwood, Lewis, *Music in Renaissance Ferrara, 1400–1505: The Creation of a Musical Center in the Fifteenth Century*, Cambridge, MA, 1984

Lowinsky, Edward E., *Secret Chromatic Art in the Netherlands Motet*, trans. Carl Buchman, New York, 1946

  '*Calami sonum ferentes*: A New Interpretation', in *Music in the Culture of the Renaissance and Other Essays*, ed. Bonnie J. Blackburn, 2 vols., Chicago, 1989, v. 2, 595–626

Luko, Alexis, 'Tinctoris on Varietas', *EMH* 27 (2008), 99–136

Lütteken, Laurenz, *Musik der Renaissance: Imagination und Wirklichkeit einer kulturellen Praxis*, Kassel, 2011, trans. *Music of the Renaissance: Imagination and Reality of a Cultural Practice*, trans. James Steichen, Oakland, 2019

Macy, Laura, 'Speaking of Sex: Metaphor and Performance in the Italian Madrigal', *JM* 14 (1996), 1–34

Magro, Agostino, '"Premierement ma baronnie de Chasteauneuf": Jean de Ockeghem, Treasurer of St Martin's in Tours', *EMH* 18 (1999), 165–258

Man and Music: The Renaissance from the 1470s to the End of the 16th Century, ed. Iain Fenlon, London, 1989

Mapping the Motet in the Post-Tridentine Era, ed. Esperanza Rodríguez-García and Daniele V. Filippi, Abingdon and New York, 2019

Materialities: Books, Readers, and the Chanson in Sixteenth-Century Europe, ed. Kate van Orden, New York, 2015

McCarthy, Kerry, *Liturgy and Contemplation in Byrd's Gradualia*, New York, 2007

McClary, Susan, *Modal Subjectivities: Self-fashioning in the Italian Madrigal*, Berkeley, 2004

McCreless, Patrick, 'Music and Rhetoric', in *The Cambridge History of Western Music Theory*, ed. Thomas Christensen, 847–879

McKinnon, James W., 'Representations of the Mass in Medieval and Renaissance Art', *JAMS* 31 (1978), 21–52

Meconi, Honey, *Pierre de La Rue and Musical Life at the Habsburg-Burgundian Court*, Oxford and New York, 2003

  'The Range of Mourning: Nine Questions and Some Answers', in *Tod in Musik und Kultur: Zum 500. Todestag Philipps des Schönen*, ed. Stefan Gasch and Birgit Lodes, Tutzing, 2007, 141–156

The Medici Codex of 1518: A Choirbook of Motets Dedicated to Lorenzo de' Medici, Duke of Urbino, ed. Edward E. Lowinsky, 3 vols., Chicago and London, 1968

Mengozzi, Stefano, *The Renaissance Reform of Medieval Music Theory: Guido of Arezzo between Myth and History*, Cambridge, 2010

Milsom, John, '"Imitatio", "Intertextuality", and Early Music', in *Citation and Authority in Medieval and Renaissance Musical Culture: Learning from the Learned*, ed. Suzannah Clark and Elizabeth Eva Leach, Woodbridge, 2005, 141–51

  'Josquin and the Combinative Impulse', in *The Motet around 1500*, ed. Thomas Schmidt-Beste, 211–46

'Sense and Sound in Richafort's Requiem', *EM* 30 (2002), 447–63

'The T-Mass: quis scrutatur?', *EM* 46 (2018), 319–31

Monson, Craig, 'The Council of Trent Revisited', *JAMS* 55 (2002), 1–37

Disembodied Voices: Music and Culture in an Early Modern Italian Convent, Berkeley, CA, 1995

Moroney, Davitt, 'Alessandro Striggio's Mass in Forty and Sixty Parts', *JAMS* 60 (2007), 1–70

The Motet around 1500: On the Relationship between Imitation and Text Treatment?, ed. Thomas Schmidt-Beste, Turnhout, 2012

Motet Cycles between Devotion and Liturgy, ed. Agnese Pavanello and Daniele V. Filippi, Basel, 2019

Motet Cycles (c.1470–1510): Compositional Design, Performance, and Cultural Context, ed. Agnese Pavanello, *JAF* 9 (2017)

Music and Culture in the Middle Ages and Beyond: Liturgy, Sources, Symbolism, ed. Benjamin Brand and David J. Rothenberg, Cambridge, 2016

Musical Theory in the Renaissance, ed. Cristle Collins Judd, Farnham, 2013

Music and Musicians in Renaissance Cities and Towns, ed. Fiona Kisby, Cambridge, 2001

Music Education in the Middle Ages and the Renaissance, ed. Russell E. Murray Jr., Susan Forscher Weiss, and Cynthia J. Cyrus, Bloomington and Indianapolis, 2010

Newcomb, Anthony, *The Madrigal at Ferrara, 1579–1597*, Princeton, 1980

Noone, Michael, *Music and Musicians in the Escorial Liturgy under the Habsburgs, 1563–1700*, Rochester, 1998

Nosow, Robert, *Ritual Meanings in the Fifteenth-Century Motet*, Cambridge, 2012

'Song and the Art of Dying', *The Musical Quarterly* 82 (1998), 537–50

Oettinger, Rebecca Wagner, *Music as Propaganda in the German Reformation*, Aldershot, 2001

Orlandus Lassus and his Time, Colloquium Proceedings, Antwerp 24–26.08.1994 (*YAF* 6), ed. Ignace Bossuyt, Eugeen Schreurs, and Annelies Wouters, Peer, 1995

Owens, Jessie Ann, *Composers at Work: The Craft of Musical Composition, 1450–1600*, New York, 1997

'Lasso's Ritual Reading of De Rore's *Scarco di doglia*', *JAF* 10 (2018), 73–93

Page, Christopher, *Discarding Images: Reflections on Music and Culture in Medieval France*, Oxford, 1993

Music and Instruments of the Middle Ages: Studies on Texts and Performance, Aldershot, 1997

Palisca, Claude V., *Humanism in Italian Renaissance Musical Thought*, New Haven, 1985

Performance Practice: Music before 1600, ed. Howard Mayer Brown and Stanley Sadie, New York, 1990

A Performer's Guide to Renaissance Music, ed. Jeffrey Kite-Powell, 2nd ed., Bloomington, 2007

Perkins, Leeman L., *Music in the Age of the Renaissance*, New York and London, 1999

Pirrotta, Nino, *Music and Culture in Italy from the Middle Ages to the Baroque*, Cambridge, MA, 1984

Planchart, Alejandro Enrique, 'Cipriano de Rore's *Da le belle contrade*: an Ovidian Work and Precursor of the *Seconda prattica*', *JAF* 10 (2018), 27–44

Guillaume Du Fay: The Life and Works, 2 vols., Cambridge, 2018

Polk, Keith, *German Instrumental Music of the Late Middle Ages: Players, Patrons and Performance Practice*, Cambridge, 1992

'Heinrich Isaac and Innovations in Musical Style ca. 1490', in *Sleuthing the Muse: Essays in Honor of William F. Prizer*, ed. Kristine K. Forney and Jeremy L. Smith, Hillsdale, NY, 2012, 349–64

Powers, Harold S., 'Is Mode Real? Pietro Aaron, the Octenary System, and Polyphony', *BJHM* 16 (1992), 9–52

'Tonal Types and Modal Categories in Renaissance Polyphony', *JAMS* 34 (1981), 428–70

Preciado, Dionisio, 'La Cancion Tradicional Española en las "Ensaladas" de Mateo Flecha, El Viejo', *RM* 10 (1987), 459–88

Rees, Owen, 'Guerrero's 'L'Homme armé' Masses and Their Models', *EMH* 12 (1993), 19–54

The Requiem of Tomás Luis de Victoria (1603), Cambridge, 2019

Reese, Gustave, *Music in the Renaissance*, rev. ed., New York, 1959

Reynolds, Christopher A., 'The Counterpoint of Allusion in Fifteenth-Century Masses', *JAMS* 45 (1992), 228–60

Rifkin, Joshua, 'The Creation of the Medici Codex', *JAMS* 62 (2009), 517–70

Robertson, Anne Walters, 'The Man with the Pale Face, the Shroud, and Du Fay's Missa Se la face ay pale', *JM* 27 (2010), 377–434

Roche, Jerome, *Lassus*, London and New York, 1982

Palestrina, London and New York, 1971

Rodin, Jesse, *Josquin's Rome: Hearing and Composing in the Sistine Chapel*, New York, 2012

Ross, D. James, *Musick Fyne: Robert Carver and the Art of Music in Sixteenth Century Scotland*, Edinburgh, 1993

Rothenberg, David J., *The Flower of Paradise: Marian Devotion and Secular Song in Medieval and Renaissance Music*, New York and Oxford, 2011

Schiltz, Katelijne, 'Adrian Willaert's Hymn to the Holy Shroud', *JAF* 4 (2012), 57–72

Music and Riddle Culture in the Renaissance, Cambridge, 2015

Schmidt-Beste, Thomas and Leitmeir, Christian, *The Production and Reading of Music Sources: Mise-en-page in Manuscripts and Printed Books Containing Polyphonic Music, 1480–1530*, Turnhout, 2018

Schubert, Peter, 'Hidden Forms in Palestrina's First Book of Four-Voice Motets', *JAMS* 60 (2007), 483–556

Modal Counterpoint, Renaissance Style, 2nd ed., New York, 2008

Segerman, Ephraim, 'A Re-Examination of the Evidence on Absolute Tempo before 1700', *EM* 24 (1996), 227–48 and 681–90

Senfl-Studien, ed. Stefan Gasch, Birgit Lodes, and Sonia Tröster, Tutzing (Vol. 1) and Vienna (Vols. 2 and 3), 2012–

Shephard, Tim, 'Constructing Identities in a Music Manuscript: The Medici Codex as a Gift', *RQ* 63 (2010), 84–127

Sherr, Richard, *Music and Musicians in Renaissance Rome and Other Courts*, Aldershot, 1999

Small, Christopher, *Musicking: The Meanings of Performing and Listening*, Middletown, CT, 1998

Smith, Anne, *The Performance of Sixteenth-Century Music: Learning from the Theorists*, Oxford, 2011

Sparks, Edgar H., *Cantus Firmus in Mass and Motet, 1420–1520*, Berkeley, 1963

'Problems of Authenticity in Josquin's Motets', in *Proceedings of the International Josquin Festival-Conference ... New York City, 21–25 June 1971*, ed. Edward E. Lowinsky, London, 1976

Stevens, Denis, 'A Song of Fortie Partes, Made by Mr. Tallys', *EM* 10 (1982), 171–81

Stevenson, Robert, *Spanish Music in the Age of Columbus*, The Hague, 1960

Stras, Laurie, *Women and Music in Sixteenth-Century Ferrara*, Cambridge, 2018

Strohm, Reinhard, *Music in Late Medieval Bruges*, Oxford and New York, 1985; rev. ed., 1990

The Rise of European Music, Cambridge, 1993

Studies in the Performance of Late Medieval Music, ed. Stanley Boorman, Cambridge, 1983

Taruskin, Richard, *Text and Act*, New York, 1995

Thomas Tallis & William Byrd: Cantiones Sacrae 1575, ed. John Milsom, London, 2014

Tomlinson, Gary, *Music and Renaissance Magic: Toward a Historiography of Others*, Chicago, 1993

Tonal Structures in Early Music, ed. Cristle Collins Judd, New York, 1998

The Treasury of Petrus Alamire: Music and Art in Flemish Court Manuscripts, 1500–1535, ed. Herbert Kellman, Ghent, 1999

van Benthem, Jaap, 'A Waif, a Wedding and a Worshipped Child: Josquin's *Ut phebi radiis* and the order of the Golden Fleece', *TVNM* 37 (1987), 64–81

Vander Straeten, Edmond, *La Musique au Pays-Bas avant le XIXe siècle*, 8 vols., Brussels, 1867–8

van Orden, Kate, *Music, Authorship, and the Book in the First Century of Print*, Berkeley, 2014

Vendrix, Philippe, 'L'Impossible Renaissance. La Musicologie face au concept de la Renaissance, 1868–2000', *BHR* 66 (2004), 7–22

La Musique à la Renaissance, Paris, 1999

Wagstaff, Grayson, 'Music for the Dead: Polyphonic Settings of the *"Officium"* and *"Missa Pro Defunctis"* by Spanish and Latin American Composers before 1630', Ph.D. Diss. (The University of Texas at Austin, 1995)

Weber, Edith, *Le Concile de Trente et la musique*, Paris, 1982

Wegman, Rob C., 'Another Mass by Busnoys?', *M&L* 71 (1990), 1–19

Born for the Muses: The Life and Masses of Jacob Obrecht, Oxford, 1994

The Crisis of Music in Early Modern Europe, 1470–1530, New York, 2005

'From Maker to Composer: Improvisation and Musical Authorship in the Low Countries, 1450–1500', *JAMS* 49 (1996), 409–79

'Johannes Tinctoris and the "New Art"', *M&L* 84 (2003), 171–88

'New Music for a World Grown Old: Martin Le Franc and the "Contenance angloise"', *AM* 75 (2003), 201–241

'Petrus de Domarto's Missa Spiritus almus and the Early History of the Four-Voice Mass in the Fifteenth Century', *EMH* 10 (1991), 235–303

Williamson, Magnus, *The Eton Choirbook: Facsimile and Introductory Study*, Oxford, 2010

Wistreich, Richard, *Warrior, Courtier, Singer: Giulio Cesare Brancaccio and the Performance of Identity in the Late Renaissance*, Aldershot, 2007

'Singing and Sociability', *SM* 18 (2011), 230–46

Women Making Music: The Western Art Tradition, ed. Jane Bowers and Judith Tick, Urbana, 1986

Wright, Craig M., 'Dufay's Nuper rosarum flores, King Solomon's Temple, and the Veneration of the Virgin', *JAMS* 47 (1994), 395–441

The Maze and the Warrior: Symbols in Architecture, Theology, and Music, Cambridge, MA, 2001

Music and Ceremony at Notre Dame of Paris, 500–1550, New York, 1989

Young Choristers (650–1700), ed. Susan Boynton and Eric Rice, Woodbridge, 2008

Index of compositions

Agricola, Alexander
   Allés regretz 198–9 (Ex. 13.3), 199
   Cecus non iudicat de coloribus 137–8, 200–1
   Comme femme desconfortée 199 (Ex. 13.4)
   Missa In minen sinn 164, 183
   Missa Le Serviteur 183
   Missa Malheur me bat 183
   Pater meus Agricola est 137–8, 200–1
   Revenez tous regretz/Quis det 144 (Ex. 11.2)
   Salve regina I 213
   Si dedero 120–1 (Ex. 9.1), 155
   Tout a par moy 204
Allegri, Gregorio, *Miserere mei* 236
Anon.
   Confort d'amours 89 (Ex. 6.2)
   Deo gratia 146
   Fortuna desperata (Felice) 120, 185
   Missa Caput 5, 6 (Ex. 1.1), 7, 70–1, 72 (Ex. 5.2), 73, 90, 111, 143, 152, 171, 181
   Missa L'Ardant désir 213–15
   Missa Veterem hominem 5, 111
   Si vous voullez que je vous ame 184 (Ex. 12.4), 185
   Sumer is icumen in 211
   (Ockeghem?), *Ut heremita solus* 215
Arcadelt, Jacques, *Il bianco e dolce cigno* 81 (Ex. 5.11), 138

Bach, J. S.
   Goldberg Variations 210
   Musical Offering 228
ballo del Granduca (tune) 166
Binchois, Gilles
   Comme femme desconfortée 175, 185
   Dueil angoisseux 106
Boyleau, Simon, *In principio erat verbum* 122
Browne, John, *Stabat mater* 217

Bruhier, Antoine
   Ecce panis angelorum 125
Brumel, Antoine
   Missa de Beata Virgine 191
   Missa de Dringhs 192
   Missa Et ecce terre motus 141, 164–5
   Missa L'Homme armé 179
   Missa Ut re mi fa sol la 201
   Requiem Mass 118
   Sicut lilium 122, 124–5, 141
   Tous les regretz 192
Brunet, Johannes, *Ite in orbem* 128–9
Busnoys, Antoine
   A que ville et habominable 142
   Anthoni usque limina 142
   Bel accueil 142
   In hydraulis 32, 92, 152, 218–19
   Je ne puis vivre ainsi tousjours 142, 152
   Missa L'Homme armé 5, 95, 178–9, 179 (Ex. 12.3), 193, 212
   Noel, noel 90–1 (Ex. 6.3)
   Quant ce viendra 72–3 (Ex. 5.3), 74
Byrd, William
   Four-voice Mass 192
   Quomodo cantabimus 178

Carver, Robert, *O bone Jesu* 220
Cipriano *see* De Rore, Cipriano
Compère Loÿset
   Au travail suis sans espoire de confort 192, 202
   Missa L'Homme armé 178–9
   Omnium bonorum plena (Ex. 3.1), 32, 175

Davy, Richard, *O Domine celi terreque* 157
De Rore, Cipriano
   Calami sonum ferentes 64, 205
   Da le belle contrade 138–40, 151, 205
   Missa Preter rerum seriem 190–1
Delahaye, *Mort j'appelle de ta rigueur* 61–2 (Ex. 4.5)

Du Fay, Guillaume
  Alma redemptoris mater 169, 170 (Ex. 12.1)
  Ave regina celorum III 33 (Ex. 3.2), 147 (Ex. 11.4), 148
  Bien veignés vous, amoureuse lyesse 61–2 (Ex. 4.5), 209
  Flos florum 124
  Je requier a tous amoureux 68–72 (Ex. 5.1), 131, 133
  Le Serviteur 55, 56 (Fig. 4.4), 185
  Les Douleurs dont me sens tel somme 142
  Missa Ave regina celorum 33, 78, 171, 191
  Missa Ecce ancilla/Beata es, Maria 78, 171
  Missa L'Homme armé 111–12, 113–14 (Ex. 8.1), 114–15, 148, 178–81
  Missa Sancti Anthonii de Padua 111
  Missa Sancti Jacobi 23, 110
  Missa Se la face ay pale 56, 73, 172, 173 (Ex. 12.2), 175–6
  Missa sine nomine 110
  Nuper rosarum flores 3, 174
  Puisque vous estiez campeur 142
  Requiem Mass (lost) 33, 118
  Resveillés vous 110
  Salve flos tuscae gentis 128
  Se la face ay pale 56, 172–3 (Ex. 12.2)
  Vasilissa ergo gaude 220

Elimot, *Nuptiae factae sunt* 128
Eloy d'Amerval, *Missa Dixerunt discipuli* 85
Escobar, Pedro de, Requiem Mass 118
Escobedo, Bartolomé de, *Missa Philippus Rex Hispaniae* 182

Fayrfax, Robert, *Missa O quam glorifica* 213, 217
Festa, Costanzo
  Angelus ad pastores ait 129
  Super flumina Babylonis 127
Fevin, Antoine de, Requiem Mass 118
Flecha, Mateo
  La bomba 135–7
  La guerra 136
  La viuda 137
Frescobaldi, Girolamo, *Capriccio sopra La sol fa re mi* 182
Frye, Walter
  Ave regina celorum 98, 124
  Missa Flos regalis 174
  Tout a par moy 182, 204

Ghizeghem, Hayne van, *De tous biens plaine* 175, 185, 214

Gibbons, Orlando, *Cries of London* 136
Gombert, Nicolas
  Ego sum qui sum 186, 187–9 (Ex. 12.5), 190, 195
  In illo tempore 195
  Je prens congié 160
  Lugebat David Absalon 160
  Media vita in morte sumus 75, 77 (Ex. 5.6), 158
Greiter, Matthias, *Passibus ambiguis/Fortuna desperata* 205
Guerrero, Francisco, *Missa L'Homme armé* 181

Hayne *see* Ghizeghem, Hayne van

Isaac, Henricus
  La mi la sol la sol la mi 14–15 (Ill. 2.2), 98–9 (Ex. 7.1), 100
  Missa O praeclara 17 (Ill. 2.4), 99
  O decus ecclesie 201
  Rogamus te, piissima virgo 16 (Ill. 2.3), 99
  Salve sancta parens 117–18 (Ex. 8.2)

Jan, Maistre, *Lauda Jerusalem* 123
Janequin, Clément
  Il estoit une fillette 101–2
  Jouyssance vous donnerai 133
  La Chasse 136
  La Guerre 136, 177
  Le Caquet des femmes 136
  Le Chant de l'alouette 136
  Le Chant des oiseaux 136
  Les Cris de Paris 136
  Toutes les nuictz 92–3 (Ex. 6.4)
Josquin des Prez
  Absalon fili mi (or Pierre de la Rue) 154, 155 (Ex. 11.6)
  Ave Maria ... virgo serena 149, 159, 192–3
  De profundis (or Nicolas Champion) 127
  Faulte d'argent 119, 175
  Illibata Dei virgo nutrix 32, 92, 143
  Inviolata, integra et casta es 123, 151
  Miserere mei, Deus 21, 122–3, 127, 157, 163
  Missa de Beata Virgine 191
  Missa Faisant regretz 182, 203–4 (Ex. 13.9)
  Missa Fortuna desperata 173
  Missa Hercules dux Ferrariae 34, 182, 191, 200, 218
  Missa L'Homme armé sexti toni 178–80 (Ex. 12.3)
  Missa L'Homme armé super voces musicales 95, 178–9, 181, 200, 212
  Missa La sol fa re mi 182, 200

Missa Malheur me bat 213
Missa Pange lingua 148
Nymphes des bois/Requiem 33, 123, 128
Nymphes nappés 119
Pater noster/Ave Maria 146, 151
Petite camusette 146
Planxit autem David (Ninot le Petit?) 127, 157
Plus nulz regretz 163
Preter rerum seriem 190–1
Que vous madame/In pace 143, 144 (Ex. 11.1)
Quis habitat 146
Stabat mater 175
Tu solus qui facis mirabilia 176
Ut Phebi radiis 201–2 (Ex. 13.7), 203, 208
Virgo prudentissima 151
Virgo salutiferi 123

La Rue, Pierre de
  Ave sanctissima Maria 10–11 (Ill. 2.1), 31, 208
  Missa Alleluia 213
  Missa Almana 192
  Missa Cum jocunditate 182
  Missa de Septem doloribus 174, 192–3
  Missa L'Homme armé 181, 209, 210 (Ex. 13.12), 211 (Ill. 13.1)
  Pour quoy non 192
  Regina celi 56
  Requiem Mass 118, 143
Lambe, Walter
  Nesciens mater 126
  Stella celi 59, 126
Lassus, Orlande de
  Beati quorum 199–200 (Ex. 13.5)
  En un chateau 134–5
  Lagrime di San Pietro 76, 92–3 (Ex. 6.5), 225
  Magnificat preter rerum seriem 191
  Missa Jäger 109
  Missa Osculetur me 188
  Prophetiae Sybillarum 104 (Ex. 7.3)
  Quand mon mari vient de dehors 148
  Vignon, vignon, vignette 135
Le Jeune, Claude, *Qu'est devenu ce bel oeuil* 206–7 (Ex. 13.11), 208
Le Santier, Jean, *Alma redemptoris mater* 122
L'Homme armé (tune) 51 (Ex. 4.1), 52–3, 137, 176
L'Homme armé, Naples masses based on 183
Ligeti, György, *Lontano* 167

Machaut, Guillaume, *Messe de Nostre-Dame* 70, 109
Maier, Michael, fuga/emblema XLV 218–19 (Ill. 13.2)
Manchicourt, Pierre, *Regina celi* 213
Marenzio, Luca, *Tirsi morir volea* 139
Monte, Philippe de, *Super flumina Babylonis* 178
Monteverdi, Claudio, *Missa In illo tempore* 186, 189–90, 194, 195–6 (Ex. 12.7)
Morales, Cristóbal de
  Missa L'Homme armé 181
  Missa Mille regretz 186
  Missa Ut re mi fa sol la 201
Moulu, Pierre
  Fiere Atropos/Anxiatus est 122, 128, 143
  Mater floreat, florescat 32, 122
  Missa Alma redemptoris mater (Mass with two faces) 213
Mouton, Jean
  Exalta regina Galliae 122
  In omni tribulatione 122, 125, 126 (Ex. 9.2), 149, 152
  Messe sans cadence 199
  Nesciens mater 123

Obrecht, Jacob
  Hec Deum celi 221–2 (Ex. 13.14, Fig. 13.1–2)
  Missa Caput 5
  Missa De tous biens plaine 214
  Missa Fortuna desperata 172–3, 214
  Missa Grecorum 214
  Missa Hercules dux Ferrarie (lost) 182
  Missa L'Homme armé 178–9, 193
  Missa Libenter gloriabor 206–7 (Ex. 13.10), 221
  Missa Malheur me bat 95
  Missa Maria zart 95, 163–4, 183, 216, 221
  '*Missa Regina celi*' (= *Missa Sub tuum presidium?*) 35
  Missa Sub tuum presidium 145–6, 183
  Salve crux 126, 148, 149, 150 (Ex. 11.5), 152
Ockeghem, Johannes
  Alma redemptoris mater 169, 170 (Ex. 12.1)
  D'un aultre amer 176
  Fors seulement l'actente 142, 152, 185
  Intemerata Dei mater 153–4, 225
  Je n'ay dueil 157
  Ma bouche rit 72, 131–3
  Ma maistresse 184 (Ex. 12.5), 185
  Missa Au travail suis 145 (Ex. 11.3), 192
  Missa Caput 5, 143

Ockeghem, Johannes (cont.)
   Missa L'Homme armé 178–9, 212
   Missa Ma maistresse 172
   Missa My-my 192
   Missa Prolationum 95, 182, 209
   Missa Quinti toni 61–2 (Ex. 4.5), 200–1 (Ex. 13.6)
   Mort tu as navré 32
   Presque transi 192
   Requiem Mass 23
   S'elle m'amera/Petite camusette 100–1 (Ex. 7.2), 105
Orto, Marbrianus de, Missa L'Homme armé 215–16 (Ex. 13.13)

Palestrina, Giovanni Pierluigi da
   Dum complerentur 160–2 (Ex. 11.8), 193
   Missa ad fugam 210
   Missa L'Homme armé (two settings) 181
   Missa Papae Marcelli 27, 104, 192
   Missa Ut re mi fa sol la (6 v) 201
Pipelare, Matthaeus, Memorare, mater Christi 175
Power, Leonel, Missa Alma redemptoris mater 171, 217
Pulloys, Johannes, Flos de spina 124, 125

Regina celi (antiphon) 145–6
Regis, Johannes, Missa Dum sacrum mysterium 176, 178–9
Richafort, Jean,
   Quem dicunt homines 176
   Requiem Mass 119, 175, 178
Rogier, Philippe,
   Missa Ego sum qui sum 186, 187–89 (Ex. 12.5), 194, 195–6 (Ex. 12.7)

Salve Regina (antiphon) 121–2
Sandrin, Pierre, Doulce mémoire 133
Senfl, Ludwig
   Ave Maria ... virgo serena 193
   Lust hab' ich g'habt zur Musica 54, 133–4, 200
   Fortuna ad voces musicales 201
Sermisy, Claudin de
   Dont vient cela 133
   Je ne menge point de porc 135
   La la, maistre Pierre 133, 135
   Languir me fays 133
Silva, Andreas de
   Gaude felix Florentiae 128
   Il illo tempore loquente Iesu 128
   Intonuit de caelo 129
   Omnis pulchritudo Domini 128–9
   Tota pulchra es 122
Solage, Fumeux fume par fumée 63
Stabat mater 127
Striggio, Alessandro the Elder
   Ecce beatam lucem 41, 165
   Missa Ecco sì beato giorno 41, 165

Tallis Thomas,
   Four-voice Mass 191
   Gaude gloriosa Dei mater 157
   If ye love me 141
   Lamentationes Jeremiae 158, 161 (Ex. 11.7)
   Miserere nostri 141
   Missa Puer natus est 158, 220–1
   Missa Salve intemerata 158, 166–7
   Spem in alium 158, 166–7
   Suscipe quaeso, Domine 199
Taverner, John
   Mean Mass 192
   Missa Gloria tibi trinitas 99
Therache, Pierre, Verbum bonum 122
Tinctoris, Johannes, Missa sine nomine 143
Tye, Christopher
   In nomine settings 137–8
   O lux 138
   Sit fast 137–8

Urrede, Johannes, Nunca fue peña mayor 175

Veni creator spiritus (chant) 20 (Ex. 2.1)
Victoria, Tomás Luis de
   Dum complerentur 193, 194 (Ex. 12.6)
   Missa O quam gloriosum est regnum 125
   Missa pro Victoria 177
   O magnum mysterium 190
   O quam gloriosum est regnum 125
   Requiem Mass 119

Weerbeke, Gaspar van, O salutaris hostia 74–5 (Ex. 5.4)
Wert, Giaches de
   Ascendente Jesu in naviculam 106–8 (Ex. 7.4)
   Vox in Rama 106
Willaert, Adrian
   Quid non ebrietas 205–6, 208
   Saluto te, sancta virgo Maria 75–6 (Ex. 5.5), 154
   Veni sancte spiritus 122
Wylkynson, Robert, Jesus autem transiens 220

General index

'a cappella heresy' 229–31
a cappella performance 228–9
academies and music 25–6
accidentals in lute music 224
acoustics
    influence on performance 234–5
    reverberant 234
Agricola, Alexander 36, 143, 177, 182
    imitation 152
    ostinato against a c.f. 203
    scale 163; *see also* Index of compositions
air de cour 134
Alamire workshop 12
Alberti, Leon Battista 24
Aleotti, Vittoria 44
Allegri, Gregorio *see* Index of compositions
Alleluia, in motet texts 129
alteration, rule of 87
alternatim settings 115
analogies of texts in choosing a c.f. 174–7
Anne of Brittany, Queen of France 123, 128
Antico, Andrea 15
    Motetti novi e chanzoni franciose a quarto sopra doi 123
antiphons 119
antiphony 245
Arcadelt, Jacques 37, 138; *see also* Index of compositions
architecture as frozen music 24–5
Arco, Livia d' 45
ascriptions to composers 13, 18, 245
Ashwell, Thomas, Masses 157
Attaingnant, Pierre 16
    Treze motets 120
attributions to composers 18, 245
audience, change in 17–18
Augenmusik 215–6
augmentation 95
authenticity 245
Ave sanctissima Maria (prayer) 124

B flat and natural 47
Bach, J. S.
    Musical Offering 228; *see also* Index of compositions
    vocal writing 230
Bakfark, Valentin 43
ballade 131
Bartoli, Cosimo, *Ragionamenti accademici* 159
bass as fundamental voice 73–74, 78
basso continuo 4–5, 73, 165
Bellini, Gentile 41
benefices 28–9, 43
Bent, Margaret 206
Benthem, Jaap van 220
Berg, Adam 17
Berger, Karol 60
bergerette 131
Binchois Consort 234
Binchois, Gilles 3, 33; *see also* Index of compositions
Blackburn, Bonnie J. 31, 177
blind musicians 42
Boethius 24
    on musical space 47
borrowing, musical 168–96, 247
    concealed 216
    inaudible 193–6
    from plainchant 168–71
    from a polyphonic model 172–96
    more than one voice 173
borrowing, textural 193
Boyleau, Simon *see* Index of compositions
Brahms, Johannes 227
Browne, John 156–7; *see also* Index of Compositions
Bruhier, Antoine *see* Index of compositions
Brumel, Antoine 33, 122
    polytextual motets and masses 101
    printing of his Masses 36; *see also* Index of compositions
Brunelleschi, Filippo 3
Brunet, Johannes *see* Index of compositions

Burckhardt, Jacob 2
Burroughs, William S. 214
Busnoys, Antoine
  excommunication 30
  imitation 152
  as model 177; *see also* Index of compositions
Buxheimer Orgelbuch 40
Byrd, William 27, 31, 33, 38, 64, 161
  Gradualia 117
  Masses 116; *see also* Index of compositions

cadences 56–9
  cadential function 68–70
  double leading-note 70 (Fig. 5.2)
  embellished 57–8
  English, 58, 80–1 (Ex. 5.10)
  evaded 197–8 (Ex. 13.1–3),
    199 (Ex. 13.4)
  'fermata' 80 (Ex. 5.9)
  four-voice 78–82 (Ex. 5.7–8)
  and mode 58 (Ex. 4.4), 59
  octave 57
  ornaments 57 (Ex. 4.3)
  with pedal point 81 (Ex. 5.11), 82
  as rhetorical gesture 199–200 (Ex. 13.5)
  Satzfehler 80–1 (Ex. 5.10)
  suspensions 57–8
  third in final 80
  two-voice 57 (Ex. 4.2)
  under-third (Landini) 57
Calvin, Jean, on music 27
Cambrai Cathedral 29
canon 119, 151, 164
  extemporized 21
  fugal 208–12, 245
  and imitation 208
  mensuration 208–11
  non-fugal 212–15, 245
  on plainchant 123
  and texture 142–3
canons
  3-in-1 181
  4-in-1, 181, 123, 209, 211 (Ill. 13.1)
  enigmatic 212
  on hexachords 202
  instructions 212–14
  at the minim 179–80
  large-scale 146
  prejudice against 215
  resolutions of 212–13
  as riddles 212–15
cantus (voice-part) 68

cantus firmus (cantus firmi) 4, 245
  canonic 151
  in English Masses 111, 114
  monophonic song 111
  multiple 145–6, 191
  plainchant 111
  from polyphony 172–85
  role of 146–51
  secular 119, 172–5
cantus prius factus 169, 245
  and notation 172
canzonet 139
Capirola, Vincenzo 43
Caput texture 70–4, 91, 141
Carpentras, Egidius *see* Genet, Elzéar
Carver, Robert 156; *see also* Index of
  compositions
Castiglione, Baldassare, *Book of the Courtier*
  25
Casulana, Maddalena 44
Caurroy, Eustache du 161
Cerone, Pietro 20
  Il melopeo y maestro 185
Certon, Pierre 135
Chansonnier Cordiforme 12
chansons 245
  'Parisian' 17
  performance of 230; *see also* songs
chant *see* plainchant
chapel-master, audition for 21–2
Charles the Bold, Duke of Burgundy 25, 29,
  174
  chapel ordinances 231
Charles V, Emperor 30, 168, 176,
  190
Charles VII, king of France 29, 175
Charles VIII, king of France 128
chiavette 74–8
  and pitch-levels 224–5
choirboys, training and careers 28, 35
Choralis Constantinus 117, 228
chordal writing 125
chromaticism 63–4, 138, 140, 205–8
  and textual considerations 205
Church, conflicting attitudes to music 27
Ciconia, Johannes 35
Cipriano *see* De Rore, Cipriano
Claude, Queen of France 122
clausula see cadences
clefs , 47, 66–7 (Fig. 5.1)
  high and low 76–7
  low 128, 163, 225; *see also chiavette*
Clemens non Papa, Jacobus 30, 33

Codex Chantilly 234
Colebault, Antoine (Bidon) 21
coloration 87, 89–90
combinative songs 100–1
comes 245
Compère, Loÿset 33, 143
  motetti missales 120
  scale 163; *see also* Index of compositions
composers
  and publishers 16–17, 37
  status of 34–5
  women 44
composition
  and extemporization 19–20, 22–3
  status of 34
compositions
  attributions 38
  ownership of 38
  payments for 35
concerto delle dame 45
conjunctae 61–3
'contenance angloise', interpretation of 4
contrafactum/contrafacta 98, 101–2, 245
contrary motion 57
contratenor 69, 74–5
  contratenor altus 71
  contratenor bassus 70–4
  style of 228
  vocal or instrumental? 230
copying of music and text 102
cori spezzati 164
Council of Trent 245
  and music 27, 117–18
counter (musical technique) 19
counterpoint 54–6
Counter-Reformation 245
Crecquillon, Thomas 159
Credos, free-standing 115
cycles *see* Mass cycles; *motetti missales*; Plenary cycles; Proper cycles

Davy, Richard 156; *see also* Index of compositions
De Rore, Cipriano 33, 38, 64, 138
  chromaticism 205
  first book of madrigals 76; *see also* Index of compositions
dedications of printed music 37
deductions 52–4; *see also* hexachords
Delehaye *see* Index of compositions
descant 19
devotion, music for 124–7
diminution 88

discantus 68
dissonance treatment 60, 64–5, 159
dot of addition 87
dot of division 87
double choir 163
Du Fay, Guillaume 3
  at Cambrai 29
  canonic works 142–3
  consulted on and composed plainchant 56
  illegitimate birth 28
  imitation 152
  Mass Propers 116
  mensural practice 90
  polytextual Masses 104–5
  self-memorialization 33
  two-tier scoring 145; *see also* Index of compositions
Dunstaple, John 4
  isorhythmic motets 217
duos 69, 156
dux 246
Dürr, Alfred 220

Early Music Consort of London 229
early music movement 229
editing music 60–1, 223–6
Edward VI, king of England 31
Egenolff, Christian 16
Egidius de Murino 176
  On the manner of composing tenors in motets 174
elevation 183, 246
  music for 115, 125
Elimot 122; *see also* Index of compositions
Elizabeth I, Queen of England 25, 31
Elizabeth of York, Duchess of Burgundy 174
Eloy d'Amerval *see* Index of compositions
emblema 217
'emic' and 'etic' approaches to musical culture 7, 246
emulation and authority 190–1
England, five-voice music in 155–8; *see also* contenance angloise
Ensemble Organum 233
ensembles, instrumental
  before 1500 39–40
  after 1500 40–1
epigrams 134–5, 246
Erasmus, Desiderius, on music 27
Escobar, Pedro de *see* Index of compositions
Escobedo, Bartolomé de *see* Index of compositions
Este, Alfonso I d', Duke of Ferrara 164

Este, Ercole I d', Duke of Ferrara 29, 123, 177, 182
   hires Josquin and Obrecht 34–5
   Josquin's *Missa Hercules Dux Ferrarie* written for 34, 191
   requests Obrecht 34
Este, Ercole II d', Duke of Ferrara 191
Este, Isabella d', Duchess of Mantua 40
Eton Choirbook 12, 63, 155–7, 213, 225
   antiphons 163
   style in 155
Eton College 121
extemporization 18–21, 43
   attitudes towards 22
   basis of 39–40
   on instruments 39–40
eye-music 215–6

faburden 19–20
Faenza Codex 40
Fallows, David 130
false relations 159
falsettists 231
fantasia
   compositions 119, 137, 193, 200
   style 99, 121, 193, 201, 222
fauxbourdon 20–1, 127
   associated with lamentation or antiquity 23
Fayrfax, Robert, Masses 157; *see also* Index of compositions
Festa, Costanzo 122, 138; *see also* Index of compositions
Festa, Sebastiano 138
Févin, Antoine de 33
   printing of his Masses 36; *see also* Index of compositions
Ficino, Marsilio 42, 105
fifths, consecutive 58, 65
Finck, Hermann, *Practica musica* 159
flats
   and affect 148
   for expressivity 127
   in signature 61–2
Flecha, Mateo 136–7; *see also* Index of compositions
form and text 96–102
format
   choirbook 9–13
   partbook 13–18
   score 9
formes fixes 106, 130–4, 184–5, 246
Formschneider, Hieronymus 16, 38, 117
Fouquet, Jean 175

Francis I, king of France 43, 122, 136, 176
freely composed 246
Frescobaldi, Girolamo 227; *see also* Index of compositions
fricassée 136
frottola 100, 133
Frye, Walter 156; *see also* Index of compositions
fuga 151, 158–61, 208
   fuga subjects 155, 189–90
function
   ambiguity of 120–1
   classification of music by 97
   and style 100

Gabrieli, Andrea and Giovanni, polychoral music 164
Gaffurius, Franchinus 54
   on writing in parallel 10ths 152
Galilei, Vincenzo 106
Gallus (Handl), Jacobus 161
   Moralia 163
   Opus musicum 117
   Proper cycles 117
games, musical
   evaded cadences 197–200
   hexachord 200–3
   ostinato 203–5
gamut 46–7 (Fig. 4.1), 49
   and hexachords 52, 53 (Fig. 4.3)
Gardano, Antonio 16, 37
gematria 220, 246
genera, Greek 206
Genet, Elzéar (Carpentras) 37, 129
genre in Renaissance music 96–108
Gesualdo, Carlo 64, 138
   chromaticism 205
Ghiselin, Johannes 36
Ghizeghem, Hayne van *see* Index of compositions
Gibbons, Orlando *see* Index of compositions
gimell 156
Giotto di Bondone 3
Glarean, Heinrich 38, 182
   reordering of modal system 55–6, 59
gloss 246
Gombert, Nicolas 80, 124, 128
   scoring 163
   style 158–60
   text sensitivity 104–5; *see also* Index of compositions
Goscalcus on *conjunctae* 62–3
Gothic Voices 230, 233

Goudimel, Claude 31
Gregory I, Pope, and music 27
Greiter, Matthias *see* Index of compositions
Guarini, Anna 45
Guerrero, Francisco 64, 168; *see also* Index of compositions
Guido of Arezzo
  on musical space 47
  and solmization syllables 52–4
Guidonian hand 47, 48 (Ill. 4.1), 49
guilds 31
gymel 19

Hacqueville, Jacqueline de 30, 142
head-motif 4, 110, 114, 116, 191
hemiola 87, 89–90
Henry VIII, king of England 25
hexachords 52–4
  in canons 202
  expanded *see conjunctae*
  and gamut 53 (Fig. 4.3)
  as musical features 200–3
  syllables 182
  transposition of 62, 205
Heyden, Sebald 55
H.I.P. 246
Hofhaimer, Paul 115
homage, musical 119
homophony 246
Horatian odes 105
Huguenot 246
humanism 246
  and music 105

iconography, evidence for performance from 229, 234
imitation 123–6, 135, 151–5, 246
  paired 148
  pervasive 158–63
  in songs 152; *see also* Masses, imitation; motets, imitation
improvisation *see* polyphony, extemporized
In nomine 99
incremental expansion 200–1 (Ex. 13.5)
indulgences 247
  earned through singing 31
instrumental music 137–8
instrumentalists
  before 1500 39–40
  after 1500 40–1
instruments
  after 1500 40

loud and soft 39
and voices together 40
use of 227–32
intabulations 43
intelligibility of the text 103–5
intermedii 165–6, 235–6
  of *La Pellegrina* 41–2
intertextuality 192, 247
intervals, consecutive 58
intonation 206, 225–6
  just 247
Isaac, Henricus 36, 134
  alternatim settings 115
  appointment as court composer 35
  imitation 152
  Mass Propers 116–17
  ostinato against a c.f. 203
  Proper cycles 117–18
  teacher of Senfl 133; *see also* Index of compositions
isomelism 247
isorhythm 247

Janequin, Clément 135, 137; *see also* Index of compositions
Jeppesen, Knud 64–5
John, Duke of Berry 234
John XXII, Pope, and music 27
Josquin des Prez 35, 36, 122, 143
  canons 146
  dissonance treatment 65
  imitation 152
  as model 178, 182, 191–3
  ostinato against a c.f. 203
  ostinato masses, 182
  scale 163
  style 159
  text sensitivity 104; *see also* Index of compositions

keyboard instruments
  enharmonic 63
  tuning of split keys 226
Kirkman, Andrew 176
Kyrie, troped 111, 115

L'Homme armé tune as a model 177–81; *see also* Index of compositions
La Fage, Johannes de 122
La Pellegrina 165–6
La Rue, Pierre de 31, 33, 36
  plainchant-based Masses 174
  imitation 152

La Rue, Pierre de (cont.)
  polytextual Masses 105; see also Index of compositions
Lambe, Walter 156; see also Index of compositions
laments for composers 33
Landini cadence 57
Landini, Francesco 34
language, choice of 103
Lassus, Orlande de 17, 35, 135, 159–60
  career 38–9
  copy of Brumel's 'Earthquake' Mass 165
  imitation Magnificats 191
  Masses on chansons with risqué texts 177
  Patrocinium musices 117
  Proper cycles 117
  text sensitivity 105; see also Index of compositions
Le Franc, Martin, *Le Champion des dames* 3–4
Le Jeune, Claude 104, 163; see also Index of compositions
Le Roy & Ballard 17
Le Santier, Jean 122; see also Index of compositions
leading note 224
Leo X, Pope 122, 128, 176
  and music 27
Leonardo da Vinci 25
ligatures 10, 88
Ligeti, György see Index of compositions
listeners 190
liturgy 247
Lobo, Alonso 215
lof 121
Loire Valley chansonniers 12
Louis IX, king of France 29
Louis XII, king of France 128
Lowinsky, Edward E. 205
Ludford, Nicholas, Masses 157
Lusitano, Vicente 20
lutenists 42
  patrons of 43
Luther, Martin, and music 27
Luzzaschi, Luzzasco 45, 138

Machaut, Guillaume de 34; see also Index of compositions
Macque, Giovanni de 64
madrigalism 103, 106
madrigals 138–40
  early 18

Maier, Michael, *Atalanta fugiens* 216–17, 218–19 (Ill. 13.2)
Maistre Jan see Index of compositions
Manchicourt, Pierre 159; see also Index of compositions
manuscripts
  copied from prints 18
  formats of see format, choirbook
  heart-shaped 12
  personal 13
  polyphonic 9–18
  for presentation 12
  structure of 13
  for use 12
Marenzio, Luca 45, 138; see also Index of compositions
Mary I, Queen of England 31
Mary of Hungary, Queen 30
Masses
  alternatim settings 115
  cantus firmus 4, 111
  as a cycle see Mass cycles
  ferial 191
  with enigmatic titles 192
  hexachord 201
  imitation 185–91
  length of 109–16
  'Missa brevis' 109
  omission of text 105
  ostinato 182
  paired movements 110–11
  parody or imitation 115–16
  polyphonic settings 105, 109–16
  polytextual 105
  segmentation 182–3
  shared material 110–11, 110
  'sine nomine' 116, 191
Mass cycles 5, 109–16, 181–5
  analogy with symphony 183–4
  English 4–5, 110–12, 181–2
  formal layouts 111–15
  liturgical reconstruction 235
  on plainchants 191
  'symphonic' reading 235
Mass Propers 110–11
Maximilian I, Emperor 115
  and music 35
maximodus 85
Medici Codex 122–4
Mengozzi, Stefano 52, 54
mensuration
  consecutive 91–2, 94
  cut 88

and style 88–93
mi against *fa* 60
Milsom, John 154–5
mimesis 136
minor color 87
'Missa brevis' 109
models 247
  designation of 192
  for Masses, choice of 174–7
Moderne, Jacques 16
modes
  and affect 55, 106, 178, 190
  classification of 49–50
  eight church 50 (Fig. 4.2)
  melodic formulae 50
  mixed and commixed 51, 55, 127
  organization according to 76
  Phrygian, different behaviour of 59, 78, 132
  reciting tone (tenor) 50
  transposition of 61
modus 85
Molinet, Jean 30
Molza, Tarquinia 45
Monte, Philippe de 35, 38, 160; *see also* Index of compositions
Monteverdi, Claudio 45, 103, 138; *see also* Index of compositions
Morales, Cristóbal de 16, 160; *see also* Index of compositions
motet cycles *see motetti missales*
motet-chanson 143
motets 120–9
  devotional 124–7
  for the elevation 125–6
  imitation 193
  isorhythmic 3, 6, 131, 171, 172, 182, 183
  occasional 128
  penitential 127
  performance of 120
  secular 128
motetti missales 120–1, 125–6
Moulu, Pierre *see* Index of compositions
Mouton, Jean 33, 122
  imitation 152
  imitation Masses 185
  printing of his Masses 36; *see also* Index of compositions
music
  effects on humans 25
  as inferior to painting 25
  knowledge of as mark of good breeding 25
  and number 217–22
  and the passions 26

penitential 127
and public morals 25–6
in the *quadrivium* 24–6
as a science 24–7
of the spheres 24–6
and status 29
music making, domestic 17–18
musica falsa or *ficta* 60–3, 224
  in lute music 224; *see also* accidentals
musica mundana, humana, and *instrumentalis* 26
musica recta or *vera* 60
Musica Reservata 233
musici and *cantores,* distinction between 26
musicians, migration from north to south 35–6
mutation 54

Newes, Virginia 208
Notation, mensural 83–95
note-values
  under different mensurations 83, 84 (Fig. 6.1), 85, 86 (Ex. 6.1), 86–8
  vary by context 86
number symbolism 220
numbers in music 217–22
nuns and music 44

Obrecht, Jacob 36
  canonic writing 214
  dissonance treatment 65
  imitation 152
  ostinato against a c.f. 203
  polytextual motets and Masses 101, 105
  segmentation Masses 182–3
  spelling of name 220; *see also* Index of compositions
Ockeghem, Johannes 29–30
  36-voice canon 164
  bass voice 74
  canons 146
  dedicatee of Busnoys' *In hydraulis* 32, 218–19
  laments for 33
  mensural practice 90
  as model 177
  scoring for five voices 143–4; *see also* Index of compositions
octaves, consecutive 58
onomatopoeia 136
oral vs written culture 223
Ordinary 247
organs 226
  banned in some institutions 229

organists 42
'oriental hypothesis' 233
Orlando Consort 230, 234
Orto, Marbriano de 36, 152; see also Index of compositions
ostinato technique 134; see also Masses, ostinato

Pacioli, Luca 25
Paix, Jacob, *Missa parodia* 115
Palestrina, Giovanni Pieluigi da 16, 37–8, 165
   apology for writing madrigals 177
   Masses 174
   Song of Songs madrigals 225; see also Index of compositions
Paminger, Leonhard 39
   Proper cycles 117
paraliturgical 247
paraphrase 247
   of plainchant 120–1, 169–71
Paris, Sainte-Chapelle 29
parody 115, 139, 247
patronage
   civic 43
   of instrumentalists 43
   of music by rulers 25, 29–30
   of musicians by the Church 28
   of printed music 37
Paul IV, Pope 37
Paumann, Conrad 42
penitential music 127
Penitential Psalms 127
perfection, rule of 86–7
performance, 'authentic' 229
performance practice 223–36
Petrarca, Francesco 139
Petrucci, Ottaviano 13–15, 36
   Lamentations of Jeremiah 127
   Motetti C 14, 16
   Motetti de Passione 126–7
   Motetti libro quarto 202
   Odhecaton 14, 227
   publications of *frottole* 130
   publications of instrumental music 43
   resolution of canons 212
Peverara, Laura 45
Philip the Good, Duke of Burgundy 116
Pietrobono 42–3
Pipelare, Matthaeus see Index of compositions
Pisan, Christine de 106
pitch 46–67, 74–8
   absolute and relative 224–5
   experiments with 205–8
   pitch-levels 75–8, 224–5
plainchant
   adornment of 168–71
   as c.f. 171
   and extemporization 20
   migrating 169
   paraphrased 169–71
Plenary cycles 110–11; see also Propers of the Mass
poetic forms 139; see also *formes fixes*
Polk, Keith 42
polychoral music 164–7
polyphony
   extemporized 18–22, 233
   hostility to 27
   and mode 54–6
   re-purposing of 98
   terms for 19
Pontio, Pietro, *Ragionamento di musica* 185
Power, Leonel 4; see also Index of compositions
prayers, musical settings of 124
printing
   with moveable type 15–16
   privileges for 37
   single-impression 16
   of vocal music 36–9
   woodcut engraving 15–16
prints, polyphonic 13–18; see also under Antico, Andrea; Petrucci, Ottaviano
production, vocal, 'oriental' hypothesis 233–5
prolations 83, 84 (Fig. 6.1), 85–8
   and time signatures 85–6
pronunciation, period 234
Propers of the Mass 247
   performance of 235
   polyphonic cycles 116–18
   use of plainchant 117; see also Plenary cycles
proportions 88, 217–20
   between the planets 24
   as intervals, rhythms, and tempo relationships 24
   and tempo 94–5, 226–7
psalms 119
Pulloys, Johannes see Index of compositions
puzzles, musical
   visual 215–16; see also games, musical

quinta vox 74
quotations of music, isolated 192

Rabelais, François 136
Ramos de Pareja, Bartolomeo 54
ranges 142
   three-octave 63, 225; *see also* scale
reciting tone 50
reconstruction, liturgical 235–6
recycling of music 98–100
Rees, Owen 168
Reese, Gustave 215
Reformation 247
   effect on music 30–1
refrains 131–2
Regis, Johannes
   polytextuality 101, 105
   scoring for five voices 143–4; *see also* Index of compositions
Renaissance, definition of, and music 2–4
repertory, musical, for instruments 40–1
Requiem Masses, polyphonic 117–19
res facta 19
retrograde 112, 114, 135, 179–80, 182, 213
Richafort, Jean
   imitation Masses 185
   quotations from Josquin 178; *see also* Index of compositions
Ripa, Alberto da (Albert de Rippe) 43
Robertson, Anne Walters 175–6
Rogier, Philippe *see* Index of compositions
rondeau 131–2
Ronsard, Pierre 39
Rore *see* De Rore, Cipriano
Rosicrucians 217
Rudolf II, Emperor 216

Salve services 121
Sandrin, Pierre *see* Index of compositions
Satie, Erik 217
Satzfehler 80, 81 (Ex. 5.10a)
scale 141
   extended 163–7
   of Masses 183
   music for 12 voices 164
   music for 24 voices 165
   music for 40 voices 165
   works for more than 7 voices 220
Schiltz, Katelijne 216
Schubert, Peter 64
Schubinger, Augustein 40
scoring 141–6
   for 3 voices with c.f. 143–4
   for 5 voices 143–4, 146
      in English music 155–8
   for 6 voices 146
   for 7 voices 145–6
   for 24 voices 146
   for 36 voices 146
   for 40 voices 158
   addition of voices 145–6
   canonic 142, 146
   duos 159–60
   equal voices 142
   gimell 156
   for high voices 156
   length 157
   for low voices 143
   paired imitation 148
   panel structure 156–7
   placement of c.f. 143–4
   and texting 227–32
   thick 159
   two-tier 145
   unusual 142–3
Scotto firm of printers 16
Senfl, Ludwig
   acrostic in tribute to Isaac 133
   alternatim settings 115
   Mass Propers 117
   ostinato against a c.f. 203; *see also* Index of compositions
Sermisy, Claudin de 135; *see also* Index of compositions
Sforza, Galeazzo Maria, Duke of Milan 29
Shroud of Turin 175
Sicher, Fridolin 13
sighting 20, 62
signatures, key, mixed 61–2
signs, simultaneous mensural 94–5
Silva, Andreas de *see* Index of compositions
'Sine nomine' Masses 116, 191
singer-clerics before 1500 28–30
singers
   careers of 28–9
   lay, in churches 37–8
   singers' motets 32–3
   standards of morality 30
   travels of 177
singing *super librum* 19
Sixtus IV, Pope 31
soggetto cavato 182, 203
Solage *see* Index of compositions
solmization syllables 52
soloists, instrumental 42–3
songs
   epigrams 134–5
   in *formes fixes* 130–3
   narrative 135–7

songs (cont.)
    with plainchant c.f. 143–4
    polytextual 100–2
    strophic 133–4
sonnet 139
sopranos, female 231
Sorel, Agnès 175
Speciálník Codex 35–6, 115
species 49–50
Spinacino, Francesco 43
squares 19, 115
stave notation 47
Stoltzer, Thomas 30–1
strambotto 21, 100, 133
stretto fuga 151, 154
Striggio, Alessandro, the Elder 165–6; see also Index of compositions
stroke, meaning of 88
Studio der Frühen Musik 233
superius 68
supremus 68
syllables, solmization 52
symbolism in music 175–6, 216

Tallis, Thomas 33, 158, 166; see also Index of compositions
Tallis, Thomas, and William Byrd, *Cantiones sacrae* 158
Taverner, John 157; see also Index of compositions
teleology, teleological 248
temperament 248
    equal 225; see also tuning
tempo 226–7
    and proportions 94–5
    slowing of 92
tempus 85
tempus perfectum, absence of 124
tenor
    as foundation 56, 68, 73
    motets 174
tenorist 22, 34
tetrachords 49
text, intelligibility of 103–5
text painting 106
text setting 102–3
texting and scoring 227–32
texts
    analogies between 174–7
    and form 98
    with hexachords 201–3 (Ex. 13.8)
    poetic 130–3
    risqué 101–2, 134–5, 177

texture
    alternation of 147–51
    with c.f. 146–51
    without c.f. 151–2
    chordal 149
    and imitation 151–5, 186
Therache, Pierre see Index of compositions
timbre, vocal 233
time signatures 85–6
Tinctoris, Johannes 4
    on aesthetic properties of music 26
    on age of music worth hearing 73
    Book of the Art of Counterpoint 5
    on canon 212
    on the effects of music 25
    on mode of *Le Serviteur* 55
    on modes in polyphony 55–6
    on music as incitement to devotion 27
    on the tenor 68
    on three types of polyphony 97
    on variety 153–4; see also Index of compositions
top lines, voices for 231
Tours, Saint-Martin 29
transposition 224
trebles, child 156, 231
Trent Codices 13, 116
triplum 70–1, 78
Tritonius, Petrus 105
trope 248
tuning systems 206
    enharmonic 225
    mean-tone 225–6
    Pythagorean 225; see also equal temperament
Tye, Christopher see Index of compositions

Urrede, Johannes see Index of compositions

Vaet, Jacobus 160
vagans 74
van Eyck brothers, Ghent altarpiece 234
variety 153–4
Vasari, Giorgio 2
Verdelot, Philippe 138
vers mesurés à l'antique 104, 163, 208
Vespers 119
Vicentino, Nicola 54
    archicembalo 63, 206
    on bass as fundamental voice 78
Victoria, Tomás Luis de 38; see also Index of compositions
villancico 100, 102, 130
villanella 21, 139

viols 134
  viol consort 137
virelai 131–2
Vivanco, Sebastian de 215
vocalization, untexted 230
voice-names and ranges 66–78
voices, added 21, 74, 191, 193
voice-types, change in 4–5

Webern, Anton 228
  orchestration of Bach 230
Weerbeke, Gaspar van 36
  imitation 152
  motetti missales 120; *see also* Index of compositions
Wert, Giaches de 45; *see also* Index of compositions

Wilder, Philip van 157
Willaert, Adrian 17, 33, 38, 64, 122, 129, 138, 163
  imitation Masses 185
  Musica nova 143, 160
  polychoral music 164
  style 160; *see also* Index of compositions
Winchester Troper 116
wind ensembles 39–41, 137
Wiser, Johannes 13
women and polyphony 43–5
word-painting 135
wordplay 134–6
words and music 102–8
Wylkynson, Robert *see* Index of compositions

Zarlino, Gioseffo 59, 182

Cambridge Introductions to Music

'Cambridge University Press is to be congratulated for formulating the idea of an "Introductions to Music" series.' *Nicholas Jones, The Musical Times*

Each book in this series focuses on a topic fundamental to the study of music at undergraduate and graduate level. The introductions will also appeal to readers who want to broaden their understanding of the music they enjoy.

Books in the series

Renaissance Polyphony Fabrice Fitch
Music Sketches Friedemann Sallis
Program Music Jonathan Kregor
Electronic Music Nicholas Collins, Margaret Schedel and Scott Wilson
Gregorian Chant David Hiley
Music Technology Julio D'Escrivan
Opera Robert Cannon
Postmodernism in Music Kenneth Gloag
Serialism Arnold Whittall
The Sonata Thomas Schmidt-Beste
The Song Cycle Laura Tunbridge

For EU product safety concerns, contact us at Calle de José Abascal, 56–1°,
28003 Madrid, Spain or eugpsr@cambridge.org.

www.ingramcontent.com/pod-product-compliance
Lightning Source LLC
LaVergne TN
LVHW080311260326
834688LV00038B/1059